Living By the Power of God

Rev. Dr. John A. K. Bonful

xulon PRESS

Living By the Power of God
by Rev. Dr. John A. K. Bonful

Printed in the United States of America

ISBN 1-594677-04-2

www.xulonpress.com

"GYE NYAME"
(EXCEPT GOD)

A Symbol of the Supremacy of God
with all His Attributes:
omnipotence, omniscience, omnipresence, sovereignty, holiness, majesty, justice, faithfulness, unconditional love, mercy and peace.
In the African concept of God, the "Gye Nyame" Symbol represents God in His totality.

DEDICATION

**TO THE
GLORY OF GOD,
OUR MAKER.**

And to Calvary Redeeming Methodist Church, Rockville, Maryland, U. S. A., which is a part of the Living Witness of the mighty work of God being done in the name of Jesus Christ through the ministry of the Holy Spirit in an earthen vessel.

TABLE OF CONTENTS

Introduction 17

1) God Created All Humans Equal 27
   There is Power in Unity 28
   Godless Americans 29
   Every Nation is Gifted with Some Knowledge about God 37
   Ghanaian Artistic Symbols 38
   Each Symbol Bears a Sign of a Cross 39
2) The Hindrance to Africa's Success and Prosperity 43
   The Partition of Africa 44
   Bribery and Corruption 47
   What God Did our Ancestors Worship? 49
3) Ancestral Worldview 51
   The Elite and Occultism 53
4) We Came into this World with Nothing 65
5) Libation in the Old Testament 67
6) Traditional Chiefs Entrusted with Authority 71
   The Only Hiding Place 76
7) God Answers Prayers 79
   Catholic Schools Prayed for Peace 80
   God Reveals in order to Redeem 81
8) Ghana: A Typical Example 87
   The Rise and Fall of Nkrumah 87

9) Idolatry of the Heart....99
    Idolatry is Foolishness....102
10) Areas of Ghanaian Life in Conflict with Scriptures....105
    The Traditional Role of the African Wife in the Home....107
    The King of Ashanti Sets An Example....108
    Same Sex Marriage....112
    Naming Ceremony....113
    Ritual for Twins....115
    Funeral Ceremony....116
    Installation of a Chief....117
11) Leaders who Fear to Lose their Position....121
    Life without God is Fruitless....123
12) Christians are Part of the Problem....129
    Worshipping God and Traditional Spirits....129
    The Failure of Okomfo Damua....132
    God Does Not Want Anyone to Perish....141
13) Carnal Christians....145
    Church Goers....145
14) There are Two Kinds of People in the World....149
15) The Way Forward....153
    The Solution to the Problems....155
    Come to God with a Penitent Heart....156
    The Cross is the Greatest Miracle of God....157
    The Purpose of the Miracles....160
    The Bitter Turns to Sweet....162
16) The Resurrection of Jesus Christ....165
    What the Resurrection Means to Believers....166
17) Empowerment by the Holy Spirit....171
    Who is the Holy Spirit?....171
    The Holy Spirit is for All Believers....172
    The Work of the Holy Spirit....174
    The Fruit of the Holy Spirit....175
18) New Life for All who Believe in Christ....177
    Case Stories of Those who Believe in Christ....177
19) The Christian Hope....183
    What is Hope?....183

The Biblical Hope....184
20) Living in Hope As Faithful Disciples....187
Jesus Taught the Religious Leaders Scriptures....188
The Question about Resurrection....191
Living By the Word of God....191
21) The Benefits of Knowing the Scriptures....195
The Word Leads to Success and Prosperity....195
Neglecting the Word Results in Defeat....197
Jesus Defeats Satan with the Word of God....198
The Key to Victorious Christian Life....199
The Word Equips Believers for Spiritual Warfare....200
22) Take with You the Full Armor of God....203
The Belt of Truth....203
The Shoe of the Gospel of Peace....204
The Shield of Faith....204
The Helmet of Salvation....205
The Sword of the Spirit....206
23) Know Your Enemy....209
The Duty of Angels....209
Lucifer's Rebellion in Heaven....210
Activities of Satan and Evil Spirits....211
They Slander God and Believers.......213
They Plant Evil Thoughts in the Mind of People....213
They Ill-Influence National Leaders....214
The Devil Can Control the Mind of Unbelievers....214
24) Resisting the Devil....219
What is Prayer?....220
Prayer is a Priority and Discipline....223
Prayer is a Ministry unto God....223
Prayer is a Communion with God....224
Prayer Opens our Spiritual Eyes....225
Prayer Makes a Way for God's Will on Earth....226
Prayer Enables Believers to Receive Revelation....228
Prayer Must Be in Accordance with God's Word....231
25) Prayer and Fasting....233
Prayer and Fasting by Household and Church....236
Fasting Acceptable to God....238

Hindrances to Prayer....................................240
26) Prayer As a Substitute for Libation....................................243
Drumming, Singing and Dancing....................................243
27) Africans Shall Rise and Shine....................................247
When Will This Happen?....................................249
How is God Going to Do This?....................................253
Africa is a Place of Refuge for God's People....................................256
The African Enterprise....................................259
28) Ghana – As the Star of Africa....................................263
Examples of Fulfilled Prophecies....................................265
How to Pray to Become a Christian....................................266
Many of the Youth Flock to Church....................................267
Traditionalists Preach 'Sankofa'....................................268
Caution: Do Not Look Back....................................269
Those Who Look Back Are Not Worthy....................................271
Total Commitment....................................274
God Answered Their Prayer....................................276
Meeting the Needs of Believers Today....................................278
It Calls for a Team of Prayer Warriors…....................................280
The East Africa Revival—A Living Example....................................284
The South Africa Example—A Ray of Hope....................................285
Conclusion....................................293

FOREWORD

The writing of this book was inspired by a vision the author, Rev. Dr. Bonful strongly believes, came out from God. Thus, he is speaking from the heart. I have known Rev. Dr. Bonful as a seasoned minister of God for several years, but most importantly, because this book carries a simple, but soul stirring message, very vital to our humanistic world today. There is more to this book than meets the eye. It has a very illuminating message about the necessity of reliance on the Almighty God, the Maker of this universe. Rev. Dr. Bonful has done a great job at presenting a very poignant message about the love, peace and power of God. He uses a powerful Ghanaian/African symbol, "*Gye Nyame*" (*Except God*), that speaks of the supremacy of God with all His attributes of omnipotence, omnipresence, omniscience, sovereinty, majesty, holiness, love, goodness, mercy, truth, righteousness, peace, etc., which we very much need in these times for the transformation of Africa in particular, and also of the world in general.

It is important that the message this book brings is received in good spirit. The message covers a plethora of issues, but I will highlight a few with the hope of wetting your appetite to read the whole book. Rev. Dr. Bonful's message flows like a journey -a journey that takes you through some of his personal experiences, and through God's will for our lives and the way forward.

First, he points out the fact that the concept of God is universal and that we are all created equal in the image of God. This point is very basic to our understanding of what God can do for us and what He can do through us. It is important that we understand this fact if we are to consider the essence of this book. If we understand that God is there for us, and that He has made us in His own image, and that He seeks what is best for us, then we will acknowledge that we cannot succeed in the world we live in without His role in our lives.

Another point worthy of mention, and which has been a bane to human beings throughout the centuries and man's relationship with God, is the issue of idolatry. Throughout the Bible, we read of many people who initially had God's approval but lost it because of idolatry. The list includes Saul and Solomon, and yet, to date, many people have not recognized that idolatry and worship of God are at par with each other. This point is stressed in the book, and from the perspective that idolatry is not only the worship of idols, but also the craving of materialistic things. In today's materialistic world, many Christians find themselves craving things, most of which they rarely need. They turn all their attention to material things so much that God, or the things of God, are pushed to the background. For example, many of us will be willing to use our money to buy things we do not need, yet will grumble when it comes to giving tithes and offerings for God's work. The point being made is not that we should not desire things that make life easy for us. Rather, we should not let them consume our attention so much that the things of God are forgotten or become secondary.

Finally, a very practical solution is provided, and that is, reliance on the Almighty God, our Maker, the Creator of heaven and earth. The point does not need much emphasis, because that is the essence of the book. Even the title tells it all-that we have to go back to God, for we are nothing without Him. As human beings, we have tried all ways and methods to be self-reliant but all of our efforts have not yielded the desired result. Despite our failures, some of us have still not come to the realization that our lives are meaningless without our Maker.

This book raises that poignant fact and it is my prayer that by the time you finish reading this book, you will come to acknowledge the fact that you need God more than ever in your life.

In conclusion, I want to thank Rev. Dr. Bonful for putting

together this great book and for allowing me to be part of this great endeavor. Thank you. God bless and guide you in your reading.

The Most Rev Dr. Robert Aboagye-Mensah
Presiding Bishop of the Conference
Methodist Church-Ghana,
Accra, Ghana.

ACKNOWLEDGEMENT

In the first place, I am eternally grateful to the Almighty God for His grace through His Son, Jesus Christ, in enabling me by the power of the Holy Spirit to serve Him in His vineyard for the past thirty-two years. Indeed, no words are adequate to express my gratefulness to God, for His providence, particularly, for this great vision, which He had gradually, under His guidance, led me to commit to writing for all to read.

Secondly, I want to express my heart-felt gratitude to my wife, Georgina, for being with me all these years, and for the spiritual, moral and financial support she constantly offered me, especially, when I quit my full-time secular job two years ago to concentrate on writing this book.

Thirdly, I want to express my deep appreciation to the Presiding Bishop of Conference of the Methodist Church, Ghana, the Most Rev. Dr. Robert Aboagye-Mensah, who, despite his busy schedule, managed to write the Foreword to this book. His work sets the tone for the book for which I am most grateful.

Also, my sincere thanks and appreciation go to Prof. Alex Kobina Armoo of the Baltimore International College, Baltimore, Maryland, USA, who was the first to read the manuscript, worked on the design, and put the pieces together into a printable format. Without his help this would have been a totally different book. Prof. Armoo, may God bless you for your efforts and in all your endeavors.

Furthermore, I am wholeheartedly grateful to Professor Albert

Wright, chairman of the Africa Water Task Force and Caretaker of the Ghana Wesley Methodist Church, Virginia, USA, Dr. George Ebo Bonney, Professor of Genetics at the School of Medicine of the Howard University in Washington, D.C.; Rev. Dr. Emmanuel Lartey of Atlanta Theological Seminary; Rt. Rev. Ebenezer K. Dadson, senior pastor of the Ghana United Methodist Church in Bronx, New York, as well as Mr. Otoo Kofi and Jeffrey Marshall for helping me with my computer problems and also for their excellent work in terms of corrections, comments, and sound advice, which helped to enhance the contents and quality of the book.

The leadership and members of my local church, the Calvary Redeeming Methodist Church of Rockville, and also, the New Creation Gospel Church, headed by Pastor Albert Amo-Mensah, deserve to be mentioned here, for standing together with me all the way in prayer and with initial financial support.

To my senior brothers, Rev. Father Joseph K. Bonful, and Dan, including my sister, Mrs. Agnes Harvey Ewusi, and my children-James, Emma, Esther, together with their spouses, I extend grateful thanks and appreciation for keeping me in their thoughts and prayers.

Finally, to Iyse Lee, my Author-Liaison, for her advice and guidance and the Xulon Press team, who designed, printed and helped to get the book on the market, including all and sundry, who worked behind the scene, in one way or the other, in support of this divine project, I say, Thank you with all my heart! May God Richly bless you all !!

Rev. Dr. John A. K. Bonful
July 7, 2004

INTRODUCTION

The date was December 9th, 2001. My wife and I were on the flight from the Baltimore-Washington International Airport (BWI) heading to Accra, Ghana. This was a very important flight, because we were on our way to attend the wedding ceremonies of our children. Our son, Jim, was getting married on December 22, 2001, while our daughter, Emma, was having her wedding on January 5, 2002. We were really feeling blessed, because two weddings, of two children, two weeks apart, rarely come anyone's way.

I looked out the window at the dark sky–no stars, no clouds, just pitch darkness, and wondered what was out there. I soon realized, all over again, how awesome God is. He had created everything, the entire universe out of nothing. How awesome! How wonderful! How marvelous! That is the God I serve!

After a while I looked into my hand luggage and pulled out a book. It was Bruce Wilkinson's book entitled, "*The Prayer of Jabez*". The book, about the story of the prayer of Jabez, had gained much public attention within Christian circles. I started to read the book. As I read, my mind kept drifting back to Jabez's prayer. Jabez had cried out to the God of Israel, saying, "*Oh that you would bless me, and enlarge my territory! Let your hand be with me, and keep me from harm so that I will be free from pain*" (1 Chronicles. 4:9-10). The rest of the text reads: "*And God granted his request.*"

I was so touched by this prayer, that I began thinking about it more and more. I could relate to what Jabez had gone through.

When I look back at my life while in Ghana, and my present situation in the US, I found myself relating to Jabez's prayer in a lot of ways, and therefore, I adopted the prayer as my own. "*Oh that you would bless me, and enlarge my territory! Let your hand be with me, and keep me from harm so that I will be free from pain.*" I believed that the Lord, "*Jesus Christ,* (who*) is the same yesterday and today and forever*" (Hebrews 13:8)—the Lord who never changes—*would grant my request.*

For the past five years, I have been ministering to the Calvary Redeeming Methodist Church, a congregation of about 100 members. The church was started, in obedience to a vision the Lord had given me on the night of Sunday, February 2, 1997. My prayer has always been that the Lord would increase the membership of His Church, so that I might undertake a full-time ministry. As I read the book, I prayed that the Lord would 'bless me and increase my territory', that is, increase the membership of the church. I continued with this prayer through my trip to Ghana, and continued even after my return to the United States on Sunday, January 20, 2002. However, that was not all I was praying about, for I was also praying for Africa, my beloved continent.

My Prayer for Africa

My thoughts and prayers, for quite sometime, had been concerning the lack of political, technological, economic, spiritual development in Africa. This lack has created a condition of extreme hardship in many countries in Africa today. Rwanda, Ethiopia, Liberia, Sierra Leone, Nigeria, and Ghana, to mention only a few, are notable examples. Hence, many have left their countries for places, where they can make a living. The result is reduction of labour force and personnel in almost every profession: Engineering, Medicine, Nursing, Teaching, skilled labour, etc. The brain drain syndrome has compounded the already existing underdevelopment of Africa. With these disturbing thoughts on my mind, sometimes, I could not help asking God the following questions. Why is it difficult for most Africans to make progress in life? Why are we at the bottom rung of the ladder in terms of development— politically, technologically, and economically? You made all human beings equal in your image as declared in your Word [e.g., Genesis 1: 26], what is the problem with Africans? Why is it so difficult for African nations to develop? Why is Africa, which is so endowed with natural resources, so underdeveloped? What do the advanced nations have that Africa is missing?

Every now and then my mind wonders to the story my roommate told me several years ago. My roommate at the Seminary, who was from the Philippines, had told me an amusingly ridiculous Filipino folk story. We had been discussing the creation account in Genesis. He said there was a Filipino folklore that told the story of how God had created all human beings with clay, and baked each batch in a big oven. According to the story, after God had put the last batch in the oven, He became so busy with other creative activities that He forgot about the batch he had left in the oven. When He finally remembered to take the creatures out of the oven, they had turned black. Those black creatures, according to the folklore, were Africans, or people of African descent. Can you believe this? What a ridiculous story!

Frankly, you and I know that the story is not true, and that of course, my friend was telling the story not to make fun of me (a black African), but rather to highlight one of the misconceptions some people have of the black race. Like all folklores, the story has no Biblical or theological basis. Even if, (and that is a big 'if'), there is any truth in it, the story only answers the question of color, and not the situation black people find themselves in. After all, the Almighty God, "*will neither slumber nor sleep*" (Psalms 121:4), and He "*will not forget*" (Isaiah 49:15) His own handiwork and leave them to burn in an oven. Above all, I know that black people are as beautiful as any other group of people. At the end of His creation, God observed " . . . *all that He had made [including all human beings], and it was very good*" (Genesis 1:31). Hence, I reproduced the Filipino folklore merely to stress the fact that all human beings were made in the image and likeness of God and that no race is better or worse than the other. We are merely different from one another, yet each one of us bears the same imprint of God on the soul.

I am not as bothered about my color as I am about the living condition or situation in which we (black people) find ourselves today. There are many theologians and Bible believers who hold the view that Africans are the descendants of "*Ham, the father of Canaan*," who "*saw his father's nakedness*" and was cursed; as it is written, "*When Noah awoke from his wine and found out what his youngest son had done to him, he said, "Cursed be Canaan! The lowest of slaves will he be to his brothers. May God extend the territory of Japheth; and may Canaan be his slave*" (Genesis 9:24, 27). According to Warren Baker, "the curse pronounced by Noah was fulfilled when the Canaanites became 'woodcutters and water carriers' for the Israelites" (Baker, Warren, Ed. *The Hebrew-Greek Key Bible Study Bible: Commentary on Genesis 9:20-27*).

Whatever might have given cause to the African situation, it became one of my chief concerns, and therefore, one of my constant prayers to God. I am believing God for a lasting solution. I am, however, always comforted, and strengthened, by the great truth that God revealed to Peter when he went to the house of Cornelius. He said, "*I now realize how true it is that God does not show favoritism but accepts people from every nation who fear him and do what is right*" (Acts 10: 34-35). This Scripture has been encouraging me to believe that there is a lot of spiritually talented Africans that God could use for His glory, and for the blessing of the entire continent, and the world at large, just as He had done long ago.

There are other instances in the Bible that support the importance of mother Africa and her people to God. For instance, the role of Egypt in the history of Israel is unquestionable, particularly in the life of Abraham, Joseph, Moses and even Jesus. The infant Jesus, together with His parents, took refuge in Egypt when King Herod sought to destroy the child (Matthew 2:14). Other examples include, the role of Simon from Cyrene, an African, who was called upon to bear the cross for Jesus on the way to His crucifixion. Several scholars claim that Simon (referred to as 'black' in Acts 13:1), one of the leaders of the Church of Antioch, who consecrated Paul and Barnabas for their missionary work, was the same person from Cyrene. There are many other historical records, which prove that Africans had not always been at the receiving end. Significant men like Simon and the Ethiopian official were biblically indisputable among the first Africans to be baptized, linking them to the Church in Africa. It is not known for certain who established Christianity in Africa. However, the records point to the city of Alexandria in Egypt. According to Noel King, it was John Mark (the writer of Mark's Gospel), who was the first to plant the Church in Africa before the turn of the first century (Taryor, Religions of Africa, 1984, p. 30). Christianity in Africa spread and from the second century onwards, the Church in Africa was strongly established that it became part of the universal Church. Again, according to Taryor, the first theological Seminary was founded in Alexandria in the second century; while the monastic movement owed its origin to Egypt through the devotion of a black African called St. Anthony, born in 250 A.D. It is worthwhile to mention further that three of the Popes of the early Church hailed from Africa. They were Pope Victor 1 (A.D. 189-199), Pope Mechaiades (A.D. 311-314), and Pope Gelasius 1 (A.D. 492-496).

It is significant to note furthermore, that some of the most prominent early Church fathers like Tertullian (A.D. 220), Origen (A.D. 254), Cyprian (A.D. 258), and Augustine (A.D. 430), were Africans (Taryor, p. 171-3). Both Taryor and Fotland maintain that those were the Church fathers, who took pains to formulate the Christian doctrines and practices. If these Church fathers of Africa, indeed, were part of the early Christian community, who trusted in God, the Owner of the entire universe with all its fullness and riches, and *"righteousness exalts a nation"*, then, why is Africa not as developed as other parts of the world? *Why are Africans still lagging behind in many areas of life? What went wrong with the faith of our fathers?* I sought the Lord in my daily prayers for answers to these mind-boggling questions.

The Vision

Then, finally, about 4. 00 a.m. on Thursday, January 24, 2002, while meditating on Jeremiah chapters 16 & 17, I felt the anointing of the Lord mightily upon me. Instantly, the room was filled with the presence of the Lord, and the Holy Spirit began ministering to me in the spirit. He illumined my mind, giving me a deeper insight (i.e. revelation) about the spiritual condition of Ghana, as well as

Africa and the world at large. God revealed to me (i.e. God enlightened my mind, as it were, to understand) the reason why there is so much fear, mistrust and a strong feeling of insecurity in the world today. Why there is no peace, or stability; and why many are poor, suffering and dying out of diseases (e.g. HIV-AIDS, etc.), hunger and poverty in the world, especially in Africa.

Since the Lord reveals in order to redeem, He taught me what must be done to effect a change in this miserable condition of humankind. I quickly grabbed a pen and a notebook and wrote down the message. The message, according to the Lord, was to be delivered first to my fellow Ghanaians, then to other Africans, and then finally, to the world at large. Just as in the past, God graciously revealed His secrets to the Prophets to be delivered to His people Israel, so the "*immortal, and the invisible, the only wise God*" (1 Timothy 1:17), who "*is the same yesterday, today and forever*" (Hebrews 13: 8), continues to speak to His church and all people everywhere. He does so through His anointed servants in visions and dreams today, as Amos declared, "*Surely the Sovereign Lord does nothing without revealing His plan to His servants the Prophets. The lion has roared–who will not fear? The Sovereign Lord has spoken–who can but prophesy*" (Amos 3: 7-8b)? Therefore, what follows is a divine message worthy of serious attention of all people under the sun, irrespective of race, color, gender or rank, who sincerely desire to be saved from their sins in order to "*flee from the coming wrath*" (Matthew 3:7c).

It must be noted for the purpose of clarification that although the vision was received on a particular day, writing down the entire message took me many months, almost two years (January, 2002-December, 2003). Before dawn each day, I would be awakened from sleep and the Lord would draw my attention to the message, and would add to it or straighten up what needed to be corrected. It is, therefore, very important to note, before going any forther that this vision is consistent with Scripture. Now, I invite you to read on with an attitude of humility, and openness of heart and mind. Expect the Lord to speak to you personally, so that you may "*know the truth and the truth shall set you free*" (John 8:32) from sin and from whatever entangles you. Then you will be able to serve and worship the Living God with joy and enthusiasm under the inspiration of the Holy Spirit.

'Gye Nyame'

The Akan compound word '*Gye Nyame*' is the name of a Ghanaian art pattern or symbol. Its meaning arises from the Ghanaian notion that "*nyimpa nnye, gye Nyame*". That is to say, "*humans are bad, except for God*" (i.e. only God is good), or "*with the exception* of *God, no one else is good.*" It is the same as the Ghanaian proverbial expression: "*Nyame nntse de Odasanyi*" ("*God is not like a human being.*"). This Ghanaian notion is commensurate with what the Scriptures say about God. For example, Numbers 23:19 states that, "*God is not a man, that He should lie, nor a son of man, that he should change His mind. Does He speak and not act? Does He promise and not fulfill?*" Psalms 92:15 *also states that, "The Lord is upright, He is my Rock, and there is no wickedness in Him."*

According to Professor Kwame Gyekye, Africans in general hold the religious concept that, "*goodness is the prime characteristic of God*" (*African Cultural Values*, 1996, P.9). This notion is in line with the Holy Scripture, which affirms that God is good and what He does is good (Psalms 119:68). But concerning human beings, it is written that, "*There is no one righteous, not even one*" (Romans 3:10). In other words, only God is good. Jesus echoed the same truth in His response to the rich young ruler, who came to Him with a burning question: "*Good teacher, what must I do to inherit eternal life?*" (Luke 18:18). Jesus answered him, saying: "*Why do you call me good? No one is good-except God alone*" (Luke 18:19). When the young ruler claimed to have obeyed the commandments from his youth, Jesus finally said to him: "*You still lack one thing. Sell everything you have and give to the poor, and you will have treasure in heaven. Then come, follow me*" (Luke 18:22).

But the man could neither sell his goods nor follow Jesus. Instead, "*he became very sad, because he was a man of great wealth*" (Luke 18:23). By failing to follow Jesus, the rich man portrayed his selfishness and greed, and lack of concern for the poor in his community. Thus, the Ghanaian/African expression,

'G*ye Nyame'*, is biblically and theologically sound. Another meaning of 'G*ye Nyame'* emerges from the African recognition of the unpredictability of the unforeseen, changing scenes of life. Thus, in saying "*Gye Nyame*", the Ghanaian/African is acknowledging the truth that we (humans) have no control over the daily affairs and circumstances of our earthly existence, except God, as the Scripture declares:

> *Unless the Lord builds the house, its builders labor in vain.*
> *Unless the Lord watches over the city, the watchmen stand guard in vain.*
> *In vain you rise up early and stay up late, toiling for food to eat—*
> *for God grants sleep for those He loves (Ps. 127: 1-2).*

James, the Apostle of the Lord, also underscores the same truth as he writes:

> *Now listen, you who say, "Today or tomorrow we will go to this or that city, spend a year there, carry on business and make money. "Why, you do not even know what will happen tomorrow. What is your life? You are a mist that appears for a little while and then vanishes. Instead, you ought to say, "If it is the Lord's will, we will live and do this or that." As it is, you boast and brag. All such boasting is evil* (James 4: 13-16).

In this connection, James calls everyone's attention to the necessity of submitting our plans to God, and to depend on Him for wisdom, guidance and strength to accomplish our aim in life. '*Gye Nyame*' stresses the African notion that God is powerful ('*Nyame ye tumfo'*), but humans are frail, and that without God, no human being is able to achieve or realize his dream/goal in life. An Akan (Ghanaian/African) maxim puts it this way: '*Ikwatsir kokromatsir a, renntum mmbo pow*', meaning, "*Without the thumb, one cannot tie a knot."* In the African concept, *"to tie a knot"* is to succeed in reaching a particular target or one's goal in life. Thus, when used in a full sentence, 'G*ye Nyame'* could be expressed as follows: *"Without God, all human efforts are fruitless."* Or to put it in another way, *"We (creatures) cannot make it without, our Maker (God)."*

Now, we may ask the question: "How were our ancestors, in their traditional religion, able to know or arrive at this truth about human beings on one side, and God on the other? I am convinced that our ancestors learned or gained this insight through intuition, as well as daily human experience, including observation of the environment or natural theology. Professor Kwame Gyekye expresses his view on this as he wrote, "Traditional African religion, not being a revealed religion, can only be regarded as a natural religion arising out of the people's own experience and view of this world" (*African Cultural Values, 1996, p.56*).

Hence, in Africa in general, and Ghana in particular, unlike other parts of the world, there are no atheists. The African believes in the existence of God, as well as other deities or spirits. Thus, every aspect of the African's life (e. g. birth, work, marriage, death, etc.) is permeated with religion. *"As a people,"* writes Appiah Kubi, *"the Akans make little or no distinction between religion and culture, which has religion at its base*" (Kofi Appiah—Kubi, Man Cures, God Heals, p. 5).

Now, with this introductory background, I warmly invite you to read on, and may you be richly blessed, as the Lord gives you insight into the truth revealed in this book.

CHAPTER ONE

GOD CREATED ALL HUMAN BEINGS EQUAL:

Through the ministration of the Holy Spirit, God confirmed to me (in the vision) the truth that all human beings, whether white, or black, or brown, male or female, all were created equal in the image of God as declared in the Holy Scriptures:

> *From one man (i.e. one blood) he made every nation of human beings, that they should inhabit the whole earth; and he determined the times set for them and the exact places where they should live. God did this so that human beings would seek him and perhaps reach out for him and find him, though he is not far from each one of us. For in him we live and move and have our being, . . . we are his offspring* (Acts 17:26-28; see also Genesis 1:26, 2:7).

On the same biblical principle of equality of the human race, 15 men representing 13 states of America, boldly wrote down the 'Declaration of Independence' on July 4, 1776, in the city of Philadelphia:

> *We hold these Truths to be self-evident, that all men*

> *are created equal that they are endowed by their Creator with certain unalienable Rights that among these are Life, Liberty, and the pursuit of Happiness. (Encyclopedia Americana-International version, by Grolier Incorporated-Vol. 8-p. 591).*

Therefore, as humans, we must realize that the physical differences we find among one another: either in our race, color, rank, or gender, like the various colors of the rainbow, altogether are intended to reveal the beauty of the handiwork of God, and also of the unity that exists among the Godhead—God, the Father, God, the Son, and God, the Holy Spirit (the Trinity), and also among humankind and the creation as a whole.

There is Power in Unity

Again, as we carefully observe ***"the white and black keys on the keyboard of the organ/piano,"*** we realize how much they *"illustrate the beauty and unity of the human* ***race,"*** declared the late Dr. Kwegyir Aggrey, a great son of Africa, born in Anomabu in the Central Region of Ghana. In their separate ways, each key (black or white) exists alone, producing a monotone whenever touched or played by anyone. But when played together by a competent musician, these same black and white keys produce sweet sounds of harmonious, melodious music capable of restoring peace in the mind and soul. It does impart healing to the sick both spiritually and physically, and eventually sets the troubled heart at rest.

Similarly, when we live in our various places with one purpose under God, there is no limit to what we can achieve for the benefit of the entire human race. For, God recognized power in unity when He saw the people united together to build the Tower of Babel and said:, "*If as one people speaking the same language they have begun to do this, then nothing they plan to do will be impossible for them*" (Genesis 11:6).

Nevertheless, the builders of the Tower of Babel failed, because they were full of pride, and determined to reach great heights without God, "*so that we may make a name for ourselves*", they said (Genesis 11:4b). But they failed miserably. For, it is written,

"Unless the Lord builds the house, its builders labor in vain. Unless the Lord watches over the city, the watchmen stand guard in vain" (Psalms 127:1).

Are There Godless Americans?

As I write, there are people in America, who, to my utter surprise, speak and act without reference to God, because they do not believe in the existence of God. For instance, an article published by the Washington Post on Sunday, November 3, 2002, showed pictures of people carrying placards, some of which read: *"Godless Americans March On Washington"; "Their Religion Our Money, No Way!!", "God is a Fairy Tale"; "Keep Your Gods Out Of Our Schools."* According to the report, the group consisted of *"atheists, agnostics, and other secular humanists"* numbering between 2000 and 3000 people with Ellen Johnson as their President. Here is part of what she said, *"Ladies and gentlemen, I see a sleeping giant that is waking up and is ready to assert its political and cultural influence."* She was reported to have announced, *"the creation of a 'godless' political action committee, which will henceforth be responsible for making their views heard on any political platform in America."*

Can you believe this? Who would have thought that America, of all nations, would have in its midst such a large number of people declaring themselves as "atheists." This is a nation whose founding fathers believed in God and boldly witnessed the same to the world by declaring their faith on their currency: "*In God We Trust.*" What has happened over the years to cause America to breed such a number of atheists, who have the inkling to raise their puny fists to the face of God? Are they not fearful of the Almighty God, who has the power to reduce humans to dust and ashes in a second by sniffing His life-giving breath out of us? (2 Kings 19:32-35; Luke 12:16-21).

The call to remove God, and for that matter, the Bible, out of schools is detrimental to our children, community, as well as the entire nation. Objection to teaching religion, especially, the Christian religion in schools was first made by a woman atheist and her advocates in the mid-sixties. Since then, the Bible has been taken out of the hands and bag-packs of school children, and from classrooms. Yet, it is written: *"The fear of the Lord—that is wisdom, and to shun evil is understanding"* (Job 28:28).

Taking God out of Schools Spells Danger

Now, if children are being educated to acquire just academic knowledge without "*the fear of God*", what do we expect the children to do with morality? It is obvious from what we are hearing that there are many homes where the Bible is not taught or read for family devotions. Since God is the source of all goodness and morality, what do we expect from these innocent school children brought up and trained in homes and schools, where the Bible or God has no place? Instead of Bibles, what do we find in the hands and bag-packs of these children nowadays? We find drugs and guns, by means of which school children have murdered their mates, teachers and parents. A typical example is the recent case of a 15-year old student, who shot and killed a fellow student— a good football player, of the same high school. When God is driven out of the classroom, the Devil sets up his kingdom there and reigns in the hearts and minds of innocent children and influences them to commit all kinds of evil deeds at home, schools, and streets, making every place unsafe for everyone.

Sharing his thoughts on America's schools in comparison with those of Ghana, Kwabena Aaron Jeter of Ohio University said, *"Living and teaching in Ghana the past four months has allowed me to compare many of the educational similarities and differences to those in America. Lack of funding, oversized classrooms, understaffed, and under paid teachers and administrators are all issues that burden many of America's school systems.*

"Unfortunately," Jeter continued, *"over the years as a result of legislation because of frequency of lawsuits, the word 'discipline' has been nearly erased in many of America's schools. Gangs, metal detectors, probation officers, and pregnant students are just some of the many challenges teachers are faced with on a daily basis.* The 1999 Columbine High School incident that occurred in Littleton, Colorado (where two students walked into school with semi-automatic rifles killing 12 students, one teacher, and then themselves)

will probably forever illustrate just how far America's schools and families have morally decayed. . . . That is not to say all of America's schools are suffering from these problems. But what I have noticed," says Jeter, "in my experience teaching and talking with many teachers is that despite the economic hardships that many people of Ghana endure everyday, they would never resort or accept the type of chaos that exists in many of America's schools" (Kwabena Aaron Jeter, *Wesley Grammar School Magazine — "Abrempon"*, 2000, p. 36).

I strongly hold the opinion that America is the strongest nation in the world today, because some of the founding fathers of the nation, if not all, believed in God and built their families, their communities, and their hopes on the Almighty God. For instance, *"John Witherspoon, James Madison, and George Washington," according to Leonard, "were practicing churchmen" (Bill J. Leonard, Early American Christianity*, 1983, P. *13).*

Being firm believers, they trusted in God as their Maker, Lord and Saviour, Provider, and Sustainer of their lives. They did not consider it a shameful act or a sign of weakness to acknowledge God and to practice their Christian faith publicly, as Leonard has pointed out in his book. Why? The basic reason was because they knew that they could not govern America and make it a strong nation without God's strength and guidance. Therefore, they relied completely on God in their leadership of the nation. Hence, God was on their side and they were able to withstand several trials of their time, such as the war for independence, the civil war, and more recently, the Cold War.

The September 11, 2001 Attacks

I am convinced it was the same faith, that the founding fathers had in God, that motivated thousands of Americans to hold on to God after the September 11, 2001 terrorist attacks on the World Trade Center in New York, and the Pentagon in the State of Virginia. That attack, which caused the loss of thousands of lives, and valuable property, was intended to destroy what I have come to describe as *"The Three Strong-holds of America"*, namely, *the Economic Power*—represented by the World Trade Center; *the Military*

Power—represented by Pentagon; and the Capital City, Washington, D. C., —representing *the Political Power of America.* The terrorists were aware that America's influence over the world depended on these most important sectors. Nevertheless, there is one other stronghold, and the most important of them all, which eluded the attackers, and that is "***Trust in God***," upon which the founding fathers built this great nation, and which is still held by millions of Christians in America today. That trust or faith in God causes many to pray to God daily for proection, unity and peace for America. Thus, by God's intervention, the plan to hit Washington was foiled by brave men and women on the hijacked-plane, who put their lives on the line, and crashed the plane before it could reach its target. May the souls of such loving, courageous, patriotic, departed citizens rest in perfect peace!

Commenting on the September 11 incident, Bishop John Bryson Chane of the Episcopal Diocese of Washington had this to say:

> *Those who carried out these attacks and killed so many innocent victims had deserted God and had, out of their own ignorance, fear and hatred chosen to desert the God of compassion, unconditional love and peace to follow a God they had created in their own minds—a graven image, an idol and a misrepresentation of the true God, who is at the center of Judaism, Christianity and Islam. They deserted the God of life and created a god of death (Washington Window, Vol. 73, No. 11, p.2).*

Though the loss of property together with precious lives created a deep wound in the souls of many families and homes, it could not break United States of America. As I have already pointed out, what the terrorists did not realize was that the soul of America, as far as believers are concerned, is hidden "*with Christ in God*" (Col. 3:3), and kept by the power of God. Therefore, no one can destroy America. "*For in Him we live and move and have our being*" as God's children (Acts 17:28). As some of us observed, the Sunday following the September 11 attacks, saw many churches full of worshippers praying to God, through Christ, to sustain America, and to comfort the families of those who had lost loved ones in the attacks. Thus, despite the enormous damage to human lives and the economy, America still goes on, upheld by the mighty hand of God.

Furthermore, the goodwill of the American people, moved by the love of God and compassion, coupled with the generous contributions from various companies and the hard work of agencies such as the Fire Service, Red Cross, and many individuals—all of these together, played a significant role in maintaining the morale of the bereaved families. All this, I believe, was a fulfillment of God's promise to meet the needs of all who trust in Him, and call on Him in time of trouble, as it is written in the Psalms: *"Call upon me in the day of trouble; I will deliver you, and you will honour me" (Ps. 50:15).* That is why *"Those who trust in the Lord," says the Psalmist, " are like Mount Zion, which cannot be shaken but endure forever"* (Psalms 125:1).

A Loud Wake-Up Call

What have we learned from these brutal, merciless attacks on America? I consider the attacks of September 11 as a loud, wake-up call to America, the most powerful nation in the world today, not to rely on its military, political, or economic power, or boast of what we are or can achieve. Neither should the leaders forget to look to God, who is the source of all power and wisdom for direction in their deliberations. For the Lord wants us all to understand that every nation is made up of imperfect, sinful human beings, and so whatever security system is put in place has a loophole, which the enemy can discover and use to destroy lives and property. That is why the Scripture admonishes us: *"Trust in the Lord with all your heart and lean not on your own understanding; in all your ways acknowledge Him, and He will make your paths straight. Do not be wise in your own eyes; fear the Lord and shun evil"* (Proverbs 3:5-7).

Unlike the builders of the Tower of Babel, and the emerging atheists of our time, we, who are American Christians, together with every true believer and lover of God and his neighbor, must not depend on our own ability in striving for justice, peace, nobility and success. Rather, we must depend on *the "Rock of Ages", "The*

Unmoved Mover", the Maker and Giver of all good things (both visible and invisible), who will supply whatever strength, wisdom and power we need to reach the zenith of our goal in this life, and in that which is to come. We must keep the tradition of the faith of our fathers by practical, daily living in close fellowship with Christ in order to *"obtain grace to help in time of need."* Writing to the Corrinthians about the hardships he and his team encountered in their missionary work, Paul shared the following:

> *We do not want you to be uninformed, brothers, about the hardships we suffered in the province of Asia. We were under great pressure, far beyond our ability to endure, so that we despaired even of life. Indeed, in our hearts we felt the sentence of death. But this happened that we might not rely on ourselves but on God, who raises the death. He has delivered us from such a deadly peril, and He will deliver us. On Him we have set our hope that He will continue to deliver us, as you help us by your prayers (2 Corinthians 1: 8-11).*

St. Paul and his team learned to trust in God and not in themselves. He asked for support in prayers from his fellow Christians for a successful ministry. Likewise, Americans, as a people seeking to stand for freedom, justice and peace, cannot achieve this lofty goal by themsselves, unless the Lord, the Source of life, freedom, justice and peace, is on their side. For *"apart from Me,* says Jesus, *"you can do nothing" (John 15: 5).*

Realizing the need for God in governance, George W. Bush, the 43rd president of the United States of America, looks to God for direction. He recounts instances of his predecessors, who relied on God in their hours of need. He wrote: *"the first president to live in this house composed a prayer on his second evening here for all who would follow him. Our 16th president, Abraham Lincoln, knew that his burdens were too great for any man, so he carried them to God in prayer. Over the radio on D-Day in 1944, Franklin Roosevelt prayed for God's blessing on our mission to 'set free a suffering humanity'" (Bush, George W., On God and Country, 2004, p.68).*

According to Thomas M. Freiling, President Bush is a practicing Christian, who *"believes in the God of the Bible, and His Son Jesus Christ. He believes in the power of prayer, and that all men and women are created equal by God. He believes the Bible commands us to love our neighbor and have compassion. He believes that evil exists in the world, that freedom is our God-given right, and that as Americans we have a duty to protect the rights of all people to be free.. . . He uses the Bible and prayer to find comfort and help, not to condemn or discriminate. Most importantly," says Freiling, "his religious beliefs are what drive his 'compassionate conservative' policies on issues like AIDS and his faith-based initiatives to help the poor and needy" (Ibid. p. 12).*

Thus, there is evidence that this great nation of ours—America, did not rise to greatness overnight, but by means of the power, wisdom and guidance of God, which the predecessors and successors together diligently and resiliently sought through daily prayer in Christ, including personal integrity, human dignity and hard work. The founding fathers have left a lasting legacy for the present and posterity to follow. Being a Christian, President Bush too, has learnt to lean upon God, and not solely on the strength of America. The following expresses his faith in the power, wisdom and guidance of God through prayer.

"Prayer teaches humility. We find that the plan of the Creator is sometimes very different from our own. Yet, we learn to depend on His loving will, bowing to purposes we don't always understand. Prayer can lead to a grateful heart, turning our minds to all the gifts of life and to the great works of God. Prayer can also contribute to the life of our nation. America is a strong nation, in part because we know the limits of human strength. All strength must be guided by wisdom and justice and humility. We pray that God will grant us that wisdom, that sense of justice and humility in our current challenges, and in the years ahead" (Ibid. p. 71-72).

It is gratifying to note here that President George W. Bush, as a firm believer in Christ, is determined to follow the path of his predecessors, who laid the foundation of this nation on a solid ground through faith in God. Like those who came before him, Bush has learned that to succeed as a Leader, he must wait on the Lord in prayer always. In that, he believes strongly that he will find strength, comfort and peace from the Word of God. As the Prophet, Isaiah declared:

> *He* [the Lord] *gives strength to the weary, and increases the power of the weak. Even youths grow tired and weary, and young men stumble and fall; but those who hope in the Lord Will renew their strength. They will sour on wings like eagles; they will run and not grow weary, they will walk and not be faint* (Isaiah 40:29-31).

It is, therefore, the wisest thing to do to put God first in all our plans and to look to Him, who alone, is the Source of our life, strength, wisdom and power, for achieving our purpose in life. My dear friend, are you working with God today, or are you going along without Him? God is interested in all the good things we want to do to make life meaningful and profitable. Knowing our human frailty, God is more than willing to help us reach our target; as He declared to the Prophet Jeremiah: *"I am the Lord, the God of all humankind. Is anything too hard for me?"* (Jeremiah. 32:27). This message from God came as an answer to Jeremiah's prayer, when he was unable to understand why God would ask him to buy from his uncle a land in Jerusalem, which God had declared was shortly to be destroyed.

Nevertheless, God's promise surely came through for Jeremiah, in that when the Babylonian army came down to destroy Jerusalem, and to take the Jews captive, he was spared, and given a captain who took good care of him. Besides, the copies of the deed of purchase of that plot of land was kept in a clay jar, which lasted for a long time -that is, seventy years—it was protected by the power of God—until the return of the Jews from captivity (Jeremiah 32:6-16). Just as God proved faithful to Jeremiah, because he trusted in Him, so will God be faithful to anyone or nation, who will trust in Him. But, unless we give God a chance in our lives as individuals, and as a people, regardless of who we are, and where we live under the sun, we cannot experience God's presence among us, let alone His love and faithfulness.

Every Nation is Gifted with Some Knowledge About God

The Holy Spirit further made me understand that since God made every human being in His own image, everyone of us has the ability to recognize the existence of God (Rom. 1:20); because God has planted within each person's soul the spark of the divine seed (Gen. 1:26). Therefore, no one is ignorant of the existence of God. However, due to the broken human condition (i.e. our sinful nature through the Fall of humanity), we cannot, by our own human effort, know God, love God, and serve God, or do His will (Psalms 53:2-3; Romans 3:23).

Unfortunately, there are people, who deny the existence of God because of pride, rebellion and selfishness. They do not want anybody, not even God, to tell them what to do or not to do. They want to have their own way of life, and be the captains of their own ship. To such people, the Word of God declares that:

> *. . . what may be known about God is plain to them, because God has made it plain to them. For since the creation of the world God's invisible qualities—his eternal power and divine nature-have been clearly seen, being understood from what has been made, so that people have no excuse* (Romans 1:19-20).

The different names by which God is called by different tribes and people throughout the world, underscores the truth that majority of humans, if not all, believe in the existence of God. For example, before the Gospel reached the shores of the West Coast of Africa through European missionaries, ancestors of Ghana believed in the existence of God. In his book, "*African Cultural Values*", Kwame Gyekye echoed this truth: "The African world into which European Christian Missionaries entered in the late seventeenth century was a religious world in which the idea of God as the

Supreme Being was already known and held by the people. Their idea of God is proved by the various names and appellations they attribute to God according to their various religious experiences." For instance, the Akans call God, *'Boadze/Boadee'* (Creator); *'Enyiansombea'* (All -Seeing); *'Totrobonsu'* (The Giver of sun and rain); *'Nyankopon'* (The best of all friends); *'Twerduammpon'* (Dependable One-the unmovable Tree capable of supporting all who lean upon Him); *'Nyame'* (Fante/Twi); *'Nyomo'* (Ga); *'Mawu'* (Ewe); *Allah* (Hausa/Islam), *'Olu'* (Yoruba), *'Chineke'* (Ibo).

Ghanaian Artistic Symbols

Beside the various names, our ancestors used symbols and artistic patterns to speak of God or present a theological message (e.g. Fig. 1 below). I have learnt through this vision that of all the names assigned to various African symbols, the most important one to which we must give our deepest thought is "Gye Nyame".

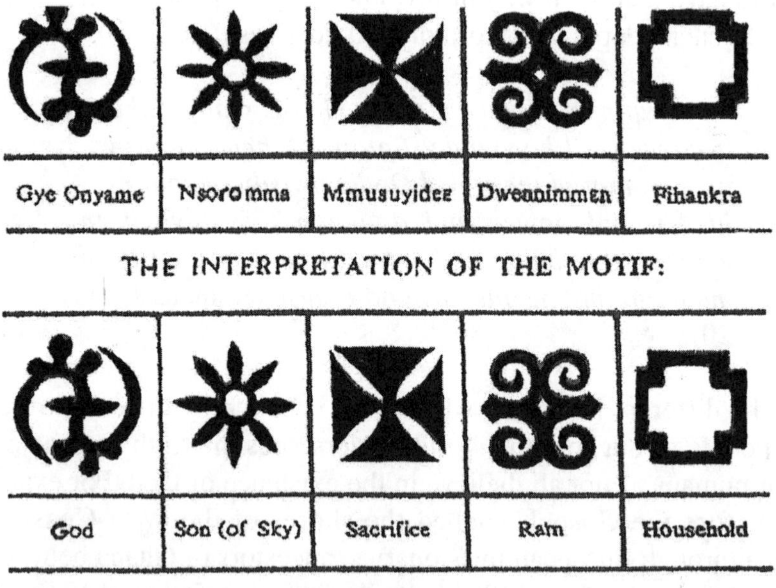

GOD'S SON BECAME A SACRIFICIAL LAMB FOR THE HOUSEHOLD

FIG.2

That expression means, just as we cannot tie a knot without the thumb, so we cannot tie up or put our broken life together or succeed (in life—according to God's standard) without God, Who is "*The Alpha And The Omega, Who is, and Who was, and Who is to come*" (Revelation 1: 8). As the Lord spoke with John at Patmos, so the Lord gave me insight to know from this vision that due to the Fall of Adam and Eve, every human being, as a descendant of Adam and Eve, is contaminated with sin. Therefore, every aspect of our life is affected by sin, and it is only God, our Maker, (like the potter), who can put us back together again. That is to say, God is the only One, who can recreate us in His image. It is God alone, whose prime characteristic is goodness, who can make us whole again as before, and as good and upright as He wants us to be, so as to fulfill His eternal purpose, which is good, for every human being on earth. Apart from God, our Maker, nothing can transform humanity to achieve their divine purpose or realize their God-given destiny.

Each Symbol Bears a Sign of a Cross

Did you notice a sign of a cross in each of the symbols in fig. 1 at page 37? Take a careful look at each symbol from the first to the last, and you will strangely see a croos in each of them. Isn't that wonderful? Just as all the five symbols together convey the message that ***"God's Son became a sacrificial lamb for the household,"*** even so each individual symbol bearing a cross conveys to all readers **the GOOD NEWS of the message of Christ's death at Calvary for the salvation of humankind.** Thanks be to God for giving our ancestors the creative ability do design these powerful symbols with such divine messages. Though they did not realize the full benefits of these symbols, I strongly believe they were divinely led to create them for us and our posterity. It was to understand these sybolic messages and to treasure and derive from them their full benefits that God graciously gave me this vision. Otherwise, we would still be ignorant of the blessings God has instore for us. *"In the past God overlooked such ignorance," says Paul, "but now He commands all people everywhere to repent*" (Acts17: 30).

That is why the Lord asked me to put in writing the message of this vision, so that all people every where, particularly, my fellow

Africans, may get hold of the power of God in Christ that has overcome the world, namely, faith in God's love revealed in Jesus Christ on the Cross (John 3: 14-16). We shall discuss the Cross later on in much detail. Let us now return to our discussion on the various names of God as discovered by the Hebrews.

The Hebrews (i.e. the Israelites) also have different names for God as a result of the various encounters they had with God in their history. For instance, Hagar called God: "*Beer lahai Roi*", meaning, "*You are the God who sees me*" (Genesis 16 13-14). This happened when God graciously sent His angel to rescue Hagar and her child from imminent death. She thought no one cared for her, but God did. Gideon, too, called God *"El-Shalom,"* which means *"God is Peace"* (Judges 6:24).

In a booklet, "*God Is*", written by the World Church of God, there is further information, explaining various names ascribed to God by the Hebrews/Jews, which we find in the Holy Scriptures, as follows: *'Yahweh'* or *'Jehovah'* designates God in a covenant relationship with those He created. *'Yahweh'* means 'the Eternal-the Immutable One-the Everlasting God' (Genesis 21:33); *'Yahweh-Tsidkenu'('Yahweh,* our righteousness') (Jeremiah 23:6); "*El*" (The Almighty, the Omnipotent); '*Elohim'* (in all his strength, the God who possesses all) (Genesis 14:18-22); *'El Shaddai'* (The God Almighty, is the all-bountiful giver of grace. He supplies all the needs of his people) (Genesis 17:1)" (Thomas Nelson, Inc., *God Is*, 1992, pp. 12-13).

These names, to mention only a few, should be enough to indicate that throughout human history, from one generation to another, God has graciously revealed Himself in diverse ways to humanity in our different situations and cultures in the world. Therefore, the phrase, *"Gye Nyame"* is loaded with meaning. More importantly, the title of this book, *"Living by the Power of God"* expresses the fact that the life of all human beings, as creatures of God, is so much rooted in God that unless the Lord be with us at every step of our earthly life, every human effort is vain. In other words, every successful venture by any person or group of people or nation is not possible without God's Power. For without His 'breath', i.e., His life-giving Spirit, {Genesis 2:7}) in us, we on our own are but dust and ashes. Indeed, without our Maker, we can do nothing. For many centuries, one nation after another had failed to make their mark, because they abandoned the Maker of this world, whose kingdom rules over all. This is the message, which the Lord, God Almighty, wants me to communicate not only to Ghanaians, but also, to all Africans, and the world at large.

CHAPTER TWO

HINDRANCES TO AFRICA'S SUCCESS & PROSPERITY

It was further revealed to me that the majority of African countries, including Ghana, are lagging behind in development, because the national builders, namely, our ancestors-the founding fathers, traditional chiefs, political leaders, priests, people in authority, including all of us as human beings, did not put God first in our plans. Though in Ghana, for instance, our ancestors believed in the existence of *"Nyame"* (God), and called Him by different names, they did not really know God in the biblical sense of the word; neither did they seek Him with the view to worshipping Him "*in spirit and in truth*" (John 4: 24).

Kwame Gyekye wrote the following: "*A European traveler to West Africa around the end of the seventeenth century observed that the Africans believed in a supreme God, that they had 'an idea of the true God, and ascribe to Him the attributes of Almighty and Omnipresent; they believe He created the universe, but they do not pray to Him or offer sacrifices to Him.*'" (Gyekye, Kwame, *African Cultural Values*, 1996, pp.3-4).

When the Bible speaks of *'knowing God'*, it refers to *having a close relationship with God*. For instance, in Genesis chapter 4:1, it is written, "*And Adam knew Eve his wife; and she conceived and gave birth to Cain.*" That is to say, Adam entered into 'intimate relationship' or had sexual intercourse with his wife and the result was a product of a child, which is also a gift from God and not from any other god, goddess or ancestors, as heathens are made to believe. Thus, to know God, is to have a close and personal relationship with Him, comparable, in a sense, to the relationship between husband and wife.

Another example could be cited from the message of the prophet Hosea, expressing God's lamentation over His people: *"my people are destroyed for lack of knowledge"* (Hosea 4:6). That means, Israel's rejection of instruction from God's Word through the Prophets of God, has made them so ignorant that they do not know how to live in a covenant relationship with God. They were no longer following God's way of righteousness, or His commandments. Their rebellious attitude had separated them from God, and were no longer under God's arm of protection. As a result, they were being destroyed by their enemies (Deuteronomy 28:25f.). Similarly, the failure of our ancestors to know and worship the true God (Nyame), made it impossible for them to build the land of Africa on a firm foundation, which could stand the storms and turmoils of life. Consequently, like Israel, the African continent crumpled under various attacks from European traders, who scrambled for the riches of Africa, which we shall discuss in the next paragraph.

The Partition of Africa

This is what Europeans did in partitioning Africa, as R. R. Palmer and Colton wrote:

"The Berlin conference of 1885 had laid down, for expansion in Africa, certain rules of the game— a European power with holding on the coast had prior rights in the back country; occupation by administratotrs or troops; and each power must give proper notice to the others as to what territories it considered its own. A wirld scramble for 'real occupation' followed. In fifteen years the entire continent was parceled out" (R. R. Palmer and J. Colton, *A Modern History of the World*, p. 623). How was the land distributed? The writers continue: "First, somewhere in the wilderness, would appear a handful of white men, bringing their inevitable treaties— sometimes printed forms. To get what they wanted, the Europeans commonly had to ascribe powers to the chief which by the customs of the tribe he did not possess—powers to convey sovereignty, sell land, or grant mining concessions" (Ibid. p. 623). The only African nation, which stood against the whites was Ethiopia, as Palmer reports: *Some 80,000 Ethiopians, however, slaughtered and routed 20,000 Italians in pitched battle at Adowa in 1896. It was the first time that native Africans sucessfully defended themselves against the whites, and it discouraged invasion of Ethiopia by the Italians (or other Europeans) for forty years(Ibid.626).*

The rest of the African continent was taken with ease by the Europeans. Let's take the following example: between 1882 and 1884, H. M. Stanley, who returned to the Congo from Europe, *"concluded treaties with over 500 chiefs, who in return for a few trinkets or a few yards of cloth put their crude marks on the mysterious papers and accepted the blue-and-gold flag of the Association,*" known as 'an International Congo Association, founded at Brussels in 1878, with a few financiers,' including Leopold II, king of Belgium (Ibid. p. 621).

The next question to ask is, What happened to the natives after their lands had been taken away from them? Palmer provides us with the answer as follows: *"Labor was the overwhelming problem....The result was that Europeans all over Africa resorted to forced labor. Or the new government, once installed, might allocate so much land to Europeans as private property(another foreign conception) that the local tribe could no longer subsist on the lands that remained to it. Or the whole tribe might be moved to a reservation, like Indians in the United States*" (Ibid. 624). Thus, Africans were not only dispossessed of their native lands, but also, displaced and demoralized by the European settlers. Read again, the follwing report:

> *In any case, while the women tilled the fields or tended the stock at home, the men would move off to take jobs under the whites for infinitesimal pay. The men then lived in "compounds," away from family and tribal kindred; they became demoralized; and the labor they gave, unintelligent and unwilling,*

> *would scarcely have been tolerated in any more civilized community. In these circumstances everything was done to uproot the Africans, and little was done to benefit them. The old tribal or village society collapsed, and nothing replaced it* (Ibid. p. 624).

This ill-treatment of Africans by Europeans must help my fellow Africans and all other readers of this book to understand why Africans are lagging behind in many areas of development—spiritually, economically, politically, and technologically. What can we do to avert the situation? We don't have to continue to live in this quagmire of degradation the rest of our lives. Or like the story of the four leprous men sitting outside the gate of Samaria, we have to ask ourselves the question: *"Why (must we) stay here until we die?"* (2 Kings 7:3b). The four lepers, as the story goes, gathered up courage and rose up at dawn and went in faith to the camp of the Arameans, who had besieged the city of Samaria for weeks. When they reached the camp, the Aramean soldiers had ran away for their lives, deserting the camp, *"for the Lord had caused the Arameans to hear the sound of chariots and horses and a great army, so that they said to one another, 'Look, , the king of Israe has hired the Hittite and Egyptian kings to attack us!' So they got up and fled in the dusk and abandoned their tents and their horses and donkeys. They left the camp as it was and ran for their lives*" (2 Kings 7: 6-7). We know from the rest of this story that, not only did the Good Lord save and provide the four leprous men with enough food for themselves, but also, through their witness, the entire city of Samaria and its surrounding towns, were saved from the Aramaen domination, and food was in abundance. In his comment, Haddon Robbinson put it this way:

> *You and I have discovered that salvation is found in Jesus Christ. It is a breakdown of basic integrety to keep that truth to ourselves. If we have found the cure for a guilty conscience, If we have found the food of life, we are obligated to share it with others. Evangelism is one hungry beggar telling another*

> *beggar where to find bread.*
> (Haddon Robinson, Daily Bread, February 23, 2005).

Therefore, despite our present predicament, let those of us who believe in Christ, rise up with faith, and boldly approach the throne of God with a plea for deliverance, and the Lord, Who delivered Samaria from war and hunger through the faith of four, sickly outcasts—the lepers—is still a miracle-worker and in the business of deliverance, and will certainly deliver us, too.

Bribery and Corruption

In many cultures of the world, black or white, it is customary for individuals to express their gratitude to their benefactors by presenting to them gifts in cash or kind for kindness done. However, if the gift precedes the act of kindness, it is tantamount to bribery, because the person concerned is naturally influenced by the weight of the gift to act contrary to his will or conscience. This happens in various circumstances of life. For example, if three people—*Abudoso, Bolewa*, and *Cuboro* (not using their real names) have applied for the same job position as *salesmen* in a corporation, it is up to the management to choose the best out of the three applicants. During the interview, *Abu* proves to be the best, yet *Cuboro* is hired for the job, because prior to the interview, he had offered a gift of substantial amount through a friend to the chief executive. So *Cuboro* starts work, but fails to measure up to expectation. Sales drop considerably and the corporation encounters losses of income/profit. Under normal circumstances, *Cuboro* should be fired immediately, but the chief executive cannot do it due to the bribe he had received. If the situation is not remedied, it will result in the closure of the entire business, simply because of someone's incompetence, selfishness and greed.

This has happened to countless sectors of the resources of the African continent and thus hindered our progress as a people. A notable example was cited by Palmer and Colton in the following report:

> *All Africa inland from the coasts was considered to*

> *be, like America in the time of Columbus, a "terra nullius," without government and claimed by nobody, wide open to the first civilized persons who might arrive. Stanley, returning to the Congo in1882, in a year or two concluded treaties with over 500 chiefs, who in return for a few trinkets or a few yards of cloth put their crude marks on the mysterious papers and accepted the blue-and-gold flag of the Association* (Ibid. p. 621).
>
> It is for this reason that the Scriptures offer strict warning to judges, kings and people in authority against receiving gifts, as follows:
>
> *Do not deny justice to your poor people in their lawsuits. Have nothing to do with a false charge and do not put innocent or honest person to death, for I will not acquit the guilty. Do not accept a bribe, for a bribe blinds those who see and twists the words of the righteous* (Exodus 23: 6-8). *Follow justice, and justice alone, so that you may possess the land the Lord your God is giving you (Deuteronomy* 16: 20)

We are aware that the majority of countries in Africa are politically independent, yet for many reasons, notably, bribery and corruption, mismanagement and nepotism, they are still tied up to the apron strings of their colonial masters or governments. As stated in the above Scriptures, we shall not possess the land, unless we follow justice, because "*righteousness exalts a nation, but sin is a disgrace to any people*" (Proverbs 14: 34).

It has also been noted that lack of faith in God through Christ, reliance on the powers of other gods and ancestral spirits, the practice of occultism by the elite, as discussed in the previous passages, had plunged the continent of Africa into darkness and poverty.

What can we do to rise out of this darkness and poverty to follow the light of God, which leads to peace and prosperity? Since *"all have sinned and fall short of the glory of God,"* none of us is exempted; we are all part of the problem. Therefore, we must repent, and turn to the Lord for the answer to our problem. Let's always remember the Truth, which the Lord has spoken and which will never be altered: *"I am the Way and the Truth and the Life. No one can come to the Father except through Me. Without Me, you can do nothing"* (John 14: 6, 15: 5). *"Come to Me,"* He says, *"and I will give you rest"* (Matthew 11: 28).

In order to understand our past and to come out clean to seek the Living God with all our heart, and soul, and mind, as one people, we need to explore further the religious background of our ancestors, as we discuss the following subject.

What God Did our Ancestors Worship?

This is a legitimate question, which needs to be considered. "If our ancestors did not worship God, the Creator of the universe, then, what kind of god did they worship and call upon in times of need?" The undeniable, honest answer to this probing question is that our ancestors worshipped other gods and goddesses (as some still do today). They called on these gods in times of trouble. Anyway, could these gods/goddesses save anybody from sin, misfortunes, poverty, disease, or death? The answer is capital NO!

Just as the people of Israel fell prey to their enemies for forsaking the true God, (*Yahweh*), so have we become victims to capitalist nations of Europe, selfish, political leaders in Africa, demonic forces, and our arch-enemy, the Devil, *"who comes only to steal, to kill, and to destroy" (John 10: 10).*

In this connection, the Lord reminded me of my studies on African Traditional Studies, under the tutorage of Reverends Joseph DeGraft Johnson (deceased) and Dr. J. K. Agbetie, both of Trinity College, Legon, in Accra, Ghana (1968-72), now known as Trinity Theological Seminary. Furthermore, both my Masters and Doctoral Studies, which were completed at Wesley Theological Seminary in Washington, D. C., under Professors Josiah Young, Recinos, James Shopshire and James Logan (1988-93), to mention only a few, gave me access to books on African Theology. These studies enabled me to understand the religious world-view (cosmology) of our African ancestors, which is discussed in detail in the next chapter.

CHAPTER THREE

ANCESTRAL WORLDVIEW

Our ancestors viewed the world as consisting of a hierarchy of spirit-beings with the Supreme Being at the apex. Below the Supreme Being (*"Nyame"*) are the ancestors, followed by other gods, then lesser gods (such as dwarfs). At the bottom of the hierarchy of spirit-beings is Satan-the Devil, called in Akan "*Sasambonsam.*" Besides, there is an Akan myth about the transcendence of God. The story has it that long ago, God (*Nyame*) was so close to human beings that one could easily reach out to Him in the sky. However, one day an old woman accidentally hit *Nyame's* dwelling place with a pestle while pounding *"fufu"* (mashed plantain/yam/cassava). She apologized to God, and begged Him to move up a little further. God agreed and went up a little as requested. Then the pestle hit God again, and again. Therefore, *Nyame* went up so high that no human being could or can ever see or hit God anymore, forever. Funny and unrealistic as this story may seem, it does explain for the African the transcendence of God—the reason why no one can see or reach God.

"In traditional African religion," says Gyekye, *"God is the Supreme Being but not the object of direct worship. Worship is directed to trees, rocks, rivers, and mountains, and rivers. . .. It is believed that objects of nature are inhabited by spiritual beings or deities who are thought to exist in the universe as intermediaries*

between God and humans but who cannot be seen by the human eye" (Ibid. p.6-7). Whatever reason that might have prevented our forefathers from worshipping the true God, the Lord made me understand that it was a choice they made themselves. Nobody forced them to make that choice or decision to worship other gods. Just as our first parents, Adam and Eve, made a conscious decision to obey the voice of the serpent (i.e. Satan) instead of God's, so our ancestors, having observed their environment, decided to worship other gods and spirits. They poured libation and sacrificed to them and the dead ancestors with the hope that they would receive both spiritual and material support from them. In his book, Towards African Theology, J. S. Pobee, wrote:

> *The idea of mediator between God and man is not foreign to him (i.e. the African). The West African nature gods are said to be children of God, sent by Him as His representatives in human form*; they can *be seen, whether in the natural phenomenon or in the symbol placed in their shrine (e. g. rock, tree, or river) and so it is easier for man to approach them with offerings and prayer than the invisible high God. (John S. Pobee, Towards African Theology, p. 48).*

Indeed, what Pobee has said in the above passage is quite true, and I have a personal testimony to substantiate it.

A few days after my graduation from the Trinity Theological Seminary in Accra, Ghana, I went home to visit with my mother and the family. The entire family members of my dad and mom had gathered in the family room to welcome me home. After a few words of welcome, the elder of the family (Nana Kojo Kum, not his real name) took a cupful of schnapps (called "akpeteshie"— a hard liquor brewed locally) ready to pour libation as a-thank-offering to the gods and ancestors. But, I respectfully restrained him, because the Lord had made me know the Truth that pouring libation to gods and ancestors is tantamount to idol worship. Though I have great respect for Nana Kum as the elder of the family or clan, I decided, like Peter, to "*obey God rather than men*" (Acts 5: 29). Therefore, I offered a prayer, thanking God, Who had saved me from sin and imminent death, and graciously prepared me for His ministry. After praying, I invited them to join me in saying the Lord's Prayer, which they did amicably.

The following morning, when I was about to leave for Kumasi, Nana Kum asked me for a bottle of schnapps/whisky as a fee for juju/voodoo, which he said would give me protection and power for a successful ministry. Once again, I politely refused his seemingly good offer. I strongly assured him that the Almighty God, Who called me into the ministry of His Son, Jesus Christ, would never leave me nor forsake me. He will ever be my Guide, my Strength, my Wisdom, my Salvation and my All-In-All. At this point, realizing that I was fully dependent on the Lord for everything, he shook hands with me, and wished me success. Indeed, I knew he meant well and wanted to help me succeed in life, but, his source of power for success (i.e. juju/voodoo), was completely in conflict with my Christian Faith. One year later, while on vacation, I went back home and shared the Gospel with my people, including Nana Kum. For the Scriptures forbid us to worship any other gods (Exodus 20: 1—6). Therefore, it is the duty of those of us who are privileged to know God through Christ to reach out with the Good News to our pepole in oder that Christ may draw them from the power of darkness into the marvelous light of His kingdom.

The Elite and Occultism

I have been made to know by God's revelation that whereas some of our ancestors or people in authority consulted diviners, or medicine men or spirits of the dead, some of the elite of our African societies and most countries of the world delve in occultism. According to Webster's Dictionary, the *"elite*" refers *to "a socially superior group; a powerful minority group —inside government*" or ruling class of the community, including others in institutions, corporations, the army, the police, the church, etc. Then, what is occultism? It is *"belief or study of the action or influence of supernatural powers*" (Webster'sNew Collegiate Dictionary, p.794). Owing to their high positions in government or society and the respect accorded them, they indulge in these practices secretly.

Hence, no member dares to divulge what takes place behind their closed doors. Norman Mackenzie writes that for most of them, the purpose of joining the group is mainly for *"self-development,"* which is not wrong in itself. However, since members seek power or influence or success from other spirits or angels and deities other than God, the Creator, and the Father of our Lord, and Savior, Jesus Christ, and the Holy Spirit, they violate the Word of God, and incur the anger of God. As it is written:

> *Ahab, son of Omri did more evil in the eyes of the Lord than any of those before him. He not only considered it trivial to commit the sins of Jeroboam son of Nebat, bur he also married Jezebel daughter of Ethbaal king of the Sidonians, and began to serve Baal and worship him. He set up an altar for Baal in the temple of Baal that he built in Samaria. Ahab also made an Asherah pole and did more to provoke the Lord, the God of Israel, to anger than did all the kings of Israel before him* (I Kings 16: 30-33).

We incur God's displeasure when we reject Him, Who made us in His image, to worship fallen angels, other deities or spirit beings, who are creatures other than God, the Creator. Sometimes, such supernatural beings may help one to attain certain positions of authority, but in the end, there is disappointment, and shame. That is the main reason why we have been cautioned repeatedly in this book by the following Scripture: "*Unless the Lord builds the house, its builders labor in vain. Unless the Lord watches over the city, the watchmen stand guard in vain*"(Psalm 127: 1).

The pity is that sometimes, we may not even be aware of the magnitude of our sinful behavior, until it is revealed to us. Let me share with you my own testimony here. Though I had personally not poured libation prior to my coming to Wesley Seminary, and had previously withstood the pouring of libation by my family elder, yet in my studies, I had somehow allowed myself to be influenced by opinions of other writers on African theology, and to some extent, compromised my stand on libation. Thus, in the presentation of my thesis, I wrote in favor of libation, describing it as an acceptable African way of prayer, as follows:

> *Libation is an appeal made to Nyame-the Source of all things, Before turning to any other in the hierarchy of being. After God, a portion of the wine is poured to Asaase Yaa (Mother Earth) and also to the ancestors, and finally to the other deities or gods. Libation is therefore a traditional way of praying* (John A. K. Bonful, *Applying Both Hands to the Plough: Preaching and Healing Ministries of the Church*....1993, p. 33).

Now, guess what happened next. A few weeks after graduation, while I was still in Washington, I had a dream in which I saw myself sitting together with idol worshippers on a bench before a diviner's shrine back home in Ghana. In my confusion, I asked the Lord during my early morning meditation for the meaning of the dream. He said to me: *"Since you have written in favor of libation, and are willing to teach others to do the same,* aren'*t you just like one of those heathens, who worship other gods.?*" That was an eye-opener to me. I realized that it is always necessary for believers to stick uncompromisingly to the Truth revealed in God's Word, instead of following a tradition or opinions of theologians, or respectable people in authority. Traditional rites or opinions of people, however high, HAVE NOT and WILL NEVER SAVE anybody. The only exception is when such an opinion or tradition does not conflict with the Scriptures. I thank God that using the dream, He made me realize my mistake and quickly drew me away from it before I could impart it to anybody else. We must always be on the alert, lest we fall or be deceived (1 Corinthians 10: 12).

Here is another example. The most senior leader of an elite group has been selling books on *occultism* to new members. Then, on one occasion, the Lord sent me to convey the following message to him:*"If you have been selling Bibles to your members, you will have helped to lead some to heaven. But since you have been selling books on occultism, you have sent more people to hell than you can imagine*". Naturally, this *big boss* was upset on hearing these words. But I assured him that the Lord loves him and does not want him and others to be condemned and destroyed in hell fire; that was why He sent me to him. Besides, as a messeger of the Lord, I love him, too; hence, I did not hesitate to bring him God's message of warning and of salvation—salvation which is possible through faith in Jesus Christ alone, and none else. At this point, he seemed to have calmed down and, after a few words of conversation, I prayed with him. But, lest I forget, I want you to know that this man was *a leader and a preacher* in a local church in Ghana, yet God knew that he had not surrendered his life to Christ. Years later, the *big boss* of the elite group died, and only God knows where he will spend eternity—whether with God in heaven or with Satan in hell.

A third example was the case of a seasoned minister, who gained fame in the healing ministry. After several years of ministry in various places, complaints reached his Bishop and church authorities that he was indulging in occultism and that his powers of healing were not of the Lord. Investigations conducted on him, including other witnesses proved him guilty of violating the Church's dotrinal principles of ministry. The minister was prematurely retired from the ministry.

At this juncture of our discussion, I think Isaiah's question to his fellow Jews when they delved in idolatrous practices is relevant: "*And when they shall say unto you, seek unto them that have familiar spirits, and unto wizards that peep, and mutter: should not a people inquire of their God? Why consult the dead on behalf of the living*?" (Isaiah 8:19).

My brothers and sisters, there are two questions in the above passage that require answers:

(i) *Should people not inquire after their God?* The answer is emphatic "Yes!" The Good God graciously invites all the people of this world to seek Him, saying, *"call upon me in the day of trouble; I will deliver you and you will honour me"* (Psalm 50:15).

Again He says, *"Turn to me and be saved, all you ends of the earth; for I am God and there is no other"* (Isa.45: 22). In other words, there is no other god or power that can deliver human beings from the original problem of sin, insecurity and chaos, except God, ('Gye Nyame'), *Jehovah, The "I AM WHO I AM"* (Exodus 3:14), *the UNCHANGEALE ONE.*

(ii) The second question is, *"Why consult the dead on behalf of the living?"* (Isaiah 8:19). The reason is that human beings want quick answers to their problems; and they want always to follow the path of easy resistance to obtain their heart's desire. But, it is demonic, and those who follow such ways soon fall into the snare of the Devil, as we have noted in the previous passages.

King Saul Consults the Dead

Take, for example, the case of Saul, the first king of Israel. Samuel, who played the double roles of priest and prophet of Israel at that time, had died. God no longer spoke to Saul through a prophet, or dream or Urim, because of his disobedience to the Word of the Lord, which He had previously sent to him through Samuel. Besides, Saul was embittered against David and wanted to kill him, because David had killed Goliath and won more praises from the women than Saul had done. The women danced as they sang: *"Saul has slain his thousands, and David his tens of thousands."* (I Samuel 18:7). Saul was very angry with this and said, rather jealously, *"They have credited David with tens of thousands, but me with only thousands. What more can he get but the kingdom?"* From now on, the cordial relationship between Kind Saul and David turned to hatred and jealousy as stated in the following text, *"And from that time on Saul kept a jealous eye on David"* (1 Samuel 18:7-9). He knew that David would be the next King of Israel instead of his son, Jonathan; so Saul was not only jealous of David, but he hated him and wanted him dead.

What made matters worse still for King Saul was that the Philistines were pressing on furiously against him for battle. His strong and faithful captain, David, was out of sight, hiding away from his master, Saul, knowing that Saul wanted to kill him. In his frustration, King Saul disguised himself and sought for help from a witch (medium) at Endor. There, he consulted the spirit of Samuel for advice on the impending battle. But it was too late, now. When the spirit of Samuel was called up, he said to Saul, *"Why have you disturbed me by bringing me up?"* Saul replied, *"I am in great distress. The Philistines are fighting against me, and God has turned away from me" (1 Samuel 28:15*). Then Samuel continued:

> *Why do you consult me, now that the Lord has turned away from you and become your enemy? The Lord has done what He predicted through me. The Lord has torn the kingdom out of your hands and given it to . . . David. Because you did not obey the Lord, the Lord will hand over both Israel and you to the Philistines, and tomorrow you and your sons will be with me (1Samuel 28:8-19).*

It is worthy of note that, though through divination of the witch at Endor, the spirit of the Prophet Samuel was consulted by Saul, he could not offer Saul the help he very much needed, namely, power to overcome the invading, Philistine army, because God has neither commanded human beings to seek help from the dead, nor empowered the spirit of the dead to help the living.

We need to be reminded here that earlier on in his reign, when King Saul was in good standing with God, he courageously carried out a religious reformation during which he purged the land of Israel of all wizards, witches and all acts of witchcraft and divination (See 1 Samuel 28:3) in accordance with God's commandment in Leviticus 20:27f.,"*A man or woman who is a medium or spiritist (that is, a wizard) among you must be put to death. You are to stone them; their blood will be on their own heads"*.

Saul was therefore aware of the Scriptures that God wanted His people to depend totally upon Him at all times for fulfillment of their needs, and not to turn to any other god or goddess or spirit of the dead for help. God says, *"Call upon me in the day of trouble; I will deliver you and you will honor me"* (Psalms 50:15). Then, also, in I Peter 5:7, we have another comforting promise, *"Cast all your anxiety upon him because he cares for you."* With these and many other wonderful promises of our faithful God, the Father Almighty, whose promises are ever sure, we must not turn to any other god or ancestors, who cannot save or help us in anyway. We must trust in God alone. Yet, King Saul violated the very principles of God, which could have saved his life and his people.

The following lessons, which I observed from Samuel's stern message to Saul, should deter us from calling on the dead or diviners.

i. Calling on the dead is a disturbance to their peaceful rest. For example, in the book of Revelation, we read, *"Yes", says the Spirit, "they will rest from their labour"* (Revelation 14:13). Hence, the last sentence pronounced by a priest over the dead at a burial service is: *"May the soul of the faithful departed rest in peace"*. Therefore, these three words: "Rest In Peace", are the most important words all relatives and loved ones leave with the dead. They are often abbreviated on most tombstones as "R.I.P." Please, for God's sake, let the dead rest in peace; and do not disturb them!

ii. Calling on the dead is an act of disrespect to the ancestors. Our ancestors deserve to be honored, even when they are dead. For example, children or adults, who honor their parents and elders, will dare not make any noise in a house or room, where dad/mom or an elder is sleeping. If it is Dad who is sleeping, Mom will warn us not to do anything to wake up Dad. If Mom is asleep, Dad will give similar warning. To disregard such a vital warning from our parents is not only a sign of disrespect, but also arrogance, which is met with due punishment. Hence, the Bible commands us to honour our father and our mother, including both the dead and the living, that our *"days may be long"* (Exodus 20:12).

iii. Calling on the spirits of the dead is provocative to their souls.
The reason is that by so doing, we are demanding from them what God alone can provide. For instance, in Luke 16:19f. , Jesus tells the story of a greedy, selfish, rich man, who died and found himself being tormented in hell fire. But, poor Lazarus, when he died, went to rest in Abraham's bosom in heaven, because he trusted in the Lord. Then, the agonizing, formerly rich man, not wanting his five living brothers, who were equally unbelievers as he, to suffer in hell after death, begged Abraham to send someone from the dead to warn his five brothers on earth. Abraham responded: *"They have Moses and the Prophets; let them listen to them."* But, the man still insisted that a witness from the dead would prove more credible to his brothers than Moses and the Prophets. Then, Abraham finally said: *"If they do not listen to Moses and the Prophets, neither will they be convinced, even if someone rises from the dead"* (Luke 16:19-31).

That statement stresses the fact that the dead cannot help the living, and therefore, we should not call or depend on them for any help or guidance, apart from the Living God.

The Psalmist wrote:

> *"Do not put your trust in princes, in mortal men who cannot save. When their spirit departs they return to the ground; on that very day, their plans come to nothing. Blessed is he whose help is the God of Jacob, whose hope is in the Lord his God, the Maker of heaven and earth, the sea and everything in them-the Lord who remains faithful for ever"* (Psalm 146:3-5).

One Advantage of the African Christian

The only advantage, if any, however, which the African concept of libation offers to the African Christian is that it reconciles with the Christian belief in life-after-death (i.e. Resurrection). For instance, Moses and Elijah showed up at the Transfiguration of Jesus and spoke with Him (Matthew 17: 3-6; Luke 9: 28-35). Again, Luke wrote that there was communication between the spirits of Abraham in heaven, and the rich man in the spiritual realm in hell (Luke 16:19-31). Also, when Jesus rose again from the dead, He revealed Himself to Mary Magdalene and spoke with her outside the tomb (John. 20:11-17). All of these evidences confirm the fact that *'the dead are still alive,'* but not to be worshipped or consulted for anything. God is our Provider, Refuge and Strenth for ever.

With this in mind, the African Christian, finds the doctrine of the resurrection of Christ, His Second Coming, and the Hope for everlasting life for the righteous (i. e. believers), and hell for the wicked (unbelievers), as taught in the Scriptures, tenable. Nevertheless, one thing is certain, and that is, the Scriptures forbid us from calling on the dead, because the dead CANNOT help the living. That is why both Peter and Paul invite us, as taught by Christ Himself, to come to God, our heavenly Father, with all our concerns, because He cares; He will give us rest (peace), and "*will meet all our needs according to His glorious riches in Christ Jesus*" (Matthew 11:28; 1 Peter 5:7; Philippians 4:6-7, 19).

As Kwame Gyekye put it, *"In Africa, . . . the belief that the ancestors are always around to provide help of various kinds has led to excessive and incessant attention to the ancestors. We must surely remember, and praise our forebears for their achievements. But we must not expect them to bestow favors on their descendants." Gyekye emphasizes the point that "the post-colonial problems of Africa clearly show that the ancestors cannot be helpful. The greatest reverence we, the descendants of the ancestors, can give to them is to let them rest in peace" (Kwame Gyekye: African Cultural Values, p.167).*

Finally, the most important reason why we should not call on the dead (or ancestors) is the fact that it is forbidden by God in the Holy Scriptures:

> *Let no one be found among you who practices divination or sorcery, engages in witchcraft, or who is a medium, or spiritist or consult the dead. Anyone who does these is detestable to the Lord, and*

> *because of these detestable practices the Lord your God will drive out those nations before you. You must be blameless before the Lord your God* (Deuteronomy. 18:10-13).

That means, we must trust in God alone, and no other, as did King David, who always looked unto the Lord as his Maker, Savior, Refuge and Strength, as well as his constant Provider. David was never found wanting, because God has promised everyone who sincerely trusts in Him, saying: *"Never will I leave you; never will I forsake you"* (Heb. 13: 5). Hence, in the following passage, David praises God, describing how much God means to him, *"Praise be to the Lord my Rock, who trains my hands for war, my fingers for battle. He is my loving God and my Fortress, my stronghold and my deliverer, my shield in whom I take refuge, who subdues people under me"* (Psalm 144:1-2).

We, too, like David, must cast our care upon God, and trust Him to the extent that we can depend on Him to lead us to victory over our enemies. Furthermore, we must look to Him to supply all our spiritual and material needs "*according to His glorious riches in Christ Jesus our Lord*" (Philippians 4:19). Then, each of us can boldly say with David, *"surely, goodness and mercy shall follow me all the days of my life, and I will dwell in the house of the Lord forever*" (Psalm 23: 6).

In a public address to Ghanaians on a special occasion in the month of September, 2002, Captain Effah Nkrabea Dartey, Ghana's Deputy Minister of Interior in the NPP Government, called on Ghanaians to stop pouring libation to other gods and ancestors during State functions and other occasions, because it does not yield any benefit to anybody or the nation in anyway. Instead of heeding the wise counsel of the Minister, some traditional leaders and their supporters began criticizing him in the media and local papers.

Yet, the Holy Bible declares that when the Israelites

> *abandoned the God, who made them and rejected the Rock, their Savior, they made God angry: They made*

> *him jealous with their foreign gods and angered him with their detestable idols. They sacrificed to demons, which are not God; gods they had not known, gods that recently appeared, . . . You deserted the Rock, who fathered you, You forgot the God who gave you birth* (Deuteronomy 32:15b-16b, 18).

It is therefore of great importance that we, who are privileged to be living in the last days of the dispensation of the Spirit and the spread of the Gospel, with the advantage of the use of computer, mobile phone, etc., for communication, should not worship idols or ancestors as our forefathers did in the past in their ignorance.

I am very optimistic that if they had had the knowledge of the Holy Scriptures as we do today, they would probably have been better Christians than some of us are today. For this reason, it is not my intention to pass judgment on our fathers or put them down in any way. What we all need to do in our generation is to follow Paul's sound counsel, *"Therefore, my dear friends, flee from idolatry"* (1 Corinthians 10:14).

CHAPTER FOUR

WE CAME INTO THIS WORLD WITH NOTHING

Perhaps, it will do us good to be reminded that whoever we are, black or white, male or female, we did not create ourselves; neither did we enter this world with anything in our hands. We were all made by God, and for God's purpose. Therefore, in all our ways, the Bible exhorts us to "come boldly unto the throne of grace, that we may obtain mercy, and find grace to help in time of need"(Heb. 4:16). Whoever we are and whatever we have—materially and spiritually—all of them belong to God. We are all, especially, as leaders of the nation — business enterprise or religious organization — accountable to no other god or ancestor, but to our people and finally to God—our Creator. Therefore, our help can come from no one else, but God alone, as declared in the Bible, "*For there is one God and one mediator between God and human beings, the man Christ Jesus, who gave Himself as a ransom for all human beings* (1 Timothy 2:5-6). Please note that, as we can clearly understand, these verses of Holy Scripture, written by no less an apostle than Paul, are in line with Krakye Denteh's interpretation of the theological message presented by the Adinkra patterns.

- **God's Son Became a Sacrificial Lamb for the Household.**

For this reason, we do not have to continue with the old traditions of our ancestors, always trying to pacify the gods with the blood of a sheep, chicken, including drinks, etc. Even though, God graciously gave our ancestors wisdom to make wonderful symbols, including the sign of the cross, with profound theological meanings, yet they did not fully grasp their real implications for the transformation of their lives.

The Jewish sacrificial system faced the same problem of tradition, and they had to learn to accept *"the new and living way"* (Hebrew 10: 20), which God had provided through His Son, Jesus Christ, *"the Lamb of God, who takes away the sins of the world"* (John 1: 29). The following scripture declares:

> *Day after day every priest stands and performs his religious duties; again and again he offers the same sacrifices, which can never take away sins. But when this priest has offered for all time one sacrifice for sins, he sat down at the right hand of God. Because by one sacrifice he has made perfect forever those who are being made holy. The Holy Spirit also testifies to us about this.*

First He says,

> *This is the covenant I will make with them after that time, says the Lord. I will put my laws in their hearts and write them on their mind" (Heb. 10:11-14, 16).* Then He adds, *"Their sins and lawless acts I will remember no more. And where these have been forgiven, there is no longer any sacrifice for sin"* (Hebrews 10: 17-18).

That statement seals, as it were, the assurance believers have over God's promise of eternal life through Christ's sacrificial death on the cross, because it is written, *"Heaven will pass away, but my words will never pass away"* (Mark 13:31).

CHAPTER FIVE

LIBATION IN THE OLD TESTAMENT

There are two particular instances in the Old Testament where libation was poured to God. The first example is seen as a means of memorial of a particular place or a special encounter with God in the life of a patriarch. For instance, God appeared to Jacob on his return journey from Paddan Aram, and blessed him, saying:

> *I am God Almighty, be fruitful and increase in number. A nation and a community of nations will come from you, and kings will come from your body. The land I gave to Abraham, and Isaac, I also will give to you, And I will give this land to your descendants after you.* (Genesis 35:11-12).

After God had spoken with Jacob, God departed from him. To mark this occasion as significant in the life of Jacob, he set up a stone pillar at the place where God had appeared to him, and "*. . . he poured a drink-offering on it; he also poured oil on it*" (Genesis 35:14). This example of libation is significant for the following reasons:

- It is a token of thank-offering from Jacob to the living

God for blessings received, and not to any other god or ancestor such as Abraham or Isaac, who were dead.

- It is a memorial to future generations of God's revelation to Jacob at that particular place and time in his life.
- It is a memorial to the future generation of God's loving kindness towards the patriarch-Jacob, whenever they read the story of his life.
- It marks the footsteps of the ancestors, that is, their relationship with God, and thus draws attention of children to fear, love and worship the God of their fathers.
- It is sometimes considered as a form of prayer to God as the following example shows:

Then Samuel said, "Assemble all Israel at Mizpah, and I will intercede with the Lord for you." When they had assembled at Mizpah, they drew water and poured it out before the Lord. On that day they fasted and there they confessed, "We have sinned against the Lord" (1 Samuel 7:5-6).

- It shows both the present and future generations how much their fathers trusted in God, and depended upon God alone for salvation and victory over their enemies.
- It teaches them to trust in the God of their fathers, and to learn to obey and serve God as they did.

Careful observation of both examples of libation as given above enables us to realize that unlike the Ghanaian/African type of libation, the oil/water was poured out not to other gods or spirits or ancestors, but to the only true God—the Creator of the universe—Who alone is the Source and Sustainer of our life. Therefore, God alone, according to the Scriptures, is worthy of worship by human beings (Exodus 20:1-6). Besides, God bids us to direct our prayers to Him alone (Jeremiah 33:3). There are several other places in the Old Testament, however, where a patriarch might have built an altar, and called upon the name of the Lord (i.e. worship) at that particular spot, without necessarily offering any drink or libation to God (Ref. Genesis 12:8; 35:7; Joshua 4: 1-9).

Whenever the people of God had followed the pagan practice of sacrificing or calling on other gods or spirits, or the dead, they were sharply rebuked by God through the prophets or apostles. Often, their disobedience would cause God to withdraw His provision from them. That left them helpless and hopeless at the hands of their enemies. Then, they would repent and cry to God in their trouble for deliverance. This was the type of religious roller coaster in which they found themselves during the period of the Judges (Ref. Judges 1:1-21; 1 Samuel 28:15f; 1 Kings 21:20-28; 1 Corinthians 8:4-8; 1 John 5:21).

All this happened to teach them and the future generation the truth, *See, the storm of the Lord will burst out in wrath, a driving wind swirling down on the heads of the wicked. The fierce anger of the Lord will not turn back until He fully accomplishes the purposes of his heart.* (Jeremiah. 29:23b-24). This is therefore for our warning, as well as edification, in order that we may not fall into similar situations in our time. And Paul earnestly exhorts believers, "Wake up, *O sleeper, rise from the dead, and Christ will shine on you. Be very careful, then, how you live—not as unwise but as wise, making the most of every opportunity, because the days are evil"* (Ephesians 5:15-16).

CHAPTER SIX

TRADITIONAL CHIEFS ENTRUSTED WITH AUTHORITY:

The Bible counsels all people, especially believers, to submit to those in authority, because those placed in authority are put there by God; as it is written:

> *For there is no authority except that which God has established. Consequently, he who rebels against the authority is rebelling against that which God has instituted. For rulers hold no terror for those who do right, but for those who do wrong. For he is God's servant to do you good* (Romans 13: 1-4).

That means, those entrusted with authority represent God and they are expected to exercise their authority in accordance with the Will of God for the good of the people of the land or employees of a particular business, if one happens to be the head of such an enterprise. Thus, any person in a leadership position is accountable to God, as well as to the people through whom God elevated him. The Bible has several examples of men amd women like Joseph, Moses, Miriam, Joshua, Gideon, Deborah, Esther, Peter, and Paul (to mention only a few), who had weaknesses just as we do, yet they respectively discharged their tasks successfully, because they each depended on God and not on their own ability or wisdom. For instance, when Joseph was brought from prison before king Pharaoh to interprete his dream, Pharaoh said, *"I have heard that when you hear a dream you can interprete it." "I cannot do it,"* Joseph replied to Pharaoh, *"but God will give Pharaoh the answer he desires" (Genesis 41: 15-16*). After interpreting the dream, Joseph asked Pharaoh to *"appoint commissioners over the land*" to be in-charge of the reservation of food for Egypt. Pharaoh then asked his officials: *"Can we find anyone like this man, one in whom is the Spirit of God?*" So Pharaoh turned to Joseph and declared in the presence of all his officials: *"Since God has made all this known to you, there is no one so discerning and wise as you..... I hereby put you in charge of the whole land of Egypt"(Genesis 41: 38-39,41).*

As people in authority, what lessons do we learn from Joseph. Firstly, Joseph believed in God and so God's Spirit dwelt in him (Genesis 39: 2-5, 37-8). Secondly, he feared God and obeyed His commandments (Genesis 39: 6b-10). Thirdly, Joseph did not claim to have special ability to interpret dreams on his own. He gave all the glory to God and drew Pharaoh's attention to God, who has the power to *"reveal to Pharaoh what He was about to do. God will give Pharaoh the answer he desires"* (Genesis 41:15-16).

Ghana, like many African countries, is blessed with a rich heritage of chieftaincy, a tradition of chiefs and queens, including elders who are placed in authority by God (through the people) to govern the people. It follows, therefore, that those in authority must exercise their authority not for their own personal interests, but for the well-being of all the people of the land. Hence, according to tradition, before a King/Chief/Queen takes office, he/she is given a traditional sword or scepter, which is a symbol of royal authority. Now, standing up before the assembly of king-makers, elders, and the entire people of the land, the new King or Queen swears the oath of allegiance, or vows to the elders and the people that he /she will exercise his/her authority faithfully at all times for the progress of all the people of the land.

In order for Ghanaians to maintain our cultural values and to advance as a distinct people of African descent, our ancestors/ predecessors bequeathed to their succeeding kings/chiefs and queens vast acres of land to be developed or cultivated for the benefit of all and sundry. In addition to lands and other treasures of gold and silver, our traditional chiefs were entrusted with a rich religious heritage, some of which are symbols or patterns, which present a theological message for the people. All these were precious, religious heritage, endowed upon us by God, and are intended to reveal to us the character of God through various names as discussed in the previous chapter. Similarly, it is believed that the various names that our ancestors used for God grew out of their experience and ideas about God. It was to preserve their religious tradition that they carved these names and ideas in artistic patterns and symbols in a piece of wood, clay, or cloth, for use by their successors and posterity.

Unfortunately, such rich religious heritage of "Akan—Adinkra" patterns, each of which conveys a unique theological message, were kept as secret treasures in the king's palace. Some of them were used to make beautiful designs in costly "kente" (the name of the specially-woven cloth worn on special occasions in Africa, particularly, Ghana) and various textiles, such as tie and dye, or wooden carvings and stools or on walls and gates of houses in the land. Nowadays, a good number of carpenters and potters also use them to produce attractive handiworks, which are purchased by both black and white people for decoration in their homes, offices and hotels. Though, such uses are not bad in themselves, they do not, in reality, serve their original, divine purpose, which is to draw our mind toward God, so that we might know God and walk in His ways. Unfortunately, that did not happen. The chiefs, political leaders, and those in authority, including the rest of us as Ghanaians, did not put God first in our lives.

That is why after forty-six years of independence as a sovereign nation, Ghana, like other African countries, such as Uganda, Congo, Nigeria, La Cote d'Ivoire, (formerly, Ivory Coast), Liberia, and Sierra Leone, to mention only a few, is still lagging behind in terms of spiritual, moral and economic advancement. It is important for every reader of this message to note here that Ghana has been cited because God pointed that to me as an example, knowing that I am a Ghanaian and can speak about Ghana better than any other nation. Nevertheless, what applies to Ghana, applies to every nation and people, white or black under the sun, because "*God does not show favoritism but accepts people from every nation who fear Him and do what is right*"(Acts 10:35)

Just as the ancient builders of the tower of Babel failed miserably because they chose to pursue their aim without seeking first God's power, wisdom and guidance, so will the plans of every human organization, unless they turn to God. For instance, the United Nations, Heads of States, religious and political leaders, elders of tribes, parents, teachers and students, may all set forth laudable goals, yet without God, the result will not be to the glory of God or serve God's purpose for the community. When the leaders of Israel, for instance, neglected the Holy Scriptures, they fell into a similar situation. God then, laid the blame squarely on the leaders, saying: *"Those who guide this people mislead them, and those who are guided are led astray"* (Isaiah 9: 16).

This statement of Isaiah is not different from what was made by Jesus to "the teachers of the Law and the Pharisees" of His day, whom He described as "hypocrites", because after winning a convert over to their side, He said to them, "you make him twice as much a son of hell as you are" (Matt. 23 :15). It does follow, therefore, that due to lack of the true knowledge of God, both the teachers and those being taught are in danger of being destroyed (Hosea 4: 6). It behooves us, therefore, to let these words of Christ be our guiding light and principle, in order that we might seek His wisdom and guidance, in all our ways, otherwise, those of us who hold leadership positions, together with those under us shall eventually be woefully disappointed. How can we avoid this failure? I am convinced that the inevitable answer to such a situation, is found in the Word of God, as it is written: *"Unless the Lord builds the house, its builders labor in vain. Unless the Lords watches over the city, the watchmen stand guard in vain"* (Psalm 127: 1).

For, as nations made up of people of different cultures (whether white or black), however rich or poor, strong or weak, whatever we are, and whoever we may be, we are by nature merely flesh and blood, and therefore, liable to sin. It is not within our own strength and wisdom to order our ways. The horrible events of September

11, as well as the sniper shootings of October 2002, should humble all human beings, wherever we are, to seek God and to learn of His ways through His only Son, Jesus Christ, who is the Savior of the world (Isaiah 45: 22; John 3:16-17).

Jesus has declared: *"Without me, you can do nothing"* (John 15:5). This stresses the need for us as humans to look up to Jesus Christ, who is "the power and the wisdom of God" (1 Corinthian 1:24), as well as "the light of this world" (John 8:12). With our limited human resources, we can do very little in terms of protecting ourselves from danger or our enemies. But with Christ as our Savior and Guide, we shall receive necessary direction in every aspect of this life, and beyond that find true success, happiness, peace and security. Otherwise, we are, but preys to our enemies, who, like lions, hide in the dark, looking for people to devour. The following was part of the report in the *Wheaton Gazette*, under the topic, '*In the Grip of Terror*', written by Staff writer, Manju Subramanya with a Sub title: "Indiscriminate Murder Shocks, Unsettles County":

> *Montgomery County has seen its share of bizarre and horrific crimes, but nothing has prepared the County for the random, seemingly motiveless shootings that have gripped the region with fear, locking down our schools and changing the way we conduct our daily business. Even veteran police and prosecutors who remember the Samuel Sheinbein dismemberment case, the Golf family murders in Potomac or Bradford Bishops' disappearance after he killed his family are flummoxed by the events of this past week, which have left six people dead and two badly wounded. (Note: the number of the dead had risen to ten by the following Tuesday, October 22, with the killing of bus driver, Johnson).*

What could we do as a church? Though no particular Bishop or church Leader was called upon to join hands with the law enforcement agencies in the search for the perpetrators, we could not sit unconcerned about this horrible situation. Bishops, Pastors, and various leaders of religious organizations have called their members to prayer vigil, which is the greatest weapon of the Church. So on Sunday, October 13, 2002 members of my church, the Calvary Redeeming Methodist Church in Rockville, met solely for prayers on the situation, and also for the bereaved families. It was our conviction that if we lifted up our voices with one accord and prayed unto God in Jesus' Name, the Lord God Almighty would hear and come to our rescue. For, God has said in His Word, *"Call upon me in the day of trouble; I will deliver you and you will honor me* (Psalms 50:15). He has also assured us that, *"For, it is not by might, nor by power, but by my Spirit"* (Zechariah 4: 6).

The Only Hiding Place

If one man with his teenager-companion as a gunman, could terrorize such a security-tight region as the Washington Metropolitan Area, then we must realize that there is no safe place or haven anywhere, except in God. What David Roper wrote about "The Hiding Place" is very relevant here, "In this world's misery there is only one sure refuge: God Himself. He is a shield to all who trust in Him" (Psalms 18: 30). To 'trust in', writes Roper, "comes from a Hebrew word that means 'to take refuge in' or 'to hide in' or 'to hide with.' It suggests a secret place of concealment. When we are exhausted by our efforts, when we are bewildered by our problems, when our friends hurt us, when we're surrounded by our foes, we can hide ourselves in God. There is no safety in the world. If we were to find safety here, we would never know the joy of God's love and protection. The only safe place is God Himself. When storm clouds gather and calamities loom, we run into His presence in prayer and remain there" (Psalms 57:1).

George MacDonald said, "That man is perfect in faith who can come to God in the utter dearth of his feelings and desires, without a glow or inspiration, with the weight of low thoughts, failures, neglects, and wandering forgetfulness, and say to Him, 'Thou art my refuge.'" Roper concluded with the following poem by Hennessay:

O the sweet unfailing refuge
Of the everlasting arms;
In their loving clasp enfolded,
Nothing worries or alarms.

CHAPTER SEVEN

GOD ANSWERS PRAYER

God is so faithful and so true to His promises that those who believe and call on Him surely experience His faithfulness. As many believers intensified their prayers on the killing spree by the snipers, John Muhammad (aged 41), and John Lee Malvo (aged 17), were arrested by the Police at about 3:30 a.m. on Thursday, October 24, 2002, while sleeping in their blue Chevy Caprice at a rest stop in Frederick County. We had had our prayer vigil on October 13 and the snipers were caught on October 24. Within 11 days of our prayer vigil, God had answered our prayer, using human agents to lay hands on the perpetrators.

We must give praise and glory to God for coming to our rescue through the combined efforts of the prayer-warriors of the church, law-enforcement agencies and the co-operation of the public as a whole. As Alfred Tennyson has said, *"More things are wrought by prayer than this world dreams of"*. Surely, without God, the Sovereign God's timely intervention, the snipers would not have been caught so soon; and the killings would have continued for a much longer time than it did. *"But, thanks be to God who gives us the victory through our Lord Jesus Christ"* (1 Corinthians 15:57). God, indeed, hears the prayers of His servants when they sincerely cry unto Him in the day of trouble as He has promised (Ps. 50:15).

Commenting on the case, in the Gazette Regional News after

the arrest, Mr. Parris N. Glendenning, then Governor of the State of Maryland, said, "The death penalty should be used to punish those responsible for 10 sniper-related killings in Maryland, Virginia and Washington, D.C." (Gazette—Regional News, page A-22, for Wed., October 30, 2002). The two suspects, held in police custody, were later tried separately and found guilty of murder by the Jury in Virginia. John Mohammed was sentenced to death for masterminding the crimes, while John Malvo, the teenager, had his sentence commuted to life-in-prison for carrying out the sniper-shootings.

Catholic Schools Prayed For Peace

The news of the arrest of the snipers thrilled members of churches, organizations and institutions and schools so much that special services were held in various places to give thanks to God for answered prayer. Karl Hille, staff writer for the *Montgomery Journal* reported on the front page one of such services held by Catholic Schools in the County captioned as follows:

> **Services Held in Appreciation of Police, Sniper Task Force**
>
> *Catholic Schools, across the Archdiocese of Washington, on Thursday held prayer services for peace and to show their appreciation for Montgomery County Police and other members of the sniper task force. At Mary of Nazareth School in Darnestown, more than 300 students gathered to honor the police officers of District 1, as well as their teachers and the parents who volunteered to patrol their wooded campus. Patricia Weitzel-Oneill, superintendent of the archdiocese schools, had planned to offer prayers on Thursday morning, and many classrooms composed letters to Montgomery County Police Chief Charles Moose and their local police stations (Karl Hille: The Montgomery Journal, Front-middle Page, Col.1).*

Indeed, no amount of words are adequate to express our heart-felt thanks to God for using the team work of all the law enforcement agencies and many volunteers to arrest and bring the two snipers to justice. Again, it must be noted that had the Lord not intervened in response to prayers, all human efforts would have been vain, and the snipers could still have been killing innocent people. Glory be to the name of the Lord and may His wonderful deeds be praised by His people from generation to generation.

The point, which is being emphasized over and over again in this book is the truth that human beings in general, (including those placed in authority as heads of states, prime ministers, kings and queens, governors and mayors, etc.) can neither rule nor order their lives according to God's will or expectation unless they seek divine wisdom and guidance. Why? Because, it is God, who created us, as it is written: *" in whom we live, move, and have our being"* (Acts 17:28). Just as a child cannot survive without its parents/nurse/care-giver, even so, as humans, we cannot make it without God, our Maker, Provider, and Sustainer. The Psalmist writes:

> *I lift up my eyes to you, to you whose throne is in heaven.*
> *As the eyes of slaves look to the hand of their master,*
> *as the eyes of a maid look to the hand of her mistress,*
> *so our eyes look to the Lord our God, till He shows us His mercy(Psalm 123:1-2).*

Surely, my friend, it had never been possible in the past with generations down the centuries to do without the Almighty God. Besides, God has not changed in His nature, character, or principles by which He operates or governs the universe; neither is God respecter of persons. Therefore, every head of state, president/prime minister, or king, queen including all people under the sun, who breathe *"the breath of life"* (Genesis 2:27), had better take a cue from the vision revealed in this book for their own good and for the good of all people.

God reveals in order to redeem.

Those who sincerely call on God in their hour of need receive deliverance. Those who rely on themselves or any other god or powers for success or victory end up in utter disappointment and destruction/suicide, because as humans, we did NOT create ourselves into this world, neither can we protect or redeem ourselves from sin or danger. The security man/woman, who is supposed to guard you and me, soon goes to sleep, when we go to sleep, but God "*neither slumbers nor sleeps*" (Psalms 121:4). Hence, we can confidently say with the Psalmist:

> *God is our Refuge and strength, an ever-present help in trouble.*
> *Therefore we will not fear, though the earth give way and the mountains fall into the heart of the sea . . .. The Lord Almighty is with us; the God of Jacob is our fortress* (Psalms 46:1-2,7).

It is surprising that a number of cases of suicide have been found to involve celebrities and the rich of this world rather than the poor. The reason is not hard to find. The rich pin their entire livelihood, namely, their love, family life, happiness, hope, peace, and their future on their wealth. Thus, wealth becomes as their all-in-all. Therefore, whenever they find out that money/wealth alone does not satisfy, they inevitably have no place to hold or stand. They become not only disillusioned, but also, miserable, depressed and hateful of themselves, their family, and also of society at large.

Consequently, they feel completely out-of-joint, rejected, and suddenly life is empty and meaningless. They hit rock bottom. Then, of course, life is no longer worth living. Some end it slowly through drinking and drugs and, finally take overdose and die. But the aggressive end their lives at once to curtail their shame, loneliness, and misery. A typical example was Ray, one of the greatest musicians that the twentieth century had ever known. He had his music, popularity, money, luxurious mansion, men and women friends, and everything that could make a man happy by worldly standards, yet all these things could not prevent Ray from being scared when he was diagnozed with a serious medical condition: stress reaction leading to high blood pressure. Ray's medical condition was partly trigered by a divorce from his wife, who had fallen in love with a close friend of his who was there regularly to comfort the wife, because she felt lonely due to Ray's many trips away from home. The situation was worsened by their fourteen-year-old daughter, who had fallen into a bad company and wouldn't go to school or come home. In his hopelessness, Ray decided to end his troubles rather than face them. Eventually, he committed suicide through drug overdose. This was quite an unexpected, tragic end of a man, who was not only rich by wordly standards, but also very popular by means of his extraordinary musical talent. "*Why then,*" a concerned friend may ask, "couldn't *Ray stand up to his trials?*" Because, God did not design human beings to obtain from material things the helping hand or saving grace, which He alone can provide during the turbulence of our earthly lives. Hence, it is written: *"A man's life does not consist in the abundance of his possessions"* (Luke 12:15b). Ray had everything, but God. Despite his many friends and riches, neither of them had the power that could help him deal with his problems nor save him from suicide. But I can bet with confidence that Ray would still have been alive, if he had known Jesus as his Lord and Savior, and as the One to whom to turn in times of heplessness (Psalms 46; 50:14-15; Matthew 11: 28—30).

The sad end of Ray, and other precious lives, shortened by tragic accidents, natural disasters, and wickedness of others, should cause all of us to ponder over the brevity of life now and again. As we do so, we shall realize that life is too short to be treated carelessly. Hence, Moses, after meditating over the span of our fleeting, earthly life, prayed to God: *"Teach us to number our days aright, that we may gain a heart of wisdom"* (Psalms 90:12).

My dear brothers and sisters, the truth of the matter is that human beings were not made to derive their inward satisfaction from material things. God made us in a unique way—"*in His own image*"—so that humans will live in loving relationship with God and also with their neighbors to find, through the—indwelling Holy Spirit, lasting *love, peace, joy, patience, gentleness, faith, self-control*, contentment and fulfillment(Galatians 5: 22). Anything other than God's Way revealed in the Scriptures and affirmed by

Christ's life, death, and ressurrection (Matthew 22: 37—40; Mark 10: 42-45; John 14: 6, 15: 13-14; Luke 23-24), leads humans astray, and we are faced with disappointment, frustration, emptiness, and misery, culminating in self-destruction. But, if we walk with God in obedience to His will (1 Peter 4:2), He will sustain us by His mighty hand and loving care, in the midst of the storms of our lives (Isaiah 43: 1-2; John 16: 33). This is also affirmed by both Peter and Paul: *"Have no confedence in the flesh" (Phil. 3:3);* for *"God opposes the proud, but gives grace to the humble.Humble yourselves, therefore, under God's mighty hand, that He may lift you up in due time. Cast all your anxiety on Him because He cares for you*" (1 Peter 5: 5-7).

I want to encourage you, dear reader, to believe the Scriptures, that the Lord has power to walk you through the *"Red Sea"* (Exodus 14:15-31; Job 1:42) you have to cross in the wilderness of your life. He is able to speak His WORD of power to calm down the raging storms of your life, so that you, too, like the disciples, will exclaim with wonder: "*Who is this? Even the wind and the waves obey Him*" (Mark 4:35-41).

Just remember that as human beings, we cannot do without God. Our lives, together with our goals, and fulfillment—all as one package designed according to divine plan— depends upon our relationship with God, who made us in His image. Without Him in our lives, we are never content, because nothing can fill the void God has created in the human heart for Himself. Yes, that is quite true, my friend; without God in us fulfilling the purpose of our lives, there is always chaos, and discontentment; nothing really satisfies the soul, which is the real personality.

Hence, Rev. Dr. Michael Youssef, introducing his latest *book "Divine Discontent: Pursuing The Peace Your Soul Longs For,*" said:

> *Are you convinced that if things were different, you would be happier and more at peace? Are you finding less fulfillment in the things that consume most of your time and energy? Is there a steady background hum in your life—the dull hum of dissatisfaction?*

> *This deep-seated discontentment is not limited to those who are struggling with life's hurts and tragedies. In fact, a sense of dissatisfaction with life is often more pronounced among people who—from all outward appearances—seem to have it made. One's level of success does nothing to minimize the symptoms of discontent. And Christians are not immune. Large numbers of believers are angry with God, disappointed in their church, or troubled by the requirements that Scripture makes on their lives. Their faith seems to be powerless to quiet the hum of discontent. The nagging inner voice insists, 'There has to be more. Something is still missing.*

He continues,:

> *While most people pursue earthly solutions to quiet their restlessness, God's Word makes it clear that our lack of peace and satisfaction in life is a spiritual issue. As we study the Scriptures, we see that the loss of contentment can push us in one of two directions. The search can either lead us down paths cluttered with false promises of fulfillment, or it can bring us to a place of turning, where the journey takes on a redemptive quality. Our search for contentment can ultimately lead us to the heart of God, which is the only place where we will find rest, a place of belonging, and ultimate contentment.*

In conclusion, Michael summed up: *"God wants to refresh your soul—to replace anxiety with peace, to give you rest in place of weariness, to provide a place of belonging that will quiet your restlessness. In other words, God wants you to find contentment in His love and grace" (Michael Youssef, Leading the Way, p. 1, Jan/Feb, 2004).*

CHAPTER EIGHT

GHANA: A TYPICAL EXAMPLE

The Rise and Fall of Kwame Nkrumah

Let us take another specific example in the political history of Ghana. In the early days of his political regime, Dr. Kwame Nkrumah acknowledged that he could not make it without God. He sought for God's wisdom, strength, and direction for political leadership. Occasionally, as he considered necessary, he would retire to a quiet and lonely place, reading and meditating on the Holy Scriptures with prayer and fasting. The local News Papers (e.g. Sunday Mirror, Evening News, etc.) would publish his picture, showing him dressed in his white political suit, sitting lonely and soberly on a rock or a piece of wood in silent meditation. Most certainly, that was a figure of a man who acknowledged his need of the Omnipotent God, and humbly, but fervently sought for divine counsel, and protection, and relied on God for the fulfillment of his political aspirations for Ghana in particular, and Africa in general.

Eventually, Nkrumah succeeded, bravely achieving for Ghana his long-desired goal, namely, political freedom from British Rule, on March 6, 1957, thus making Ghana the leading nation south of the Sahara to gain independence. With God, Nkrumah made strides in politics, and was highly respected both at home and abroad, becoming Africa's pioneer in the political struggle for the total liberation of the Continent of Africa.

During the first few years (1- 5), Ghana lived in peace, freedom and justice, being a leading nation south of the Sahara to have gained independence. Thus, Ghana became a shining example, showing the way for all other Leaders in the struggle for political emancipation in their country, particularly in Africa. With God, Nkrumah succeeded, becoming Africa's pioneer in the fight for total political liberation for the continent of Africa. His views, as well as his foresight, were highly respected both at home and abroad.

Briefly speaking, I dare to say that Nkrumah put the African personality in an enviable position on the world's political market place. Nkrumah proved to all and sundry, especially to the Western world that Africa, too, has a precious contribution to make toward world peace.

In pursuance of his goal, Nkrumah initiated the formation of the Organization of African Unity, (OAU) with Ghana, Guinea, Mali, as the nucleus. To further his political aspirations, he organized series of international meetings and rallies, and shared his unique knowledge of political science and organizational spirit with African Leaders to encourage them in their struggle for freedom. Among his many powerful and inspirational utterances, there was one that greatly spurred on most of his political peers: *"The independence of Ghana is meaningless, unless it is linked with the total liberation of Africa"* (the audience often responded with a resounding applause).

Nkrumah was, indeed, one of God's greatest gifts to Africa. He was able to achieve a lot for Africa. For example, he succeeded in putting Africa on the international scene, and positively projected the African personality by appearing at some of his international meetings (e.g. at the United Nations) in a gorgeous, rich, kente cloth. By his foresight, wisdom and valuable contributions at the United Nations and other International meetings, Nkrumah lifted high the image of Africans in the eyes of the world.

Then, at the zenith of his political career, Nkrumah attributed his achievement and success to his own ingenuity. Nkrumah ascribed to himself certain divine names, such as *'Osagyefo'*

(Mighty Savior), *"Nkrumah never dies",* which were often recited on the national radio by the then disbanded Young Pioneer's Movement. As if these were not enough, Nkrumah went further still, and without fear of God, twisted a text from the Holy Scriptures, which is part of Jesus' Sermon on the Mount (Matthew chapters 5-7), saying, "Seek first the political kingdom, and all other things will be given to you as well." But the actual text as Jesus put it reads: *"Seek first the kingdom of God and His righteousness, and all these things will be given to you as well"* (Matthew 6:33).

When the Christian Council of Ghana sent a delegation to him, respectfully counseling him not to ascribe divine names to himself, or twist God's Word to suit his political aspirations, Nkrumah paid no heed to their plea. His rejection of their counsel, as I see it, equally meant his rejection of God and His divine counsel. The Christian Council spoke with him as God's mouth-piece; and for Nkrumah to have ignored them, was not only a proof of his repudiation of God, but also, of the only power that could deliver him from imminent destruction. It was obvious that Nkrumah had found another god in whom to trust. He chose to rely on a newly found god *('Kankan Nyame')* to achieve his goal. Nevertheless, to his utter shock and woeful disappointment, he was suddenly and unexpectedly overthrown from his "political kingdom" by a military coup d'etat on February 24, 1966.

Since then, Ghana, the shining Star in the West Coast of Africa, which was to lead the way for the total liberation of Africa, has ceased to be the beacon of Africa; because her leaders did not put God first in the administration of the country for the good of all, and particularly, for the glory of God. Today, after many decades as a sovereign nation, instead of progressing, Ghana has retrogressed so low by the year 2000 that it has been classified among the world's poor countries, economically known as *"Highly Indebted Poor Countries' (HIPC).*

Other national leaders in ancient times, according to the Bible, suffered a similar fate when they forsook God, as Nkrumah did. It is an unfortunate human tragedy that human beings do not learn from history. The stories of king Nebuchadnezzar and his successor,

Belshazzar of Babylon in the Old Testament Book of Daniel are notable examples in this situation. Their stories were recorded in the following:

> *God gave . . . Nebuchadnezzar sovereignty and greatness and glory and splendor. Because of the high position God gave him, all the people and nations and men of every language . . . feared him. Those the King wanted to put to death, he put to death; those he wanted to spare, he spared . . .. But when his heart became arrogant and hardened with pride, he was deposed from his royal throne and stripped of his glory. He was driven away from people and given the mind of an animal; he lived with wild donkeys and ate grass like cattle; and his body was drenched with the dew of heaven, until he acknowledged that the Most High God is sovereign over the kingdoms of men and sets over them anyone he wishes* (Daniel 5:18-21).

Anyone who has read the story of king Nebuchadnezzar would have thought that his successor would take a cue from it, but he did not; he rather did worse things than his father, as the following account shows:

Belshazzar, the son of Nebuchadnezzar, succeeded him as King of Babylon. On one special occasion, in the cool of the night, Belshazzar sat on his throne surrounded by his wives and concubines and all the nobles of his kingdom. Then Belshazzar set himself up against the Lord of heaven. He had the golden goblets from the temple of God brought to him and he and his nobles and wives together with his concubines drank from them.

Furthermore, he praised the gods of silver and gold, of bronze, iron, wood, and stone, which cannot see, or hear or understand. He did not honor the God who holds in His hands the whole universe and the lives and ways of all the people in it. As a result God sent a hand with the following inscription:

MENE, MENE, TEKEL, PARSIN

Which means:

> ***Mene:*** *God has numbered the days of your reign and brought it to an end.*
> ***Tekel:*** *-You have been weighed on the scales and found wanting.*
> ***Peres:*** *-Your kingdom is divided and given to the Medes and Persians* (Daniel 5: 25-28).

That very night, after Daniel had explained to king Belshazzar the meaning of the inscription on the wall, he (Belshazzar) was slain, and his kingdom was taken over by Darius, the Mede.

These and several other instances of similar stories abound in the Bible to warn all of us, especially, those in authority, to eschew pride and arrogance in the exercise of our authority. We must take this seriously, lest we incur the displeasure of the Almighty God, who is the Ultimate Ruler and Judge of this world. He is the King of Kings, and Lord of Lords, before whom *"All men are like grass, and all their glory is like the flower of the field. Surely the nations are like a drop in a bucket; they are regarded as dust on scales" (Isaiah 40: 6; 15).*

That was why after he and the elders of the people had provided sufficient money and materials for the building of the Temple, King David saw the need to sound aloud the following warning to his son, Solomon, who had succeeded him as King of Israel.:

> *Unless the Lord builds the house, its builders labor in vain. Unless the Lord watches over the city, the watchmen stand guard in vain. In vain you rise early and stay up late, toiling for food to eat, for God grants sleep to those He loves* (Psalms 127: 1-2).

We must bear in mind that what David said to king Solomon many years ago is still relevant and applicable to all in authority today, black or white. Therefore, all who disregard this warning, do so to their own detriment and the destruction of those they govern.

The following story may serve a good example. Uzziah was just 16 when he became King of Judah and though he was so young at heart, it is recorded that *"he did what was right in the eyes of the Lord... He sought God during the days of Zechariah, who instructed him in the fear of God. As long as he sought the Lord, God gave him success"* (2 Chronicles 26: 4-5).

Uzziah's fame spread abroad and his army grew stronger and stronger than before. He had 307,500 soldiers commanded by 2,600 officers, who helped him to defeat all his enemies in the neighbouring countries.

Then, like Nkrumah in his hey days, sadly, we read, "*But after Uzziah became powerful, his pride led to his downfall*" (2 Chronicles 26:16). That was most unfortunate; wasn't it? Commenting on his downfall, Albert Lee said, "It is tragic to witness someone starting out well in life and then finishing poorly…Uzziah had failed to remember the One who had given him success and who had given godly counsel. He sinned against the Lord when he burned incense in the temple, and God struck him with leprosy (2 Chronicles 26:16-19). He remained "*a leper until the day he died*" (2 Chronicles 26:21).

"To finish well," says Lee, *"we need to avoid having a heart that is 'lifted up.' Let's remind ourselves often of the warning in Proverb16:18, 'Pride goes before destruction, and a haughty spirit before a fall.' And let's keep seeking the Lord, obeying Him, and thanking Him for all He had done"* (Albert Lee, *Our Daily Bread,* R. B. C. Ministries, Sunday, February 8, 2004).

Disobedience to God Has Disastrous Consequences

I want to cap this portion with yet another example worthy of notice. Since *"there is no authority except that which God has established*" (Romans 13:1), it follows, therefore, that those who hold authority should exercise it according to the will of God. Like Solomon, Ahab, who became King of Israel after the death of his father Omri, reigned for twenty-two years. In those years, we are told:

> *Ahab ....did more evil in the eyes of the Lord than any of those before him. He... married Jezebel, daughter of Ethbaal king of the Sidonians, and began to serve Baal (the god of the Canaanites) and worship him.... Ahab also made an Asherah pole (goddess of the land) and did more to provoke the Lord, the God of Israel, to anger than did all the kings of Israel before him* (1 Kings 16: 29f).

What was the result of his idolatrous reign upon himself, his family and the nation?

(i). There was no rain in the land for three and half years resulting in severe famine and death of people. For example, Elijah's encounter with Ahab's 450 prophets of Baal (the god of the Canaanites) resulted in their slaughter in the Kishon Valley (1 Kings 18:40).

(ii). God spoke to Ahab through Elijah: "*I am going to bring disaster on you. I will consume your descendants and cut off from Ahab every male in Israel—slave or free*" . . . (1 Kings 21:20). In the end, Ahab was killed in his war against Ramoth Gilead (1 Kings 22:35-37).

(iii). Ahab's wife, Jezebel was thrown down from a window "*and some of her blood spattered the wall and the horses as they trampled her underfoot*" (2 Kings 9:33).

(iv). Ahab's 70 sons in Samaria, were slaughtered and their heads sent in baskets to Jezreel by the command of Jehu (2 Kings 10 :7).

(v). Jehu went to Samaria and "*Proclaimed a solemn assembly for Baal. When the temple was crowded with worshippers of Baal from one end to the other. Jehu offered a sacrifice, and then, commanded the guards to kill all the Baal worshippers. "They demolished the sacred stone of Baal and tore down the temple of Baal . . . . So Jehu destroyed Baal worship in Israel*" *(2 Kings 10:19a, 20, 21b, 25, 27, 28).*

All this evil came upon Ahab and his household, and the nation as a whole, because he forsook God and His commandments and went after other gods. Indeed, this calls for great caution for all who hold positions of leadership, as it is written: "*It is a fearful thing to fall into the hands of the living God*" (10:31), "*for our God is a consuming fire*" (Hebrew 12:29).

As it has been reiterated throughout this book, the poor state of affairs in Africa, Europe, Asia, etc.,–spiritually, emotionally and economically, boils down to the fact that we have abandoned God and His commandments, and the provision He has made through Christ for the solution of our earthly problems.

Hence, the need to take God's Word seriously by all and sundry cannot be overemphasized here. It is worth our lifetime commitment. The Lord offers abundant blessings to all who worship Him and obey His commandments in their daily affairs. God's blessings make us rich so that we may be channels of blessing to our descendants and others. God laments when we miss His blessings as a result of our disobedience, as He declared through the Prophet Isaiah:

> *If only you had paid attention to my commands, your peace would have been like a river, your righteousness like the waves of the sea. Your descendants would have been like the sand, your children like its numberless grains; their name would never be cut off nor destroyed from before me* (Isaiah 48:8-9).

Knowing that disobedience to the Word of God has disastrous consequences on individual people and nations, Jesus, the Son of God, did not turn away from the Holy Scriptures, saying, "*I know that His command leads to eternal life*", Jesus declared. "*So whatever I say is just what the Father has asked me to say*" (John 12: 50). Jesus, our Lord, has set us a perfect example, and wants us to follow suit. Anything done outside God's will is sin, which brings deadly consequences.

It was for this reason that Jesus wept over the city of Jerusalem when the Jewish leaders of His day rejected Him (Luke 19:41). For, He foresaw the result of their rejection—a massive destruction of the city and death of the people, including children at the hands of the Roman soldiers–which was to come upon them forty years after

His death at Calvary. With deep sorrow and compassion, Jesus lamented for the people as follows:

> *O Jerusalem, Jerusalem, you who kill the prophets and stone those sent to you, how often I have longed to gather your children as a hen gathers her chicks under her wings, but you were not willing. Look, your house is left to you desolate. For I tell you, you will not see me again until you say "Blessed is He that comes in the name of the Lord"* (Matthew 23:37-39).

The rejection of Jesus by the Jewish Leaders meant their rejection of the Word of God and *"salvation by grace through faith in Jesus Christ"* (Ephesians2: 8). By rejecting Christ, "*the light of the world*" (John 8:12), the Jewish leaders chose to live in "*darkness rather than light, because their deeds are evil*" (John 3: 19). Furthermore, by rejecting Jesus, who is "*the light of men*" and *the only Way* to etrnal life, (John 1:4; 14:6), they chose death. What was the result of their forsaking the Son of God, the Messiah—the Lord and Savior of their lives? The city of Jerusalem was completely destroyed by the Romans in A.D. 70, as Jesus had foreseen and rightly predicted.

There are important lessons for us to learn from those statements of Jesus:

- As a nation, and as individuals, there is a limited time within which we are to receive salvation while we live here on earth. Jesus put it this way: *"As long as it is day, we must do the work of Him who sent me. Night is coming, when no man can work"* (John 9:4).
- We must be willing to accept salvation through faith in Jesus Christ at the time when it is graciously offered to us through the preachers of the Gospel. Lest, we miss that opportunity forever, and we are forever doomed. As the

saying goes: *"Opportunity once lost, is never regained."* Hence Isaiah cried out aloud to the wayward people of Judah, *"Seek the Lord while He may be found; call on Him while He is near"* (Isaiah 55:6).

- We have no control of tomorrow or our life. Therefore, whatever needs to be done, must be done NOW (John 9:4). Tomorrow may be too late. As it is written, *"In the time of my favor I heard you, and in the day of salvation, I helped you. I tell you, now is the time of God's favor. Now is the day of salvation"* (2 Corinthians. 6:2).
- It is therefore, inevitable, and irrevocable, that those who forsake God are cursed, and doomed for destruction as a result of their rebellion against God. Thus, the only choice left to them is to fall as victims to the devil, who, . . ." *comes not, except to steal, to kill, and to destroy"* (John 10:10 a). There are no two ways about it, neither is there a neutral ground in the middle. You are either for Christ or for the Devil. The choice is in your hands. I counsel you to choose Christ.
- If the leaders of Jerusalem had accepted Jesus and His teaching about the kingdom of God, the city would have been saved from destruction. As it is written: *". . . whoever finds me finds life and receives favor from the Lord. But whoever fails to find me harms himself; all who hate me love death"* (Proverbs 8:35-36).

This is a strong warning for those who reject Jesus Christ. Being a Pastor of the flock of Christ, I want to passionately counsel you to be wise enough to choose Christ, because there is no hiding place for our sins; neither can we pay the cost, because they are too costly. Besides, "*salvation is found in no one else*," says Peter to the Sanhedrin (The Jewish Supreme Court), "*for there is no other name under heaven given to men* (human beings) *by which we must be saved*" (Acts 4:12). That scripture underlines the truth that there is no human being on earth or an angel in heaven worthy enough to plead for our salvation before the presence of Almighty God, except Jesus Christ, as John wrote:

> *I wept and wept because no one was found who was worthy to open the scroll or look inside. Then one of the elders said to me, 'Do not weep! See, the Lion of the tribe of Judah, the Root of David, has triumphed. He is able to open the scroll and its seven seals. . . . He came and took the scroll from the right hand of him who sat on the throne....And when He had taken it, the four living creatures and the twenty-four elders fell down before the Lamb....And they sang a new song:*
>
> *You are worthy to take the scroll and open its seals, because you were slain, and with your blood you purchased men (people) for God from every tribe and language and people and nation. You have made them to be a kingdom and priests to serve our God, and they will reign on the earth* (Revelation 5: 4-5, 7-8a, 9-10).

Therefore, there is salvation and abundant blessings for those who fear God, and humbly receive Jesus as Savior and Lord of their lives. But calamity and destruction of precious lives await all who refuse God's gift of eternal life through Jesus Christ, "the Savior of the world" (John 3:36, 4:42c; Revelation 20: 11-14).

CHAPTER NINE

IDOLATRY OF THE HEART

The Holy Spirit further gave me insight into the fact that idolatry may not always necessarily have to do with concrete objects like gold, silver, trees, rivers, stones or clay, which are worshipped as found in the religions of other cultures, but there is also what the scripture describes in the Book of Ezekiel as *"idolatry of the heart"* (Ezekiel 14: 1-8).

When my wife joined me in the U. S. in September of 1989, I had enrolled in the Master of Theological Studies Program at Wesley Theological Seminary. We had only a few things. The furniture in our room belonged to the Seminary, because we had none of our own. After completing my Doctor of Ministry Program in 1993, we had to find our own apartment in Washington D.C., obtain work-permit and later the Green Card so that we could work to support ourselves and our children in Ghana. It never crossed my mind that we could be materialistic. After all, I was working only part-time in a grocery store, and also as an Associate Pastor in a small Ghanaian Church (formerly United Church of Ghana) in the Washington Metropolitan Area. Nevertheless, feelings of discontent began to find place in my heart. Before long, we were craving nice things and secretly feeling resentful for not having them. Then, quite recently, as my wife and I were meditating on Ezekiel 14:1-11, the Holy Spirit suddenly opened our eyes with a 'disturbing' insight:

"Materialism isn't necessarily HAVING things; it can also be CRAVING them." There we sat side by side quietly on our bed with our Bibles on our laps, convicted of materialism! The Lord had exposed our discontentment for what it really was, an idol in our heart. My friends, I am afraid that many of you reading this story, may equally be guilty of this obscure sin: *"the idolatry of the heart."*

That hour, as we each repented and humbly asked the Good and Merciful Lord to forgive us and cleanse our hearts of this subtle sin, the Lord graciously regained our hearts as His rightful throne. Right there on our bed, a deep sense of contentment and peace filled our hearts, based not on things we have or wish we had, but on God alone. Our faith was so much strengthened by the Word of God that *"If we make His service our delight, He will give us the desires of our heart"* (Psalms 37:4).

In the days of Ezekiel, the Prophet of Judah, the Lord exposed the idolatry in the hearts of His people, who came to seek His counsel as follows:

> *Son of man, these men have set up idols in their hearts and put wicked stumbling blocks before their faces. Should I let them inquire of me at all? Therefore speak to them and tell them,' this is what the Sovereign LORD says: When any Israelite sets up idols in his heart and puts a wicked stumbling block before his face, and goes to a prophet, I the Lord will answer myself in keeping with his great idolatry. I will do this to recapture the hearts of the people of Israel, who have all deserted me for their idols. Therefore, say to the house of Israel, 'This is what the Sovereign LORD says: Repent! Turn from your idols and renounce all your detestable practices!* (Ezekiel 14:3-6).

It is easy to be deceived into thinking that you have not set up any idol in your heart. I humbly appeal to you to allow the Holy Spirit to search your heart and lead you to a decisive conviction in the light of the Word of God, which is:

> ....*living and active, sharper than any double edged sword, penetrating even to dividing soul and spirit, joints and marrow; it judges the thoughts and attitudes of the heart. Nothing in all creation is hidden from God's sight. Everything is uncovered and laid bare before the eyes of him to whom we must give account* (Hebrews 4:12-13).

The truth is that idolatry is still a problem to Christians, as well as all other worshippers of God. The danger is that it is not always so open or plain to the human mind. In our so-called civilized age, idols are usually more subtle and difficult to recognize, because they set up their home in the hidden places of our heart.

Commenting on "*Idols of the Heart*", Roper of RBC had this to say:

> *If we want to know our idols, we need to consider our predominant thoughts, for what we think about most of the time may be an idol. Our last thought before we sleep, our first thought when we awake. Our reveries throughout the day are spent on the items and issues we treasure and trust.*
>
> *Any possession or person we put our hope in to bring us fulfillment, any goal or aspiration that becomes more important to us than God—these are the 'gods' that attract all our allegiance and subtly control our lives.*

Concluding, Roper emphasized, "only God can satisfy the deepest needs of our heart and make us truly alive. That is why we would be wise to heed the loving counsel of the apostle Paul, "*My beloved, flee from idolatry.*" (1 Corinthians 10: 14). Should you find yourself convicted by the Spirit as I was, you will do well rather to repent in humility and be freed from this subtle sin of the heart, which easily besets us all, even without our notice. Then, we can truly yearn for God to recapture our soul and mind as we altogether humbly turn to the Lord, our Saviour, *"in Spirit and truth"*, with a penitent heart, singing prayerfully the following hymn:

Return, O holy Dove! Return,
Sweet messenger of rest!
I hate the sins that made Thee mourn,
And drove you from my breast.

The dearest idol I have known,
Whate'er that idol be,
Help me to tear it from Thy throne
And worship only Thee.
(Methodist Hymn Book [MHB] 461 vrs. 4 & 5 by William Cowper, 1731-1800).

Like St. Augustine, William Cowper echoes in this solemn hymn (which is one of my favorites), the truth that God has made human beings for Himself, and for that reason, no earthly thing can save us or satisfy the deep longing of the heart, other than God Himself. As I meditated on this much further, the Holy Spirit made me realize, once again, the futility and foolishness of trying by our own human effort or ingenuity to solve our individual or national problems, or to find success, happiness, peace and comfort through other sources of power such as magic or voodoo. Thus, we seem to God as though we have lost our senses and can no longer think or reason aright. Indeed, we look like foolish children before Him.

- **Idolatry is Foolishness:**

Now, the logical question to ask here is this: "If nothing, apart from God, is able to satisfy the deepest need of the human heart, why then do we bother ourselves to seek refuge, success, riches, and comfort from other sources rather than God alone?" Here is the answer, "*The fear of the Lord is the beginning of wisdom*" (Psalms 111:10). Thus, when we lean on our human intellect instead of God's, our so-called wisdom turns to foolishness (1 Corinthians 1:20-21). In order to point humans to the true way of life, God revealed to His chosen people, Israel, through the Prophet Isaiah, the foolishness of idolatry in the following passage:

> *All who make idols are nothing, and the things they treasure are worthless. Those who would speak up for them are blind; they are ignorant to their own shame. Who shapes a god and cast an idol, which can profit him nothing? He and his kind will be brought to shame; craftsmen are nothing but men. Let them all come together and take their stand; they will be brought down to shame and infamy. The blacksmith takes a tool and works with it in the coals; he shapes an idol with hammers, he forges it with the force of his arm. Half of the wood he burns in the fire; over it he prepares his meal, he roasts his meat and eats his fill. He also warms himself and says, "Ah! I am warm; I see the fire." From the rest he makes a god, his idol; He bows down to it and worships. He prays to it and says, "Save me, you are my god." They know nothing, they understand nothing; their eyes are plastered over so they cannot see, and their minds closed so they cannot understand. No one has the knowledge or understanding to say, "Half of it I used for fuel; I even baked bread over its coals, I roasted meat and I ate. Shall I bow down to a block of wood? Is not this thing in my right hand a lie?* (Isaiah 44:9-12; 16-19; also Jeremiah 10:1-15).

Let us now turn to the next chapter to discuss some areas of the Ghanaian religious belief and social life, in which tradition makes void the Word of God.

> [illegible] nothing, and [illegible] worthless. [illegible] [illegible] [illegible] they understand nothing [illegible] [illegible] [illegible] [illegible] (Isaiah 40:12 to 19; also Jeremiah 10:1–16).

Let us now turn to the next chapter to discuss some areas of the Ghanaian religious belief and social life, in which traditional [illegible] the Word of God.

CHAPTER TEN

AREAS OF GHANAIAN LIFE IN CONFLICT WITH SCRIPTURES

There are several aspects of Ghanaian religious and social life where tradition conflicts with the Word of God. The following are a few examples:

Marriage:

The typical Ghanaian traditional marriage has two stages, namely, the engagement (known in Akan as *"Esiwaah"*), and the actual marriage ceremony *('Aware')*. On each of these occasions, the elder of the family pours libation to the gods and the spirits of ancestors, invoking their blessing and support for the engagement/marriage. The elder prays to the gods and ancestors to grant the newly married couple many children (twins, triplets, etc), riches and material prosperity, etc. Again, the question is: "Can the dead help the living" (Isaiah 8:19)? Is it possible for the dead ancestors or other gods, who have never, ever before created human beings, to provide couples with children and material wealth?" Of course, NOT! For the Bible declares:

- *Sons are a heritage from the Lord, children a reward from him.* (Psalms 127:3).
- *'The silver is mine and the gold is mine', declares the Lord Almighty* (Hagai 2:8).
- *. . . remember the Lord your God, for it is He who gives you the ability to produce wealth* (Deuteronomy 8:18).
- *" No one from the east or the west or from the desert can exalt a man. But it is God who judges: He brings one down, He exalts another. For the earth is the Lord's, and everything in it, the world, and all who live in it."* (Psalms 75:6-7; 24:1).

Thus, the Scriptures teach us to understand that neither gods nor ancestors have power or any other means to provide the living or any married couple with children or riches. It is high time we stopped calling on lesser gods and spirits for help. Instead, we must look to God, our CREATOR, Who alone is able to meet our needs (both spiritually and materially), *"according to His riches in glory by Christ Jesus, our Lord"* (Philippians 4:19).

We must remember that, as many marriages as have undergone traditional rituals, without the renewing power of God's Spirit, have not the blessing of God upon them. We need to know without doubt that, *"Unless the Lord builds the house, those who build it labour in vain"* (Psalms 127:1); because we know, according to the Scriptures, *that "Every good and perfect gift is from above, coming down from the Father of the heavenly lights, who does not change like shifting shadows"* (James.1:17).

Many couples can testify that such traditional rituals tend to render them childless. For instance, I know the story of a couple who came to me for counselling and prayers, because they had been married for more than two or three years, and were still childless. In their attempt to have a child, the husband had taken the wife to a fetish in a town called, Praso in the interior of the Western Region of Ghana, where the wife was made to stand naked in the River Pra, so that the god of the river would impregnate her. Two years after consulting the fetish priest, there was still no sign of a child. The husband then began blaming the wife for their childlessness. However, medical examination conducted later on both of them, proved that it was the husband's infertility that had contributed to barrenness in the wife (i.e., his sperms were too weak to fertilize the seed of his wife's). After receiving the medical report, the wife could no longer stay in that condition, and finally, divorced the man for his dishonesty and fetishism. She later got married to another man with whom she had two children. Children are blessings from God, and not from any god or ancestor.

My dear reader, let me remind you, if I may, that no god or spirit or any ancestor, has created a child at any time anywhere in this universe. It is, therefore, a deception on the part of diviners or fetish priests and priestesses to give vain promises to married couples with infertility problem that their gods/spirits can give them children. It is a big lie. Do not listen to them.

The Traditional Role of the Wife in the Home

Many African married men put heavy burdens on their wives without even knowing of any wrongdoing. For instance, in some Ghanaian homes, where there are no children or servants, it is the wife's duty to clean the house, including the bathroom. She does laundry, goes for grocery, cooks the meals, sets the table and cleans all cooking utensils and the dishes while the husband does nothing. Thus, tradition makes the woman both wife and servant in the house. I have been told that my father-in-law, the late S. O. Gaisie, perhaps, the first Ghanaian District Commissioner in the country, was very much infuriated when he saw a man coming from his farm with empty hands, while his pregnant wife, loaded with a basketful of cassava, was also carrying another baby behind her back. Commissioner Gaisie quickly had the man arrested and charged with negligence of marital responsibility. That man's irresponsible treatment of his wife is, indeed, a typical example of subjugation of women by many husbands. It is unchristian, and unfair to human dignity. Let us put a stop to it forthwith in order to maintain a healthy, and enjoyable marital relationship with our wives.

At this juncture, perhaps, Dr. Kwegyir Aggrey's concept of the value of women in society might be relevant: "Educate a man, and you educate an individual; but, educate a woman, and you educate a nation," declared Aggrey. Surely, Dr. Aggrey could not have said it better than he did. And if, it is true, and none can deny the truth that women are the foundation of nation building, how can we continue to mistreat them and disregard their precious role in community?

Addressing a group of women at the *"Revive Our Hearts"* Radio Series on the theme *"Becoming a Woman of Discretion"*, Nancy Leigh Demoss, quoted John Adams, the second President of the United States as saying, *"From all that I have read, of history, and of Government, and of human life and manners, I have drawn this conclusion: that the manners of women were the most infallible parameter to ascertain the degree of morality and virtue of a nation*." That is to say, if we want to determine the moral standard of any nation, we can get the answer by taking a closer look at the life of its women. Thus, John Adams of America made the same observation about women as Aggrey of Africa had done that God has endowed women with considerable influence, which can make or mar the moral standard of our homes, Churches, communities, and nation at large. It is therefore, imperatively necessary for us men to respect and encourage women as much as possible in the fulfillment of their role for the good of all in society.

The King of Ashanti Sets An Example For Change

It is encouraging to note further that within the Ghanaian society there are a number of people in authority who are determined to bring about necessary changes in our tradition. One of such people in key positions is the current king of the Ashantis, Nana Otumfuo Osei Tutu II. The following article was published about him by Stella Nkrumah Ababio:

A KING WITH A DIFFERENCE: TRANSFORMATION IN THE ASANTE KINSHIP

The Asantehene, Otumfuo Osei Tutu II, has forever transformed the tradition governing the role and place of the king's wife. He has caused a mini revo-

lution. Recently, very boldly and proudly, he exhibited his wife at an official gathering in Holland. Not only was the beautiful lady seated by her husband but also the king, her husband, was not embarrassed to include her in his address to the gathering.

I am confident that a lot of folks there will agree that the present Asantehene has taken Ghana by storm. In many respects, he has shown us what a dynamic leader can do with any institution. Today, we do not picture palanquins solely when thinking of the Asantehene. One rather sees the thousands of Ghanaian children benefiting from educational scholarships; brilliant conflict resolution skills among chiefs; the tourists bringing in foreign exchange as they travel from far and near, to visit the king, and his campaign against HIV/AIDS to mention a few of his laudable initiatives.

Therefore, when the dailies surreptitiously announced the new marriage of the Asantehene, I wondered how he was going to manage this aspect of his life. Additionally, a few colleagues and I spent close to 45 minutes discussing the merits and demerits of a tradition that tacitly discourages kings from appearing in public with their wives.

A popular Ghanaian maxim intimates that behind every successful man is a woman. But these women, for a large part have been faceless, formless, invisible, neutral and voiceless, especially in Ghanaian royal corridors.

In the past, the wifely advice, strategies and concepts offered to the king have been offered in private. But today, the modern king has dared to rock the boat . . . In his address, he publicly acknowledged her presence by saying "Me ne me ho kafo" (my wife and I) in a lot of the statements he made, thereby communicating that his thoughts and statements represented those of his wife as well.

> *"This public gesture",* says Stella, *"though small, is symbolically ripe with meaning. By this gesture, the Asantehene, as the lead Man of Ashantis, has re-written the code of ethics of Ashanti kings. He has made history. I want to believe that this gesture will not only occur when the king is outside Ghana.*
>
> *We the women of Ghana will love to see the king honour and acclaim his wife publicly and officially in Kumasi and, indeed, in Ghana as often as is practical. He has definitely made a statement for the ongoing gender debate and we believe all other kings, chiefs and men will take a cue from this exemplary 21st Century leader.*
>
> *The Asantehene has made women proud. He has recognized the rightful position of women and shown by example that culture need not be* static but should evolve with the times. He has also demonstrated that "Culture was made for man and not man for culture." *Nana, we look forward to more of such groundbreaking reforms in Akan kingship* (by Stella Nkrumah-Ababio: Daily Graphic, Tuesday, August 27, 2002. P.7).

To read such news about the Asantehene is very intriguing, in that Ashantis, of all the Akans, are the most traditionalistic. For instance, in order to keep the Asante chieftaincy tradition in Washington Metropolitan Area, as well as in New York, they have installed their kings and queens, who dress in their national costumes and sit in high positions on special occasions such as funerals and marriage ceremonies. That is why the example set by Nana Otumfuo Osei Tutu II is hailed by all, especially women, who want to see a change for the betterment of the traditional life.

In the rural areas, the position of a wife is worse than in the cities. For instance, in many rural towns, the usual practice is that whenever a husband and his wife visit their farm, it is the wife who carries home a basketful of foodstuffs for consumption, while the husband carries on his shoulder just a piece of wood with a cutlass in his hand. Yet, men are deemed naturally, physically stronger than women, and are supposed to bear a much heavier burden than the weaker sex. Many men are blind to this fact due to tradition; but things must change now, in order to give women some relief, as well as respect and dignity due to them.

Every husband ought to remember that God created the wife to be his better half and not his servant. Being the head of the wife, the husband has the onerous responsibility to love and cherish his wife dearly. Thus, it is understood that the wife (woman) was made for the husband (man) to love and treat tenderly and gently and not to be mistreated as though she were inferior to man. In so doing, as the Bible points out, the husband proves that he loves himself; for the wife is mystically part of his body. After all Paul says, *"No one ever hated his own body, but he feeds and cares for it, just as Christ does the church"* (Ephesians 5:28-33).

Since marriage is a sacred institution created by God for the mutual enjoyment of husband and wife, we cannot derive the full benefit of it without relying on God. For, we know that marriage thrives on love; and only *"God is love"* (1 John 4:8b), but human beings are basically selfish. Hence, no couple can enjoy their union as much as they desire, unless they both commit themselves to Christ as their Savior and Lord, and allow Him to govern their lives. For *"Without me,"* says Jesus, *"you can do nothing"* (John 15:5).

Therefore, we need always to feed fat on God—the source of life and love—in order to have love in ourselves and share in our marriage so as to keep it going smoothly. We can only give and share what we have received from the Lord. Calling on other gods and ancestors will NEVER bring us the much-needed virtue of LOVE, which is the BED-ROCK of every happy and successful marriage. Many marriages are deficient of love, and some have ended in divorce, because of too much adherence to tradition, and unforgiving spirit and bitterness haboured by the couples involved; and thereby denying themselves of a real, loving relationship with each other that should characterize every true marriage. Thus, they end up losing not only the Holy Word of God, which should nourish their soul and lighten their path in life, but also, the blessing of

God upon their marriage.

This is not, however, to suggest in anyway that customary marriage is inferior to Christian marriage. But, the most important point to note here is that marriage is a sacred institution intended to forge a lasting relationship between husband and wife. But without God, who instituted marriage, husband and wife in their own strength cannot make it, regardless of whether it is a Christian or customary marriage. This is a proven fact. It cannot be denied, whether we admit or dismiss it. It is out of God's concern to redeem our marriage and to rekindle the love between husband and wife and family as a whole that this truth has been revealed. We must all consider our marital relationship and see to make every necessary amends until our good is better, and our better, best.

Same Sex Marriage

There is a remarkable number of men and women, who have been so disappointed with traditional Christian or customary marriage (i.e., between a man and a woman as ordained by God) that they rather choose to enter into what is now known as *"same sex marriage"*, a term which, until recently, was deemed so shameful to be mentioned in public that it was hidden in the closet. Today, it has gained access in certain quarters, including the media, TV shows, and the movies. Well, such a life-style does not solve any marital problem. It rather multiplies it and makes it untenable. In the first place, it violates God's principle of marriage between man and woman. Secondly, it perverts human sexuality. God, by His infinite wisdom, and love for humanity, designed both the male and female bodies to complement and fulfill each other spiritually, emotionally, and physically (Genesis 1:27, 2 :18, 20b,-24, Matthew 19:4-6,8-9; 1 Corinthians 7:1-5).

Furthermore, *"same sex marriage"* does not fulfill God's purpose of procreation in marriage (Genesis 1:28; Psalms 127:3-5). For, if every man marries a male he likes, and each woman gets married to a woman of her choice, then there will be no children (who will grow up) to take the place of the present generation of people when we are gone. Therefore, the gay and lesbian lifestyle seeks to annihilate the roots of the family system, and of community, and nation as a whole. Therefore, it is detrimental to human existence. It is nothing, but a figment of our sinful heart, and rebellious attitude toward God, our Creator, and Savior of humankind.

It is admitted that some marital problems, such as barenness, incompatibility, and impotence (to mention only a few), may render marriage unenjoyable. However, the solution does not lie in human hands, but in God's. He is our Maker, and Provider of all our needs—spiritually, emotionally and physically. It is "God, who gives us all things to enjoy" (1 Tim. 6:17), including sex in the context of marriage. Hence, without God's providential care of His creation, we can have nothing. That is why, St. Paul, in his Christ-like, fatherly manner, counsels every one of us in these words, "*Do not be anxious about anything, but in everything, by prayer and petition, with thanksgiving, present your requests to God. And the peace of God, which transcends all understanding, will guard your hearts and your minds in Christ Jesus"* (Philippians 4: 6-7). Therefore, if you have chosen gay or lesbian life-style, it is not too late for you to turn to the Friend of sinners—Jesus, who *"came to seek and to save the lost"* (Luke 19:10). He has power to turn your life around. There are others like you, whose lives have changed, since they came to Christ. They are in support groups, working at their jobs, and enjoying normal life. Christian counslors are out there ready to help you. I encourage you to consult any of them for counseling and necessary assistance.

Naming Ceremony

As its name implies, this ceremony is conducted to enable a married couple to make known publicly to family members and friends their gift of a new baby in the family. Since many parents name their children after their great, great grand-parents, an elderly member of the family is often asked to pour libation, calling upon the spirits of ancestors to come into the child and shield it from harm. If, indeed, children are gifts from God, then why don't we pray to God alone for their safety, well-being, and fulfillment of their purpose on this earth? The Bible urges us as parents to *"bring them* (our children) *up in the training and instruction of the Lord*" (Ephesians 6:4).

Neither gods nor ancestors can create or bless our children for good; let alone to equip them with virtues, which will enable them to achieve their goals in this world. Besides, pouring libation to spirits at a naming ceremony of a child will open up avenues for evil forces to invest their diabolical plans in the life of the child. As Christians, therefore, I suggest the following pattern: In most African cultures, naming ceremonies take place in the parents' home or church hall. To begin with, a close relative or friend is chosen as the Master of Ceremony (MC). After an opening hymn or chorus, a priest or a Christian elder of the family offers prayer, thanking God for the gift of a new baby in the family and for all the invited guests assembled in the house. In Africa, a child is a gift not only to the biological parents, but also the extended family and the community as a whole. Hence, prayers are offered, touching the needs of all concerned. This is followed by the introduction of all the invited guests, and the purpose of their meeting on that particular occasion. Then, two classes filled with water and wine (not a hard liquor-usually a fruit-drink) respectively are placed on a table. The father writes the name of the child on a piece of paper and hands it over to the officiating minister/elder member of the family appointed to perform the ceremony. The priest/godfather/elder holds the child gently in his arms and announces to the people the name of the child, and explains the reasons for the choice of that particular name. Usually, a child is named after a grandfather/mother, whose life has had a good impact on the entire family. It is believed that a child named after such a great person will naturally cultivate similar characteristics and lead a virtuous life as his ancestor.

> After making known the name, the celebrant dips his forth finger into the glass of water and touches the tongue of the child, saying to him/her (he calls out the name of the child), "so and so, se ese nsu a, nna nsu a", meaning, if you say, *this is water, then it is truly water.*" This act is repeated three times. After this, he dips his finger into the liquor and touches the tongue of the child as before, saying (he mentions the name of the child), "se ese nsa a, nna nsa a," if

> you say, *"this is liquor, it is truly,liquor).* This is in conformity with Scripture, which admonishes us as follows: *"Let your 'Yes' be Yes, and your 'No' no, or you will be condemned*" (James 5: 12).

Therefore, the signicance of this ritual is to inculcate in the child the spirit of honesty and truthfulness, so that as he/she grows up, he/she will develop such traits of character and thus become a reliable and dependable citizen in the family and community.

At this juncture, final prayers are offered for the child and his/her parents, asking for God's blessings and protection for them and all the guests. Then, the father presents his gift(usually, money) to the child, followed by the rest of the guests, who also generously offer their individual gifts of cash or in kind to the baby. These gifts are all gratefully received by the MC on behalf of the parents in respect of the child. It is to be noted here that in African culture, a child is born into a community and not as a single individual belonging to a married couple living in isolation. Finaly, the ceremony comes to an end with food and refreshment for all the guests to enjoy. There is no actual closing time for this. Sometimes, the festivities continue till midnight because as some leave, others also come in to welcome the new baby with their presents. That is enough for now. Let's turn our attention to what we do for twins.

Ritual For Twins

Again, we may have to be reminded that children-whether twins, or triplets, quadruplets, or septuplets, all are gifts from God, to whom we must be thankful. However, due to false traditional belief, the Ghanaian/African has the notion that twins are special gifts from the gods of the land/clan. Hence, a special ritual is performed for the twins during the naming ceremony. A fetish priest/priestess prepares two amulets/wrist-bands (*'abam'*)—to be worn on the wrist by each of the twin children. It is believed that the spirit in the 'abam' protects and identifies them as the children of the gods, and thus maintains the relation between the twins and the gods. It is also believed that the gods speak through the spirit to parents about the children as to what they should do or not do for the twins and the gods. It is very important to note here that since these gods truly have no power to create any human being, they neither have the divine virtues of love, mercy, or compassion for any human being-adult or child. Inability to meet the high demands imposed upon the parents by the fetish priest/priestess usually results in serious illness on the children, and finally, death.

They could be likened to *Baal, the god of the Cannanites* (1 Kings 18: 25; Jeremiah 19:5), *or "Molech, the god of the Ammonites, Chemosh, the god of the Moabites, and Ashtoreth, the goddess of the Sidonians"* (1 Kings11:33), all of which demanded the sacrifice of the children of Israel by fire to pacify them, as stated in the previous passage. Therefore, the Israelites were seriously warned against such idolatrous, and wicked act of worship, because it provoked God to anger and brought disastrous consequences upon Israel whenever they indulged in it (Leviticus 20: 1-5).

That is why in the Gospel of John, Jesus, who *"came to seek and to save the lost,"* seriously cautions all Christians about the ways of the devil, saying*: "The thief comes only to steal and kill and destroy; I have come that they may have life, and have it to the full"* (John 10:10).

There are several Christian parents, who did not go through any rituals of 'abam' for their twins, but simply had them dedicated to the Lord, the Giver and Sustainer of all human beings. Their children are still living to the glory of God. Whatever God created, the world and all its fullness, including human beings, were intended to bring God glory, as stated in the following: *"I created everyone for my glory"* (Isaiah 43:7).

Even if, they fall sick and die, (because Christians are not exempted from sickness and death, etc. see John 6:33), we still believe with Job that *"the Lord gave and the Lord has taken away; the name of the Lord be praised"* (Job 1:21).

Funeral Ceremony

Usually, on such an occasion, the Master of Ceremony calls upon an elderly man from the bereaved family, accompanied by two or three other members. They stand in the middle or corner of the hall, and the ritualist lifts up the cup of drink towards heaven, supposedly showing it to God for His approval. He then pours two or three drops of liquor to the ground for '*Asaase Yaa*' (i.e. Mother Earth), and begins to call on the names of the gods, and the ancestors of the various clans, inviting them to receive a drink. He follows this with an appeal to them to provide protection and prosperity for the community, especially for the bereaved family, and the country as a whole.

Sometimes, there is suspicion that the death of the family member was caused by an enemy (through witchcraft, voodoo or curse, etc.). In this case, the spirits are called upon to retaliate, paying evil for evil. This, again, is contrary to the will of God as revealed in the Holy Scriptures. Retaliation brings neither peace nor victory, but rather further destruction of precious lives. Hence, we are commanded by the Lord, "*love your enemies and pray for those who persecute you*" (Matthew 5:43-45). For, the Bible declares: "*Vengeance is mine, I will repay, says the Lord. On the contrary, if your enemy is hungry, feed him; if he is thirsty, give him something to drink. In doing this, you will heap burning coals on his head. Do not be overcome by evil, but overcome evil with good.*" (Romans 12:19-21).

Therefore, during funeral ceremonies, elders of the people should speak words of comfort and encouragement to the bereaved family instead of invoking the powers of gods and ancestors for retaliation, which doesn't do any good to anybody; not even the bereaved family or the children within the community. The truth of the matter is that our adherence to tradition has left a bad example for posterity to follow. The time to change for the better is now.

Installation of a Traditional King/Chief

This is a very special day in the life of a people of any Ghanaian City or community. It is the day a new chief/king/queen takes office or swears the Oath of allegiance to the Head of State, paramount chief, elders and people as a whole. One of the most significant functions on the agenda for such an occasion is libation. As the elder pours libation, he prays to the ancestors and the spirits of the land to give the new king/queen the necessary strength, foresight, wisdom and courage to deal justly with all people without discrimination, fear or favour.

The question, again, is: "Who in heaven or earth or beneath the earth is able to provide the king and his elders with virtues such as wisdom, honesty, courage, which can lead a nation to success and prosperity, but God alone?" In calling upon lesser gods and the spirits of our ancestors for help, we are violating the commandments of God (Exodus 20:1-6). The pity is that neither a god nor any ancestor is able to help a people or any nation to achieve their goal honorably on earth, except God. Therefore, by resorting to other gods and spirits of the dead for help, we leave God completely out of our plans. Since God is Almighty, Holy and a Jealous God, He has declared: *"I am the Lord; that is my name! I will not give my glory to another or my praise to idols"* (Isaiah 42:8).

On the day of the installment of a chief, when we pour libation to gods and ancestors and pray to them to meet our needs, we are only provoking God to anger as declared by the Prophet Zechariah:

> *It is the Lord who makes the storm clouds. He gives showers of rain to men, and plants of the field to everyone. The idols speak deceit, diviners see visions that lie; they tell dreams that are false, they give comfort in vain. Therefore the people wander like sheep oppressed for lack of a shepherd. My anger burns against the shepherds, and I will punish the leaders, for the Lord Almighty will care for his flock* (Zechariah 10:1b-3b).

God's anger still burns against the leaders, namely, our chiefs and kings, and the religious leaders who compromise their faith, because they are the ones entrusted with authority to lead the people in the right direction, that is, to seek God and to follow His righteous ways. But unfortunately, many of our leaders follow their own selfish ways, mislead the people, and abuse the trust confined in them. We have to remind ourselves as leaders that God, Who entrusts us with authority, different gifts and talents to fulfill our different roles for His divine purpose, also knows our weaknesses as human beings:

> *He remembers that we are dust. As for man, his days are like grass, he flourishes like a flower of the field; the wind blows over it and it is gone, . . . But from everlasting to everlasting the Lord's love is with those who fear Him, and His righteousness with their children's children.* (Psalms 103:15-17).

Therefore, as Kings, Heads of nations, as well as leaders of tribes and communities, and Christian leaders, we should acknowledge not only our trespasses as human beings, but also, particularly, our inability to do without God, who is the Source of our life, and the very Power that sustains us, including every living thing. Hence, without God, we are hopeless and helpless; indeed, we are headed for failure, disgrace and complete disaster. It is like building our castle in the sand instead of upon the solid Rock; it is bound to collapse and break into bits and pieces in the face of storms of life (Matthew 7:24-27). For *"Unless the Lord builds the house, its builders labor in vain*" (Psalms 127:1).

On this, the Lord drew my attention immediately to what is written in the Book of proverbs by the wise King, Solomon:

> *Choose my instruction instead of silver, knowledge rather than choice gold, for wisdom is more precious than rubies, and nothing you desire can compare with her. I, wisdom, dwell together with prudence; I possess knowledge and discretion. To fear the Lord is to hate evil; I hate pride and arrogance, evil behavior and perverse speech. Counsel and sound judgement are mine; I have understanding and power. By me kings reign and rulers make laws that are just; by me princes govern, and all nobles who rule on earth. I love those who love me and those who seek me find me. With me are riches and honor, enduring wealth and prosperity. I walk in the way of righteousness, along the path of justice, bestowing wealth on those who love me and making their treasuries full*. (Proverbs 8:10-18, 20-21).

These are the words of wisdom coming from the lips of King Solomon, the wisest of all the kings who had ever reigned and who are yet to reign on this earth. Solomon learnt this lesson from his personal experience with God during his reign as king of Israel. The lesson here is that unless we, as humans, live our lives in submission to God's guidance, wisdom and purpose, all our wealth, together with all kinds of earthly pleasure, all is *"Utterly meaningless, everything is meaningless"* (Ecclesiastes 1:2). Such was the miserable experience of King Solomon, who, in spite of his many wives and concubines, plus riches uncountable, found life empty and meaningless, because he turned from God to worship the gods of his foreign wives. In the process, his love for Yahweh grew cold, for his heart was no longer whole toward his God, who made him King of Israel. Solomon's experience teaches all humans that joy, happiness, comfort and the peace of mind and soul that we crave cannot come from the abundance of our earthly possessions, but from God alone, who made us in His image. He blessed us with the gift of procreation, and gave us dominion over the earth and everything in it, including birds of the air, and the fish in the sea (Genesis 1:27, 28-30). It follows, therefore, that leaders of nations, as well as people in various positions of authority, who choose to worship idols or material possessions, bring trouble upon themselves, community and the people they represent. But with God, we all become channels of blessing and "righteousness, which exalts a nation."

CHAPTER ELEVEN

LEADERS WHO FEAR TO LOSE THEIR POSITION

Let us ask ourselves this question, "Why do some people in authority refuse to accept Jesus as Saviour and Lord of their lives? The truth of the matter is that "most of the people in power today", as Burke Hedges describes them, "are scared to death. Their overriding concern is the fear of loss, that is, loss of their own power! Everywhere they turn, they see the handwriting on the wall and they don't like the message. So what do they do? They shoot the messenger" (Burke Hedges in *Who Stole The American Dream*, p.107).

For instance, when Jesus raised Lazarus from death, news of this great miracle quickly spread throughout the city of Jerusalem and its surroundings. But, when the leaders of the Jews heard it, they quickly conveyed a meeting and took counsel to kill Jesus. John, the beloved disciple, reports their plans as follows:

> *Then the chief priests and the Pharisees called a meeting of the Sanhedrin. "What are we accomplishing?" They asked. "Here is this man performing many miraculous signs. If we let him go on like this everyone will believe in him, and then the Romans will come and take away both our place and*

> *our nation." Then one of them, named Caiaphas, who was high priest that year spoke up: "You know nothing at all! You do not realize that it is better for you that one man die for the people than that the whole nation perish."* (John 11:47-50).

As the leaders of Jerusalem in the olden days rejected Jesus, and secretly plotted to kill Him, and they did kill Him indeed, even so there are several countries today, whose leaders, as well as some individuals, out of pride, jealousy and selfishness, refuse Christ's entry into their lives. They have no fear of God or regard for their neighbors. They do not believe in Christ as the Son of God, neither do they want to hear His name mentioned. But, the Bible declares that . . . *"there is no other name under heaven given to human beings by which we must be saved"* (Acts 4:12), except the name JESUS. The angel of God spoke to Joseph about this NAME: ". . . *you are to give him the name Jesus, because he will save his people from their sins"* (Matthew 1:21). Jesus is, therefore, God's answer to the human condition of sin and death, and eternal condemnation in hell.

We must remember that the rejection of Jesus Christ by the Jewish leaders resulted in the destruction of Jerusalem and precious lives of its inhabitants. We also need to be reminded that being descendants of Adam and Eve, all human beings naturally inherited a sinful tendency; it is in the blood. Therefore, just as they were cursed and suffered as a result of their sin, so are all humanity under a curse and its deadly consequences. As human beings, therefore, we must realize that we cannot save ourselves (Genesis 3:16-19). We did not make ourselves in this world; God did, according to the Scriptures (Genesis 1:26-27, 2:7, 18-24). Thus, we need the Almighty God to rescue us from the mess in which we find ourselves. Hence, the Prophet Jeremiah wrote:

> *Cursed is the one who trusts in man, who depends on flesh for his strength and whose heart turns away from the Lord. He will be like a bush in the waste-lands; He will not see prosperity when it comes. He*

> *will dwell in the parched places of the desert. But blessed is the man who trusts in the Lord, whose confidence is in Him. He will be like a tree planted by the river that sends out its roots by the stream. It does not fear when heat comes; its leaves are always green . . . and never fails to bear* fruit (Jeremiah 17: 5-8b).

The point being emphasized here by Jeremiah is that God is the source of who we are, and all that we possess here and now; as well as what we shall become in future, either with God in heaven, or with Satan in hell. It is God who gives human beings power for success and prosperity. Jesus sounded the same caution: "*without me, you can do nothing*," (John. 15:5). Paul also, reminded all of us, saying, "*For we brought nothing into this world, and we can certainly take nothing out of it*" (1 Timothy 6:7). "*Whatever we have is a gift from God, who richly gives us everything for our enjoyment*" (1 Timothy 6: 17).

Life Without God is Fruitless

As Solomon, the wise King later found out, even for anyone "*to eat and drink and find satisfaction in his/her work is a gift of God, for without him, who can eat or find enjoyment?*" (Ecclesiastes 2:24). Except the Lord be with us, there is no real satisfaction or true enjoyment in any aspect of life. It has no purpose or meaning. If so, what are we here for? Or are we like those in Judah, who said, "*Let us eat and drink, for tomorrow we die*" (Isaiah 22:13b), because they saw no hope or value for life due to the impending doom for their rebellion against God? It behooves us, therefore, not to rely on ourselves or anything that we possess. Even when wealth or riches abound, we are cautioned not to cast our hope upon them as if, all our life depends on them. For, as Jesus pointed out to the rich fool in His parable, our "*life*", as individual human beings, "*does not consist in the abundance of our possessions*" (Luke 12:15). Our life is in the hands of God, our Maker and Sustainer.

The reason is that God, in His divine wisdom, and for the total good and fulfillment of each other's life and purpose on earth, did not make human beings to be independent of Him. Life, in its highest fulfillment, according to God's plan, is designed to be lived in loving relationship with God through daily obedience to God, and in loving fellowship with one another as prescribed in His Word (Matthew 22:36-40). Anything less than the divine plan is not only meaningless, but also sinful in the sight of God.

Therefore, in the following text, the Lord specifically addresses those nations and individuals, who boast of their possessions and make their riches, knowledge or wisdom, technology, military power, magic, or voodoo, as idols to be worshipped, and in which they place their trust, hope and confidence:

> *Let not the wise man boast of his wisdom or the strong man boast of his strength! Or the rich man his riches. But let him who boasts boast about this: that he understands and knows me, that I am the Lord who exercises kindness, justice and righteousness on earth, for in these I delight, declares the Lord* (Jeremiah 9:23-24).

For instance, King Solomon, the richest man that ever lived on this planet earth, had the privilege of marrying seven hundred beautiful women from all parts of the globe, including those from his own country, Israel. Besides, he had three hundred concubines and enjoyed every kind of pleasure that his heart desired. Solomon had thought, like every other man would have done, that these earthly pleasures would bring him fulfillment, but he was miserably disappointed. He wrote:

> *Yet when I surveyed all that my hands had done and what I had toiled to achieve, everything was meaningless, a chasing after the wind; nothing was gained under the sun. So I hated life, because the work that is done under the sun was grievous to me. All of it is meaningless, a chasing after the wind* (Ecclesiastes 2:11 & 17).

Oh! What a bitter experience of disappointment from the lips of a man, who thought he had it all together? If Solomon, who had never been and will never be surpassed by any man in terms of riches and worldly pleasures never found fulfillment from these material blessings, then, none of us will find satisfaction without God. Why? According to the Biblical records, among the many wives Solomon had married were foreign women-Moabites, Ammonites, Sidonians, and Hittites, who were from the nations about whom the Lord had told the Israelites not to intermarry (because God knew that they would surely turn the hearts of His people after their gods). Although God had forbidden Israel, yet Solomon did not keep the Lord's command.

Consequently, as time went on, Solomon's foreign wives turned his heart to follow their gods, as it is written:

> *He followed Ashtoreth the goddess of the Sidonians,and Molech the detestable god of the Ammonites. So Solomon did evil in the eyes of the Lord . . .. The Lord became angry with Solomon because his heart had turned away from the Lord, the God of Israel, who had appeared to him twice.* (1 Kings 11:5-6, 9).

Looking at the issues from our human perspectives, especially from the perspective of the politician, one may say that Solomon might have done well initially for his strong alliance with neighbouring nations through inter-marriage. That strategy bonded Israel to the allied nations, and consequently made Israel to be considered by outsiders as a formidable force, not only in terms of Solomon's extraordinary wisdom, but also in its economic and political power. Nevertheless, since Solomon did not seek divine guidance in embarking upon that political alliance with foreign nations through marriage tides, what looked glamorous and successful to human estimation, eventually led to inward, religious decay and apostasy, and finally, division of the formerly united, Davidic kingdom over which he was made king. Solomon's experience, like those of many leaders today, confirms the truth that "*Unless the Lord builds the city, they labour in vain that build it. Unless the Lord watches over the city, the watchmen stand guard in vain*" (Psalm 127: 1). It was that experience, among several others, that caused Solomon, under the inspiration of the Holy Spirit, to write the following proverb as a sound counsel to young people:

> *My son, do not forget my teaching, but keep my commands in your heart, for they will prolong your life many years and bring you prosperity. Let love and faithfulness never leave you; bind them around your neck . . .. Trust in the Lord with all your heart and lean not on your own understanding; in all your ways acknowledge him, and He will make your paths straight. Do not be wise in your own eyes; fear the Lord and shun evil.* (Proverbs 3:1-3, 5-7).

Solomon was no exception in what he experienced as a young, rich prince of Israel.

Earlier on in their journey through the wilderness, Israel camped in the land of Shittim, where the men indulged in sexual immorality with the women of the land. They sacrificed to their gods, ate with the people and worshipped their gods. Their act of idolatry compounded by their whoredom, caused the fierce anger of God that 24,000 of them died as a result of a plague (Numbers 25:1-9). This is a clear warning to everyone that God is the very source of our life; and to leave Him for any other god brings nothing, but disappointment, sorrow and destruction of lives. David Roper of RBC Ministries put it this way, "*We are born and we live for the express purpose of knowing and loving God. He is the source of our life*" (Daily Bread, Friday, November 14, 2003).

After scanning his lifestyle in the light of the Holy Scriptures, St. Augustine, one of the great pillars of the Roman Catholic Church also had almost a similar thing to say, "*Thou has made us for Thyself, oh God! And our souls are restless, until they find their rest in Thee.*" St. Augustine, like Solomon, spoke from his personal experience. He was born into a family of a mixed parentage of a pious, devout Christian mother and a pagan father, who belonged to the middle class of a town in North Africa. Augustine loved learning and became well educated in textual study of the major Latin classics in Carthage. He searched and tasted almost every religion, as well as every philosophy of his day, but none of them provided him with the inner satisfaction his soul needed most. It was not until he was forty that he found the truth in the Gospel of Christ, which has the power to liberate every human being from sin and from every other force that dominates human life.

His conversion took place in a garden in Milan, where he overheard a child reciting a rhyme: "Take and read, take and read." Taking hold of his Bible, Augustine began to read Paul's letter to the Romans till he came to the text, "*. . . not in orgies and drunkenness, not in sexual immorality and debauchery, not in dissension and jealousy. Rather, clothe yourselves with the Lord Jesus Christ . . . and do not gratify the desires of the sinful nature*" (Romans 13:13-14).

Thus, Augustine began his new life in Christ under the guidance and power of the Holy Spirit. Williston Walker wrote: "He was now able to see himself as a soul whose fulfillment lay in the knowledge and love of God; and not in himself or his ability." My friend, are you restless today, driven by discontentment and a longing for that elusive "something" that you know not what? "Jesus Christ," says David Roper, "is the source and satisfaction of all you seek." In 391 A. D., Augustine was ordained a presbyter by Valerius, who was the Bishop of the church in the city of Hippo in Numidia, North Africa. In 395, when Bishop Valerius went to his eternal home, Augustine was the one chosen to succeed him as Bishop of Hippo. His teachings, writings especially, his Confessions, and devotional life, which helped immensely to guide and strengthen the church in North Africa, are still highly treasured among the great doctrines of the Roman Catholic Church today.

CHAPTER TWELVE

CHRISTIANS ARE PART OF THE PROBLEM

The question is *"If Christ is able to change sinful men and women into righteous people, whose new life of hard work and integrity can help lift a nation from deterioration to progress and from disgrace to honor, why is it that the majority of countries in Africa, including Ghana, are still lagging behind in terms of development?"* For, it is written: "*Righteousness exalts a nation, but sin is a disgrace to any people*" (Proverbs 14:34). This is not by any means to suggest that Africans are the most sinful, or backward people in the world. The Word of God applies to every nation or people under the sun, who do not give God the first place in the government of their daily affairs/lives. For example, Ghana is a country, where traditional chiefs, political leaders, preachers, as well as elders of tribes, have known for years through the popular, African proverbial expression, *"Gye Nyame"*, that unless God is with you or helps you, life is vain. The sign, *"Gye Nyame"* appears among several other African artistic designs in clothes, clay and wood. Though it is a short, idiomatic expression, it is pregnant with significant meaning and wisdom as stated in the introduction.

Worshipping God and Traditional Spirits

Somehow, as members of the church, who should have been

God's instrument for change, we distanced ourselves from the traditions of the people, and were unable to help or guide the people outside the Church to find the way that leads to salvation. On the other hand, the majority of those who do not distance themselves, but get involved with traditional religious practices, do not seem to know the difference between the Christian faith and traditional religion. We can find a typical example in a story concerning a certain rich, Christian contractor, who hailed from the Central Region of Ghana. The story, as written by Brother Idan, was that this wealthy contractor was instrumental in the building of a church, as well as the erection of a shrine for their idol/god in his local community. The story continues as follows:

> *Ironically, he put a cross 'of Jesus' on the shrine similar to that he had erected on the front view of the church. While he served as an elder of the church and even had a special seating place in the church, he was also serving as 'safohene'—(chief of the tribal group) a position that involves idolatrous practices and rituals.*
>
> *After some years, the prominent man died and a struggle ensued between the Church and the shrine over the body. The fetish priests and other 'safohene' warned the church in question that on Friday, the wake-keeping day, the church should release this man's body to them at midnight to enable them take it to their shrine for rituals to be performed over the body.*
>
> *True to their word on the wake-keeping day, when the town was filled with people from all walks of life, including a delegation from the church's Headquarters, ministers from the various branches of the church, and visitors, these idol worshippers-the fetish priests and priestesses and 'Asafohene' (the leaders of the tribal groups) with their 'Asafo' Companies invaded the church grounds, demanded 'their' body and took it to their Shrine.*

> *While the church continued with wake-keeping without the body, the idolatrous rituals and ceremonies also went on at the shrine. When it was time for the burial service to begin, they went to demand the body, but had to wait because the pagan rituals were not over. The body was later released and the burial service started (W. K. Idan, Snr., Are You A True Christian, pp. 13-14).*

In the face of a critical situation like this, Evangelist Idan poses the following challenging questions to you, dear reader:

> *Who owns the body by right; the church or the shrine? What will be the destination of the man's soul—(heaven or hell)? Why is someone called a Christian? Whose fault was it, the man, the church, ministers, the society, tradition, or the government? Do you worship the God of our Lord Jesus Christ, or the god of our ancestors? You must decide and choose your stand before it is too late.*

These are real heart-searching questions that all readers need to ponder over carefully and give accurate answers for themselves. Let's take another instance, during a naming ceremony, an elder of a Christian couple usually pours libation, after which prayers are offered by a church representative for the occasion as follows:

> *O God, Almighty, we seek your approval for our libation (i. e. on our prayer). We call on you this morning, for we know that you control our destiny. Ancestors of the clan, receive your drink. We call on you to bless this child who is being out-doored this morning. Let him grow as strong and famous as his ancestor whose name he bears. Now, gods of the land, we pray you to protect this child from illness and untimely death. We pray you to prosper the work of the parents and all the families of the clan, and*

> *those abroad. 'Eguana' (name of a clan) 'abosom' (gods), receive your drink.*

If we read these words of libation carefully, we shall find that the prayer is addressed to God, ancestors, as well as other gods or spirits. We have a problem here, because the Scriptures warn us against associating God with other gods, as follows:

> *I am the Lord your God.You shall have no other gods before me.. . . You shall not bow to them or worship them; for I, the Lord your God, am a jealous God, punishing the children for the sin of the fathers to third and forth generation of those who hate me, but showing love to a thousand generation of those who love me* (Exodus 20: 3,5-6).

Libation or prayer offered to ancestors and lesser gods is not the same as prayer made to God through Jesus Christ. The two ways conflict with each other, because one is offered to God, the Creator of this world, while libation is offered to gods and ancestors. They are NOT the same, yet it happens often in several Christian homes, because the Christians involved do not really know Christ, or *"the Truth"* that has the power to *"set you free"* (John 8: 31-32). They assume that they are keeping to tradition or ancestral religious values, but in reality, they are ignorant of the Word of God. The fact is, we cannot serve God through Christ, and also bow to other gods. By so doing, we provoke God to anger. Jesus said, *"No servant can serve two masters. Either he will hate the one and love the other, or he will be devoted to the one and despise the other"* (Luke 16:13).

The Failure Of Okomfo Damuah

Another example is the case of Rev. Father Damuah, who abandoned his Catholic faith for the position of a cultic priest with the intention to indigenize Christianity. A cultic priest, in the Ghanaian African sense is *'Okomfo'*, that is, a fetish priest or diviner, who worships idols, and lesser gods and spirits. He/she is the medium through whom the gods speak. In this particular situation, as Rev.

Harrison wrote: "Damuah's role is the same as the medium at Endor, who was consulted by Saul (1 Samuel 28 :7-25). Should the church have then worked with him?" Harrison inquires. He answers his own question with an emphatic, "No!", and then adds, "I believe he lost his hope in God, which brings joy and peace…so that one may abound in hope in the power of the Holy Spirit" (Aquaah-Harrison, Victor, *Sankofa Yenkyi* 2000, p. 42). He was rejected by the Church because the Scriptures denounce such pagan practices done in the guise of keeping African religious tradition and culture (Exodus 20:4; Deuteronomy 32:16; 1 Corinthians 10:14; 1 John 5:21).

In the following passage, Jesus vehemently rebukes religious leaders, who choose tradition over God's Holy Word, "*These people worship me with their lips, bur their hearts are far from me. They worship me in vain; their teachings are but rules taught by men. You have let go the commandment of God and are holding on to the traditions of men"* (Mark 7: 6-8). Nevertheless, in reading this from the lips of Jesus, we must not in any way jump into conclusion that Jesus is against tradition. For, in another context, He declared: "*Do not think that I have come to abolish the Law or the Prophets; I have not come to abolish them but to fulfill them*" (Matthew 5:17). Jesus proved the truth of this mission-statement in one particular instance, when, after healing a leper, He sent him away with the following instructions, *"Show yourself to the priest and offer the sacrifices that Moses commanded as a testimony to them"* (Mark 1:44). This is a proof that Jesus is not against the Law as His opponents suppose. However, He rejects vehemently any additions to the Commandments the Scribes had made, which make it difficult or impossible for the people to obey God, as we have previously read from Mark 7: 6-8.

It is, therefore, very crucial that those of us who are committed Christians should uphold the True teachings of the Holy Scriptures, and to share the Gospel boldly with others whenever, and wherever necessary, so as to enlighten those who may be in darkness and are ignorant of the Bible. Unfortunately, there are some traditional elders, pastors and church leaders, who are so steeped in tradition that they cannot do anything traditionally significant (such as marriage ceremony, funeral, etc.) without pouring libation to the gods and ancestors. They regard libation as a necessary religious practice to be followed. Any attempt by committed Christians to stop them seems offensive. They see such bold stand for Christ as disrespect for tradition or African culture. This is due to lack of revelation of the knowledge of the Holy Scriptures.

Does not God strictly warn His people (all who believe in God/Christ) not to worship other gods, as it is written:

> *I am the Lord your God, who brought you out of Egypt, out of the land of slavery. You shall have no other gods before me . . . You shall not bow to them or worship them; For I, the Lord your God, am a jealous God, Punishing the children for the sin of the fathers to the third and fourth generation of those who hate me, but showing love to a thousand generations who love me and keep my commandments* (Exodus 20: 2-3, 5-6).

What happened when the people of Israel disobeyed God and got involved in syncretistic and idolatrous practices? Moses, the leader of Israel wrote:

> *They made him jealous with their foreign gods and angered him with their detestable idols. They sacrificed to demons, which are not God; gods they had not known, gods that recently appeared, . . . You deserted the Rock, who fathered you. You forgot the God who gave you birth. The Lord saw this and rejected them, because He was angered by His sons and daughters. I will heap calamities upon them and spend my arrows against them. I will send wasting famine against them, consuming pestilence and deadly plague* (Deuteronomy 32:16-19, 23-24).

My dear reader, as evidenced in the Holy Scriptures, as well as in our own individual personal experiences, disobedience to God's commandments has always brought about disastrous consequences to those involved. For, it is written, "*The soul that sins shall die*" (Ezekiel 18:4).

During the former military regime headed by Flt. Lt. J. J. Rawlings, Heads or Statesmen of other countries who visited Ghana were welcomed with the pouring of libation to the gods and ancestors. Prayers were offered to them for security and success of our guests, as if the land and the people were protected by gods and spirits. State functions were preceded with libation, indicating that the State as a whole depended upon such deities. These spirits exist, and when you call them, they will come "*only to steal, to kill, and to destroy*" (John 10:10).

Consequently, demonic spirits gained access into the decision-making processes of the governing class, and thus, succeeded in influencing their decision on public policies for the nation. In fact, during this regime, many people, including women, died a terrible death. For instance, in his book, '*The Amazing Dictator*', John Westwood writes, "General F. W. K. Akuffo, General A. A. Afrifa, Air Vice-Marshal G. Y. Boakye, Rear Admiral Joy Amedume, Major-General R. E. A. Kotei and Col. R. J. A. Feli were also executed by firing squad. Their bodies," says Westwood, "including those of Acheampong and Utuka, were put into crude coffins constructed with rough wawa wood and buried in the grounds of the prisons" (John Westwood, *The Amazing Dictator*, 2001, p.5).

Perhaps, what created a lot of tension, fear, and insecurity among Ghanaians, were the murders of Mrs. Justice Cecilia Koranteng-Addow, Justice Fred Poku Sarkodie, and Justice Kwadwo Agyei Akyeampong, and a retired Army Officer, Major Sam Acquah. They were taken from their homes under the cover of the night and murdered in cold blood. *"Each of them,"* writes Westwood, *"was made to sit on a block and they were shot several times from behind. Their bodies were doused with petrol and set alight...."(Ibid. p.4).*

When the horrible situation became unbearable, the Makola market women courageously protested with a demonstration. They were demonstrating against the brutal murders of innocent women in the streets of Accra, calling on the Government and the Law

Enforcement agencies to trace the killers and bring them to justice. Undoubtedly, those were ritual murders associated with demonic worship, confirming the words of Jesus concerning satanic activities: *"The thief (i. e. Satan) comes only to steal and kill* and destroy" (John 10:10a).

According to Westwood, a legal team headed by Justice Azu Crabbe, which investigated the case *"led to the trial and conviction of Amartey Kwei, Amedekah, Senya, Dzandu and Tekpor for murder" (Ibid. 72).* Though it was obvious that those soldiers carried out orders issued by a ranking Officer or Officers, there was not enough evidence to convict them. But, the Almighty God knows everyone who was involved in the heinous crime, because He is Omnipresent, as well as Omniscient, as the Scripture declares, "*The eyes of the Lord are everywhere, keeping watch on the wicked and the good*" (Psalm 139:1-3,7-12; Proverbs 15:3). Someday, God will bring all people to judgment, concerning the things we have done, whether good or evil (Ecclesiastes 14:13; Romans 14:12). On that day, nobody can hide from the presence of God, because He is the Maker and Governor of this world and "*holds the whole world in His hands*" (Isaiah 40: 15-17; Daniel 4:34-35).

The question bothering the mind of many Ghanaians is, "What was the motive for the killing of General Afrifa and other army officers, and the three judges? Apparently, there was fear on the part of Rawlings that Afrifa might lead other soldiers to intervene, should the PNDC fail to fulfill their commitment to the nation. The death of the judges might have been caused by their daring stand against some of the policies initiated by the Provisional National Defence Council (PNDC).

Therefore, the motive was possibly to keep the PNDC government permanently in power. Indeed, they reigned for twenty years, much longer than any other regime that had ruled over Ghana, besides the British. However, they could not remain in power indefinitely. Did the killings and the brutal murders enable them to achieve their objectives for themselves and the nation? The answer is a big "No"! On the contrary, the PNDC government left Ghanaians much poorer spiritually, economically and emotionally than they were when they first took office in 1981. This was unlike the regime of the Armed Forces Revolutionary Council (A. F. R. C.) led by Rawlings in June 1979, which was hailed by the masses. That was when the cost of living was so high that only the rich could afford three meals a day. But with Rawlings as the head of government, we saw the following changes in the condition of life of the masses for the better:

1. Traders refrained from hoarding their commodities, and prices of goods became affordable to the average Ghanaian.
2. There was a sense of accountability in respect of those placed in authority or public office. Such awareness of accountability made office-bearers extra careful in the use of public money or government property.
3. Ghanaians were made to realize that the natural resources of the nation (e. g. gold, cocoa, etc.) were meant for the benefit of all and sundry, and not only for those in authority. By these and other initiatives undertaken by the AFRC regime, *"JJ"* sought to uproot out of the system corruption ("KALABULE"), which had spread like cancer into every sector of the Ghanaian society, hindering progress and destroying precious lives.

Indeed, Rawlings was so popular with the masses, particularly, students in the universities, that he was described by many as a man with a heart for the poor, and viewed as a savior of some sort. Hence, his initials *"JJ"* became acronym for *"Junior Jesus,"* and was hailed as such by the Ghanaian public wherever he showed up to address them. Rawlings was in power for only a brief period, just about a year or so, yet he left an indelible impression in the minds of many as a selfless leader, who staged the coup not for his persnal gain, but for the poor, in particular, and the good of Ghanaians in genral.

These reasons and others, which space will not allow me to list here prompted Ghanaians to heartly welcome Rawlings when he showed up again in the 1981 coup d'etat, which toppled the Limann government. However, as things turned out, the outcome of the second one was less favourable than people had expected. By the year 2000, when Kuffour's party took over office, as I have mentioned earlier in this book, Ghana was ranked among what the World Bank describes as *"Highly Indebted, Poor Countries" (HIPC).* What happened to our gold, diamond, bauxite, manganese, cocoa, timber, etc. of the land? Where were the good qualities of compassion and selflessness that Ghanaians saw in Rawlings during his short reign in 1979? Only God truly knows the heart of a person; doesn't He?

Here, I see the relevance of the comment by Herb V. Lugt on Job described in the Bible as *"a blameless and upright man, one who fears God and shuns evil"* (Job 1: 8). Lugt said, *"Yet after all his trials, Job said, 'I abhor myself, and repent in dust and ashes' (Job42: 6). Even after reflecting on his own goodness (29: 1-25), he knew the condition of his heart. From a human perspective, many people may be described as "good." But God sees the disobedience, selfishness, and hate that lie deep within all of us. He also knows that we have spiritual blind spots. And when He opens our eyes to see ourselves as He does, we understand why a "good man" like Job said he abhorred himself."* Lugt concluded with the following prayer and a poem by Anon:

> *Lord, help us to be good but never to lose sight of our sinfulness and unworthiness. Thank you for the forgiveness You offer us in Jesus Christ —Herb Lugt.*
>
> *Teach me, Lord, my true condition,*
> *Bring me, childlike, to Your side;*
> *May I never trust my goodness—*
> *Only in Your grace abide —- Anon.*
> (Daily Bread, January 24, 2005).

Hence, the Lord has rightly declared in His Word that as humans, we cannot win the battle of life or save ourselves by our own *"might or power, but by my Spirit*, says the *Lord Almighty*" (Zechariah 4 :6). It is irrevocable, as well as irrefutable that "*unless the Lord builds the house, its builders labor in vain*" (Psalms 127 :1). That is to say, unless we give God the first place in the government of the nation, and of our individual lives, neither we as leaders nor individuals can make the best use of the resources of gold, diamond, cocoa, food, etc., which God has richly bestowed on the land. For God is the Maker and Owner of everything in this world, including all human beings, animals and birds of the air. Nothing belongs to us, neither do we have the power to maintain nor control anything. Hence, Jesus declares,"*Without Me, you can do nothing*. (John 15: 5).

What do we look for in those we put in authority—wealth, academic qualifications or divine wisdom? As we noticed earlier in chapter six, Joseph was appointed to a high office in Egypt because Pharaoh saw in Joesph such unique gifts of wisdom and discernment God (through His Spirit) had bestowed on him. When we come to the New Testament, we find similar qualifications as the criteria for the selection of seven deacons, whom the apostles appointed to the office of administration of the church while they devoted themselves to "*prayer and preaching of the gospel*" (Acts 6: 1-6).

We must take counsel from the Bible when we come to choosing leaders to fill positions of authority in the church and nation. We must be careful to prayerfully elect people who have the fear of God, and believe in Christ as their personal Savior and Lord. They must be men and women, who depend on God for wisdom, strength, direction and success in the exercise of their privileges and responsibilities. For "*righteousness exalts a nation, but sin is a disgrace to any people*"(Proverbs 14: 34). And only God can lead a nation to success and prosperity.

Dear friend, let me remind you seriously, if I may, that our salvation lies solely in our humble obedience to God, by grace through faith in His Son, Jesus Christ. "*For, there is one God and one mediator between God and human beings*" (1 Timothy 2: 5-6). Therefore, "*Salvation is found in no one else, for there is no other name under heaven given to men by which we must be saved*" (Acts 4: 12). Jesus is God's answer to all our human problems. Hence,

Jesus said, *"I am the Way, and the Truth and the Life. No one comes to the Father (God) except throuh Me"(John 14: 6).* Earlier in John, Jesus had declared to the world the purpose of His incarnation: *"I have come that they may have life, and have it to the full" (10: 10b).*

It is therefore, imperatively important that we adhere to God's exhortationn, and not allow ourselves to be deceived by blind leaders, who are groping in darkness, relying on ocultic powers or calling on the dead for assistance, lest we shall all be destroyed in the end (Matthew 23:16-17, 24, 26, 35-36). The legitimate question to ask here is: "*Can the dead help the living*?" (Isaiah 8:19). If we follow blind leaders, or depend on occultism, voodoo or ancestral spirits for success in life, we can expect nothing, but disappointment, shame and finally, condemnation before God. Jesus unequivocally rebuked as *"hypocrites,"...... "blind guides,"*..... and "brood of vipers" such leaders and those in authority who misled the people of Israel, because pride, greed and selfishness prevented them from submitting to His teaching and claim as the Christ (Messiah), the Son of God (Matthew 23: 15, 16, 30; John 8: 42-47).

Paul described those who opposed the Truth of the Gospel as, *"those who are perishing."* Why? Because, *"The god of this age has blinded the minds of unbelievers, so that they cannot see the light of the gospel of the glory of Christ, who is the image of God"* (2 Corinthians 4:3-4).

When we look further back into the history of Israel, we find that the people of God fell into apostasy in the days of Hosea, and God's wrath burned hot against the priests and elders, who misled the people due to their ignorance of the Word of God. Their ignorance led the people into all kinds of sin, the worst of which was idolatry against God, resulting finally in the captivity and destruction of a great number of the people of Israel. Hence, God's Word came to the Prophet Hosea, saying:

> *My people are destroyed from lack of knowledge. Because you have rejected knowledge, I also reject you as my priests; because you have ignored the law of your God, I also will ignore your children . . ..*

> *They exchanged their Glory for something disgraceful. They consult a wooden idol, and are answered by a stick of wood. A spirit of prostitution leads them astray.* (Hosea 4:6-7b, -10c).

As in the days of Hosea, there are a number of leaders of nations, churches and tribal groups in our generation, who are ignorant of the Truth (i. e. the Word of God), which sets humanity free from demonic forces and the power of sin with its deadly consequences. Hence, by wrong teachings and evil influence, many have been led astray or destroyed. Being followers of Christ, we must seriously be on the alert against diviners and false teachers of the Holy Scriptures, lest many will yet be deceived and led into darkness. It is for this reason that Jesus warned Christians:

> *Watch out for false prophets. They come to you in sheep's clothing, but inwardly they are wolves. Every tree that does not bear good fruit is cut down and thrown into fire. By their fruit you will recognize them* (Matthew 7:15, 19).

"*The days are evil*" (Ephesians 5:16), says Paul, and as always, false prophets and teachers are all over the place, maneuvering with their humanistic and New Age philosophies to mislead the innocent. It was with similar concern that Paul, in his usual, fatherly manner, warned his spiritual son, Timothy, "*. . . guard what has been entrusted to your care. Turn away from godless chatter and opposing ideas of what is falsely called knowledge, which some have professed and in so doing have wandered from the faith* (1 Timothy 6: 20-21). We all, like Timothy, must pay heed to Paul's wise counsel for our own good.

God Does Not Want Anyone to Perish:

I strongly believe that God is graciously showing His people, Israel and the whole world, including Africa, the way to salvation, peace, love, and prosperity, which come with showers of blessings upon all people, who "*seek first the kingdom of God and His righteousness*" (Matthew 6:33).

It is noted throughout the Holy Scriptures that whenever God sends His prophets with His Word to any people, it is a demonstration of God's love for that particular people or nation, indicating His willingness to save them from sin and its destructive consequences.

For instance, when the ancient city of Nineveh, the capital of Assyria, with its many acts of atrocities and wickedness, posed a great threat to Israel, God sent Jonah to proclaim judgment that was to come upon the city. Guess what happened: the entire nation, led by the king and his nobles, humbled themselves with prayer and fasting and sincerely repented from their sins. Jonah writes, *"When God saw what they did and how they turned from their evil ways, God had compassion and did not bring upon them the destruction He had threatened"* (Jonah 3:10).

Aren't we Christians supposed to be "*the light of the world*"? (Matthew 5:14). Are we not able to share God's Word with people, and to perform acts of charity, capable of drawing others to Christ that they might be saved by grace through faith in His name? (Ephesians 2: 8). Don't we believers have the privilege of being called "the salt of the earth" (Matthew 5:13), a people endowed with divine qualities that have the potential to preserve a city, from decay, corruption, or destruction? There are modern cities like Nineveh throughout the world today, particularly Africa, full of people led by kings and nobles, who are wicked, selfish and greedy, doomed to perish for their sins, unless they hear God's Word and repent.

I tell you what: God sees them all and *"has compassion for them, because they are harassed and helpless, like sheep without a shepherd"* (Matthew 9:36). Most certainly, it is not God's will that anybody should perish. God desires all to be saved, so that together we may enjoy the blessings that God has in store for us in His kingdom. But we must begin here and now, lest it may be too late.

God's question is: *"Whom shall I send? And who will go for us?"* (Isaiah6: 8). Isaiah responded to God's call, and through his prophetic ministry to Israel in three different phases of their history as God's chosen people, God's eternal purpose for the world was fulfilled in the birth, life, teaching, death and resurrection of Jesus Christ, the Saviour of the world. Thus, Paul wrote: *"God was reconciling the world to himself in Christ, not counting their sins against them"* (2 Corinthians 5:19).

Therefore, like Isaiah, let us as ministers of the Gospel, together with our congregations, lift high the banner of Christ, and proclaim His Word for all to come to the saving knowledge of Jesus Christ, our Lord. But, I am afraid that we cannot proclaim Christ or share His Word with others as boldly as we should, because there may be a question mark on our Christianity. And the question is: "Are we truly believers and teachers of the Gospel of Jesus Christ? Or are we false prophets—'wolves in sheep's clothing' (Matthew 7:15), intending to deceive others? If we are truly committed Christians, then we are "not ashamed of the Gospel, because it is the power of God for the salvation of everyone who believes" (Romans 1:16). Otherwise, we are nothing, but carnal Christians or perhaps, at best, only "mere infants" as those Paul addressed in his epistle (1 Corinthians 3:1ff.). We must individually ponder over these questions seriously and answer them honestly for our own spiritual advancement and, as a witness to the world and to our Lord, Jesus Christ.

CHAPTER THIRTEEN

CARNAL CHRISTIANS

Carnal Christians are immature believers. Like children, they are easily deceived by false teachers with every form of doctrine, because they do not really understand the Scriptures. They choose sides and bring divisions in the church, as it happened in the church of Corinth (ref. 1 Corinthians 3:1-9). Since they are not strong in the faith, they easily fall prey to the devil, who tempts them to indulge in all sorts of immoral behaviour.

For instance, in the church of Corinth, there was one such carnal (worldly) Christian flirting with his father's wife. When Paul received such a disgraceful report, his immediate reaction was firstly, to rebuke the leaders for their lukewarm attitude in allowing this wanton, immoral conduct, "*and of a kind that does not occur even among pagans*" (1 Corinthians 5:1b) to go on in the church of Christ. Secondly, Paul issued serious instructions to the leaders of the church to take immediate disciplinary action against that member: "*Expel the wicked man from among you*", was his Apostolic order to the leaders (1 Corinthians 3:1-9, 5:1-12).

Church goers:

The term, "church goers," refers to people who attend church service for any reason, but have not yet come to faith in Jesus Christ. Jesus said: "they call me 'Lord, Lord', yet do not do the will of my Father who is in heaven" (Matthew 7:21a). Again, Jesus describes them as "people who honour me with their lips, but their hearts are far away from me" (Matthew 7:21; Mark 7:6). We need individually to ask ourselves these questions: "What sort of a Christian am I?" "Am I a committed believer in Christ or carnal Christian?" Or "am I just an ordinary churchgoer, not knowing exactly what the church is all about?" Asking ourselves these searching questions, and answering them honestly will do ourselves and our churches a lot of good, and thus lead us to practical faith in Jesus Christ, which yields fruitful results of salvation to the glory of God. Jeremiah was bothered with similar questions when the people of Judah began to live in repeated disobedience to God's covenant. He asked:

> *Is there no balm in Gilead? Is there no physician there? Why then is there no healing for the wound of my people? . . . From the least to the greatest, all are greedy for gain; Prophets and priests alike all practice deceit. They dress the wound of my people as if it is not serious. 'Peace, Peace' they say, when there is no peace . . .. We hoped for peace, but no good has come, for a time of healing, but there was only terror.* (Jeremiah 8:22, 10b-11, 15).

When the people of Judah refused to heed God's Word proclaimed to them by the Prophet Jeremiah, they fell miserably into the hands of the invading army of King Nebuchadnezzer of Babylon in 586 B.C. That is a warning to all nations not to reject God's commandments. Being vulnerable human beings, we have learnt from the Holy Scriptures the sad, but inevitable truth that disobedience to God's Word often results in disgrace or death.

It has rightly been said: "choice determines destiny". If we choose God's Way, we have eternal life here and now; then hereafter, we shall live eternally with God and His Son in heaven. On the other hand, if we decide to go our own or Satan's way, we shall live an empty, unfulfilled life - style (i.e. life without meaning or fulfillment) throughout our earthly life. Then, of course, we will face condemnation before the judgment seat of God after this earthly life (Romans 14:12; 1 Corinthians 5:10), and finally, be cast into hell together with Satan, as declared by Jesus (ref. Matthew 25:41).

CHAPTER FOURTEEN

THE TWO KINDS OF PEOPLE IN THIS WORLD

There are people whom the scriptures describe as the children of God; and those who are classified as the children of the Devil. Does this surprise you? Let us find out from the words of Jesus Christ as He speaks to a group of Pharasees as follows:

> *I know you are Abraham's descendants. Yet you are ready to kill me, because you have no room for my word. If you were Abraham's children, then you would do the things Abraham did. As it is you are determined to kill me, a man who has told you the truth that I heard from God. Abraham did not do such things. You are doing the things your own father does* (Jn. 8: 37f).

Then, the Jews vehemently protested, saying: "*We are not illegitimate children. The only Father we have is God Himself.*" (John 8:41). Jesus replied with the final bullet that sent them wild with rage:

> *If God were your Father, you would love me, for I came from God, and now I am here . . .. You belong to your father, the devil, and you want to carry out*

> *your father's desire. He was a murderer from the beginning, not holding to the truth, for there is no truth in him. Yet because I tell you the truth, you do not believe me. He who belongs to God hears what God says. The reason why you do not hear is that You do not belong to God* (John. 8:37-42, 44-45 & 47).

Jesus proves it clearly to the Jews that in seeking to kill Him who is telling them the truth (that is, the Good News), which will save them and humankind from sin and hell, they are doing exactly what the devil always does, namely *"to steal, to kill, and to destroy."* (John 10:10a). Therefore, by plotting to kill Jesus (which they did anyway in the end), they have become indeed, the devil's agents for destruction, just as God's children, on the other hand, are agents for righteousness in the world.

My question to you as you read these words of Jesus is: "Whose child are you? Are you on the Lord's side or on the side of the devil? Are you bearing the fruit of the Spirit of God, which is "love, joy, peace, patience, kindness, goodness, faithfulness, gentleness and self-control,' (Galatians 5:22-23), which identifies the true children of God? Or are you showing traits of the devil, who manifests himself in acts of wickedness and sexual immorality, impurity, debauchery, idolatry and witchcraft, hatred, discord, jealousy, fits of rage, selfish ambition, envy, and the like? (Galatians 5:19-21).

This is the time for thorough and honest self-examination; to find out where you truly stand, in order to make a wise decision once and for all that will settle your destiny -either for God in heaven or for Satan in hell. Jesus made it clear in the Gospel of Matthew that hell was primarily created not for human beings, but for Satan and his demonic angels. What then must we do to get on the side of God, Whom to know is eternal life through His Son, Jesus Christ? The right answer may be found in the words of Pastor Scotty Smith of Christ Church in Nashville, "Instead of turning to lesser gods to fill a void, we must be willing to face our pain and trust the Lord for deliverance." (Charles Stanley, In Touch, March, 2002, p.17).

Now, brothers and sisters, as Smith experienced in his own

spiritual journey, "healing begins with realizing that our hearts are bored, discontent, anxious, empty, or restless". God's ultimate purpose, according to Smith, is "to win our hearts from things that hold no ultimate satisfaction" (Ibid. p.17). Therefore, the best way for us as individuals, and also as a people (regardless of our race), for restoring our broken relationship with God, and with one another, is to be honest with one another and before God.

Let us look briefly at the life of King David, for instance: as God's chosen King of Israel, David misused his authority. He invited Bathsheba into his palace and committed adultery with her, while her husband, Uriah, (one of Israel's loyal soldiers), was with his fellow soldiers under the command of Joab, fighting against the Ammonites on the battlefield. In his effort to conceal his sin, David sent orders to Joab to permit Uriah to come home. When he arrived, the King persuaded him to go home to his wife, but Uriah refused, because his thoughts were with his fellow soldiers on the battlefield. Since he could not get Uriah to do what he wanted, David finally sent Uriah back with orders for captain Joab, requesting him to place Uriah in the fiercest part of the battle front, where he could be killed. Joab obeyed the King's orders, and as might be expected, Uriah was, so to speak, hit by an enemy-bullet and died instantly.

Nevertheless, when God's Word came to the Prophet Nathan to confront King David with his sins of adultery with Bathsheba and the murder of her husband, David instantly admitted his sins and said to Nathan: "*I have sinned against the Lord*" (2 Samuel 12:13).

The following is part of David's classic prayer of confession and plea for forgiveness, which he passionately sought before God:

> *Have mercy on me, O God, according to your unfailing love; according to your great compassion blot out my transgressions. Wash away all my iniquity and cleanse me from my sin. For I know my transgressions, and my sin is always before me. Against you, you only, have I sinned and done what is evil in your sight.* (Psalms 51:6b, 7).

CHAPTER FIFTEEN

THE WAY FORWARD

We Must All Acknowledge Our Sins Before God

As King David sincerely admitted his sins before God and humbly asked for God's forgiveness, so must we, irrespective of race, color, rank, or gender, whenever we are convicted of sin in the presence of God. And like David, we should, without hesitation, plead for forgiveness for all our sins of pride, idolatry, selfishness, greediness, etc., which we have committed against God and our fellow human beings. For the Bible declares in the prophecy of Isaiah, *"We all like sheep have gone astray, each of us has turned to his own way; and the Lord has laid on him the iniquities of us all"* (Isaiah 53: 6).

In his classic theological epistle to the believers in Rome, Paul also reiterated the depravity of the human condition: *"All have sinned and fall short of the glory of God; there is no one righteous, not even one; All have turned away, they have together become worthless"* (Romans 3:23,10,12). This serves as a timely warning to those, who rely on their own righteousness for salvation, such as the young rich ruler, who came to Jesus with a question: "Good teacher, what must I do to inherit eternal life?" Jesus answered him unequivocally: *"Why do you call me good? No one is good except God alone"* (Luke 18:19).

Or we might be like one of the two people who went into the temple to pray, one a Pharisee and the other a tax collector. The Pharisee stood up and prayed about himself as follows:

> *God, I thank you that I am not like other men-robbers, evildoers, adulterers or even like this tax collector. I fast twice a week and give a tenth of all I get. But, the tax collector stood at a distance. He would not even look up to heaven, but beat his breast and said,'God have mercy on me, a sinner'* (Luke 18:10-13).

Jesus then concluded His parable, saying, *"I tell you this man, rather than the other, went home justified before God. For everyone who exalts himself will be humbled, and he who humbles himself will be exalted*" (Luke 18:14). We must, therefore, come before the Holy God, not with a high opinion of ourselves, but with humility, and penitent heart; and like David, ask God for forgiveness. As it is written, *"if we claim to be without sin, we deceive ourselves and the truth is not in us."* (1 John 1:8). But, God's promise is *that "if we confess our sins, he is faithful and just and will forgive our sins and purify us from all unrighteousness"* (1 John 1: 9).

The hymn writer, William Cowper, puts it this way:

There is a fountain filled with blood
Drawn from Immanuel's veins;
And sinners, plunged beneath that flood,
Lose all their guilty stains.
(M.H.B. 201, V.1, by William Cowper, 1731-1800).

As expressed in the above hymn by William Cowper, so the Ghanaian ancestors echoed the same Biblical truth shown in the Adinkra patterns in fig. 1 (a-e). *'the Son of God offered Himself as sacrificial lamb for the salvation of the household.'*

In the olden days before the dawn of Christianity, our fathers offered either a sheep, goat, or cow to pacify the gods whenever someone in the community had been found guilty of some wicked act. Almost a similar religious ritual was performed by the Jews when they sought God's forgiveness through the priests in the temple, according to the Old Testament Law or tradition. (Leviticus 17:11). However, as pointed out by the writer to the Hebrews, *"it is impossible for the blood of bulls and goats to take away sins"* (Hebrews 10:4).

Christ's Sacrifice was a Perfect Sacrifice for our sins:

Since Jesus was conceived by the Holy Spirit, and not by the seed of man, (see Luke 1:35-38; John 1: 1, 14), He did not inherit the human depravity or the natural tendency to sin, which all human beings inherited from Adam and Eve, though Jesus was mysteriously fully human and fully God. Hence, the Bible speaks of Jesus as *"one who has been tempted in every way, just as we are—yet was without sin*" (Hebrews 4: 15). Therefore, Jesus Himself declared concerning His sacrificial death for our redemption:

> *Sacrifice and offering you did not desire, but a body you prepared for me; with burnt offerings and sin offerings you were not pleased. Then I said, 'Here I am—it is written about me in the scroll—I have come to do your will, O God'* (Hebrews 10:5-7).

Thus, by setting aside the Old Covenant, with its ritual sacrifices and offerings, which could not take away sins, Jesus willingly offered His own body, which He said, *"You prepared for me*". And by that will, (Hebrew 10:5b, 7b), says the Hebrews writer, *"We have been made holy through the sacrifice of the body of Jesus Christ once for all . . . because by one sacrifice He has made perfect for ever those who are being made holy*" (Hebrews 10:10, 14).

Let me remind you, if I may, that as in the African Traditional religion, a chicken/lamb/goat/cow is slaughtered as sacrifice to the gods with the belief that the sacrifice will atone for sin or calamity (that is *'musu/musuo'* in Akan), (see fig. 1c), so did the Israelites. But, the Scriptures have made it very clear to us all—whether White or Black, Jew or Asian— that *"the blood of bulls cannot take away sins";* neither can it deliver us from Satan nor eternal condemnation in hell fire on the Day of Judgment (Ecclesiastes 12:14; Matthew 25:41-46). What then must we do to escape the eternal fire that awaits the impenitent heart or the hardened criminal?

Come with a Penitent Heart and Mind

What is repentance? Repentance, as I understand it, is more than a "feeling for wrong doing." It is an act of turning away from sin or wrongdoing. It involves confessing our sins, forsaking our own sinful way of life, and taking hold of the righteous Way of Christ, "Who was made sin for us, so that in Him we might become the righteousness of God"(2 Corinthians 5:21). Paul puts it this way: *"Do not conform any longer to the pattern of this world, but be transformed by the renewing of your mind* " (Romans 12:2).

Therefore, true and sincere repentance inevitably results in a transformation of life, as we find, for example, in the story of the prodigal son (Luke. 15:11- 24). Since he returned home with a penitent heart, he was forgiven, and clothed with "the best robe"; a ring was put on his finger and a pair of new sandals on his feet. The "best robe"("a garment of righteousness"—represents God's gift of salvation— a new life— for all who turn to Him through Christ), "the ring on his finger" (a symbol of acceptance as a son by the father), and "the sandals on his feet" (indicating that he is now ready to walk as a bearer or beneficiary of the Gospel of Jesus Christ).

Suffice it to say that what the father did for his son was an indication of his wholehearted acceptance of him as a beloved son or a precious member of the family and not as "*one of the hired servants*" (Luke 15:19b), as the son had supposed on his way home. The joyful reception or celebration that greeted his homecoming indicates *"the great joy in heaven over one sinner that repents"* (Luke 15:10). It is assurance of complete salvation that God graciously offers to all who truly repent of their sins and seek God's forgiveness and change of life through faith in Jesus Christ. Similarly, when King David came before God to confess his sins, he did so with "*a broken and contrite heart*" (Psalms 51:17b), seeking a complete renewal of life. He did not come with a lamb to offer any sacrifice for his sins. The following is a portion of David's prayer of confession:

> *You do not delight in sacrifice or I will bring it; . . . The sacrifices of God are a broken spirit; a broken and a contrite heart, O God, you will not despise. Create in me a pure heart, O God; and renew a steadfast spirit within me* (Psalms 51:16a, 17, 10).

Let us, therefore, like King David, come with true, penitent hearts, and sincerely confess our sins to the Lord, asking not only for forgiveness and cleansing, but also complete transformation of life, through faith in Jesus Christ, in response to God's gracious invitation:

> *Come now, and let us reason together, says the Lord. Though your sins are like scarlet, they shall be as snow; though they are red as crimson, they shall be like wool. If you are willing and obedient, you will eat the best from the land; but if you resist and rebel, you will be devoured by the sword, for the mouth of the Lord has spoken.* (Isaiah 1: 18-20).

Christ's Death on the Cross is the Greatest Miracle of God For the Redemption of Humanity From Sin

The Holy Spirit has taught me to understand through this vision that Christ's death on the CROSS is the means by which God has wrought on earth the *Greatest Miracle*, namely, *salvation of humankind by grace through faith in Jesus Christ*. For by that one miracle, God has redeemed for Himself all human beings—white or black, men or women, adults or children, bond or free, who truthfully repent and confess their personal faith in Jesus Christ as their Lord and Savior. By His death on the CROSS, Jesus has proved to be our Substitute, who redeemed humankind from the consequences of our sins (Romans 6:23). Also, as God's *"Sacrificial Lamb"* (Hebews 10:12; John 1:29), Christ has purged away all our sins and removed the curse or the effect of the original sin, which we all inherited from our first parents, Adam and Eve. By purging our sins through His precious blood, Christ has both justified and perfected forever all who come to God through Him as declared in Hebrews 10:14.

That's why I deem it so significant, as well as, so insightful artistry that our ancestors could, by intuision, design each of the Adinkrah patterns in fig. 1 (see ch. 1) to contain a symbol of a cross. Whether they realized it or not, I believe it was God, the Holy Spirit, who led them ingonito to produce such wonderful workmanship, which speaks so eloquently about God (Nyame) and the sacrifice of His Son—the lamb of God—for the redemption of humankind. Isn't that amazing?

Paul wrote as follows to the Colossians concerning the miracle-working power of the CROSS:

> *When you were dead in your sins and in the uncircumcision of your sinful nature, God made you alive with Christ. He forgave us all our sins, having cancelled the written code that was against us; He took it away, nailing it to the cross. And having dismantled the powers and authorities, he made a public spectacle of them, triumphing over them by the cross* (Colosains 2:13b 15).

It follows, therefore, that all of us who truly believe in Jesus Christ are no longer slaves to sin, as Paul writes, *"For sin shall no longer be your master, because you are not under law, but under grace"* (Romans 6:14). By the same grace of God, believers are empowered to lead a new life of righteousness, made possible by the in-dwelling power of the Holy Spirit. Hence, Paul boldly stated, *"Therefore, if anyone is in Christ, he is a new creation; the old has gone, the new has come. All this is from God, who reconciled us to Himself through Christ and gave us the ministry of reconciliation"* (2 Corinthians 5:17-18).

Thus, in Christ, *the sinner* turns into *a saint, while the spiritually dead person is quickened and made alive, and the sick are healed* (Isaiah 43:19-21, 53:4-5; Matthew 8: 17). These were some of the miracles that were foretold would signify the *Messianic Age* (e. g. Isaiah 11, 35:1-10). If we do not consider these as greatest miracles God has done and continues to do among humankind, then, I do not know what else can appeal to us as the greatest miracle human beings can experience on this planet. And who else is capable of making it happen? For, no one has power to do these things, except the Lord. Hence, Nicodemus recognized Christ's divine power and rightly admitted: *"Rabbi, we know you are a teacher who has come from God. For no one could perform these miraculous signs you are doing if God were not with him" (John 3:2).*

Again, St. Paul emphasized the same principle when he wrote to the converts in the city of Ephesus about the new way of life into which believers had entered by virtue of their faith in Jesus Christ. He declared:

> *You were taught, with regard to your former way of life, to put off your old self, which is being corrupted by its deceitful desires; to be made new in the attitude of your minds; and put on the new self, created to be like God in true righteousness and holiness* (Ephesians 4:22-23).

From these two references above, Paul underscores the undeniable fact that true believers, by virtue of the work of the in-dwelling Holy Spirit, really have a new lifestyle quite different from their previous way of life. It is a new life, created and controlled by the Holy Spirit. Hence, the Bible declares that *"those who are led by the Spirit of God are the children of God"* (Romans 8:14), because their new life reflects the fruit of the Spirit (Galations 5:22), similar to the character of God. Thus, believers are privileged to be partakers of the kingdom of God.

The concept of new life of the kingdom of God was the primary goal of Christ's ministry. All the miracles He performed were signs of His claim to be God, and thus, establishing in the midst of humanity the presence of the kingdom of God.

Any one in the United States, who has seen the *film, "The Passion of the Christ"* by Mel Gibson bears witness of the power of its appeal on all who have watched it. According to the Peoples Magazine, *"The Passion of the Christ"* has earned an astounding $300 million at the box office so far, defying all expectations. Nearly 45% of Americans have either seen the film or say they intend to, according to a March Gallup poll—evidence that the film's appeal extends far beyond evangelical Christians" (*People*, April 5, 2004, p.95).

There have been several testimonies of healing and conversions by people after they have seen The Passion. A guy, who murdered his girl friend and secretly kept the crime for ten years, could no longer hide his sin after watching how much pain Jesus had to suffer for the salvation of the world. On leaving the show, he confessed to the murder and handed himself over to the Police. Surely, there is power in the *Cross of Christ*, and it works wonders, far beyond our expectation or imagination.

It was anticipated that by the end of the following few week or so, the film would have brought in a record amount of more than $500 million in the box office. Thanks be to God for the marvelous gift of His Son, Jesus Christ for the redemption of humankind.

The Purpose of the Miracles Of Christ:

Jesus did other wonderful things also to encourage men and women everywhere to "believe that Jesus is the Christ, the Son of God, and that by believing, you may have (eternal) life in His name" (John 20:31). For instance, at the wedding ceremony in Cana, where Jesus turned water into wine, John wrote: *"This, the first of his miraculous signs, Jesus performed at Cana in Galilee. He thus revealed his glory, and his disciples put their faith in him"* (John. 2: 11).

After this first miracle at Cana, the New Testament Gospel writers recorded several miracles Jesus performed during the course of His ministry. He made a bed-ridden man completely whole to prove His authority both to heal the sick and to forgive sins. With a young boy's meal of five loaves and two fish, Jesus fed five thousand people, not counting women and children, and still had twelve baskets of food left over. Thus, Christ fulfilled His claim as being *"the bread of life,"* (John 6:35); and having *"streams of living water"* (John 7: 37-38).

He walked on water and stilled the raging seas to affirm His power over nature. He cast out demons to set captives free, healed the sick, restored paralyzed limbs, and opened the eyes of the blind.

He made the deaf to hear and the dumb to speak. All this was done to fulfill what was said through the prophet Isaiah: *"He took up our infirmities and carried our diseases"* (Isaiah 53:4; Matthew 8:17).

Above all, He raised a man named Lazarus from the dead after he had been buried four days in the tomb, affirming His claim to be *"the resurrection and the life"* (John 11:25). As I have already indicated, all these wonders were done to support Christ's claim to be the Son of God/the Messiah, *that "this man is indeed, the Savior of the world"* as admitted by even the Samaritans (John 4:42b). Surely, none can claim to have the power to save humanity except God, through the miracle of the death of His Son, Jesus Christ on the Cross.

John, the beloved apostle, concluded his Gospel with the following, *"Truly, Jesus did many other signs in the presence of his disciples, which are not written in this book; but these are written that you may believe that Jesus is the Christ, the Son of God, and that believing you may have life in his name"* (John 20: 30-31). The point being emphasized here is that Christ gives healing and new life to all who sincerely confess faith in Him. That is why John emphatically stated in the last chapter of his epistle: *"And this is the testimony: God has given us eternal life, and this life is in his Son. He who has the Son has life; he who does not have the Son of God does not have life"* (1 John. 5:11-12)

What does John mean by "life" in this contest? Surely, he is not talking about our temporal existence here on earth. In this passage, as in many places in John's Gospel, John is certainly referring not only to endless (that is, everlasting), spiritual life with God, but also, particularly, the quality of life, which God alone has power to give to those who turn their back to the world, and come to Him for salvation through faith in His Son, Jesus Christ.

This is eternal life, which God, the Holy Spirit, creates in us the moment we receive Jesus into our lives as Savior and Lord.

It begins here and now in this earthly life and continues beyond death for evermore with God in heaven. According to the Scriptures, nothing—not even death—is able to separate believers from that bond of eternal life, which we have with God through our Lord Jesus Christ. Thus, Paul declares with unflinching conviction in his epistle to the Romans:

> *Who shall separate us from the love of Christ? Shall trouble or hardship or persecution or famine or nakedness or danger or sword? . . No, in all these things we are more than conquerors through him who loved us. For I am convinced that neither death nor life, neither angels nor demons, neither the present nor the future, nor any powers, neither height nor depth, nor anything else in all creation, will be able to separate us from the love of God that is in Christ Jesus our Lord* (Romans 8:35-39).

That is the great assurance of security that Christianity offers to all believers in Christ—that Jesus died to save us from our sins and lives to keep forever those He has saved. For example, in the commissioning of His apostles after His resurrection, Jesus' last words were, "Behold, I am with you always to the end of the age" (Matthew 28:20).

With the Cross the Bitter Turns Sweet

Whenever believers focus on the Cross, they receive extra-ordinary grace from above to overcome their problems through the ever-abiding presence of Christ with His people. According to David Roper, this was exemplified in the life of the Israelites as they journeyed to the Promised Land. Commenting on Israel's wilderness experience, Roper said, " Joy and sorrow are often close companions. Just as the Israelites went from the thrill of victory at the Red Sea to the bitter waters of Mara just three days later (Exodus 15:22-23), our rejoicing can quickly turn to anguish.

At Mara, the Lord told Moses to throw a tree into the water, which made it *"sweet" and drinkable* (v. 25). There is *"Another 'tree'*, says Roper, *"when 'cast into' the bitter circumstances of our lives, can make them sweet. It is the cross of Jesus* (1 Peter 2:24). Our outlook will be transformed as we contemplate His sacrificial death and His submission to the will of God (Luke 22:42). *"Our pain,"* says David Roper, *"may come from the ill-will of others, or worse, from their neglect. Nevertheless, our Lord has permitted it. We may not understand why, it is the will of our Father and Friend, whose wisdom and love are infinite. When we say, 'Yes!' to God as His Spirit reveals His will to us through His Word, the bitter circumstances of our lives can be sweet. We must not grumble against what the Lord permits. Instead, we must do all that He asks us to do. Jesus said that we must take up our cross daily and follow Him (Luke 9:23). When we remember Jesus' cross and submit to the Father as He did, bitter experiences can become sweet."* Therefore, I completely agree with David Roper in concluding that, *"God uses our difficulties to make us better—not bitter"* (*Daily Bread*, January 27, 2004).

At this point, it is quite appropriate for us to turn our focus to the next chapter for a brief discussion of yet another miracle, perhaps, the greatest of all miracles that had ever been written on earth, namely, the resurrection of Jesus Christ, and its implications for believers and non-believers.

CHAPTER SIXTEEN

THE RESURRECTION OF JESUS CHRIST

The rising of Jesus Christ from death on the third day after His burial is a crucial event, as well as a remarkable dimension in His life and mission, and also of His followers, and finally, of the universal Church. Indeed, without the resurrection of Christ, the purpose of His sacrificial death on the Cross at Calvary would have been incomplete. Sin would have triumphed over righteousness, and evil over good in this world. Then, there would have been no Ultimate Moral Standard for humanity to follow; our standard of behavior would have been relative, depending on our own human judgment, which differs from one another's. In fact, without the resurrection of Christ, there would have been no hope in this life, or in any future existence. As Paul puts it, *"Then those who are fallen asleep in Christ are lost. If only for this life we have hope in Christ, we are to be pitied more than all people"*(1 Corinthians 15:18-19). Hope is what we expect for the future, for without "hope", guess who would have rejoiced and reigned as KING and LORD over humanity and the entire universe? Certainly, it would have been nobody else; not even any of the patriarchs— Abraham, Isaac, and Jacob, or any of the Prophets— such as Moses or Elijah, or any other god or ancestor of any race on earth, but the enemy of God and of humankind, the Devil. "*But, thanks be to God*" (1 Corinthians 15:

57), that in His divine wisdom, God used the death of "*His only begotten Son*" (John 3:16), Jesus Christ, to defeat forever the wicked plot of the Devil and all the enemies of Christ. It is written:

> *Death has been swallowed up in victory. Where, O death, is your victory? Where, O death, is your sting? The sting of death is sin, and the power of sin is the law. But thanks be to God! He gives us the victory through our Lord Jesus Christ* (1 Corinthians 15:54b-57).

What the Resurrection Means to Believers

In God's plan of salvation, both the death and resurrection of Christ have one purpose, namely, to redeem humankind from the dominion of Satan, power of sin and its deadly consequence. This is necessary, so that all who believe in Christ might live in the new life of righteousness, joy, peace, and hope (Galatians 5:22). This new life, implanted by the Holy Spirit, is made possible by the power of the presence of Christ Himself, who said: "*I am making everything new*" (Revelation 21:5). Let us, for example, take a look at Peter's life before the death of Jesus. To him Jesus gave the leadership of the disciples and "*the keys of the kingdom of heaven*" (that is, authority to win souls into the Church of Christ) after he had made his great confession of Christ in Caesarea Philippi (Matthew 16:17-19).

We all know how woefully Peter denied his Lord three times during the trial of Christ before the rooster crowed, just as the Lord had predicted (Matthew 26: 69-75). Realizing how much he had failed his Master, Peter wept bitterly with shame and sorrow. Nevertheless, after Jesus had risen from the dead, He appeared to Peter and six other disciples by the Sea of Tiberias. Knowing that they had caught no fish, He directed them, in His usual compassionate, but miraculous way, to make a big catch of fish. When they drew the net to the shore where Jesus was, He prepared breakfast with some of the fish they had caught, and said to them, "*Come and have breakfast*" (John 21:12). John, the beloved disciple, reports:

> *"None of the disciples dared to ask Him, 'Who are*

> *you?' They knew it was the Lord. Jesus came, took the bread and gave it to them, and did the same with the fish. This was now the third time," says John, Jesus appeared to His disciples after He was raised from the dead."* (John 21:1-13).

Then, having dined with them to regain their trust in Him that He was really the Lord, Jesus Christ, He gave Peter, the second chance to affirm his faith and position in Him by asking Peter the same question three times: "*Peter, do you love me*?" When Peter answered in the affirmative, Jesus said to him: "*Feed my sheep*" (John 21:15-19). By so saying, Jesus indicated His forgiveness and acceptance of Peter into His fold as a leader of His flock., and thus, afforded him a second chance to affirm his discipleship and loyalty to Him and His Church, regardless of his failure to stand the test of discipleship.

Here are a few essential lessons about the Resurrection that I want to share with you. Firstly, the Resurrection of Christ brings joy and peace to replace sorrow and weeping. For instance, Mary Magdalene, who was overcome with sorrow as a result of the crucifixion of Christ, stood in the graveyard weeping. But when Jesus showed up and called her by her name, *"Mary,"* in His usual, gentle tone of voice, she turned toward Him and responded in Aramaic *"Rabboni*" (meaning Teacher) (John 20 13-15). At that instant, Mary's sorrow and tears vanished like vapour into the air, and their place filled with unspeakable joy and peace, which no one could take away from her, because she had seen the risen Christ.

Furthermore, without the resurrection of Christ, there would have been no Peter of the kind that we read about in the Acts of the Apostles, let alone any Epistle, namely, 1st and 2nd Peter, written by him. For, Jesus had previously cautioned them: "*Without me, you can do nothing*" (John 15:5). Therefore, Simon Peter became somebody—the Leader of the apostles and of the Church in Jerusalem—whom the first Century world could reckon with. "Why?" Because by His resurrection, Jesus had overcome death and given His followers, led by Peter, power to be His witnesses—*"in Jerusalem, and in all Judea and Samaria, and to the ends of the earth"* (Acts

1:8; Mark 16:15: Matthew 28:18-20).

Then also, with the resurrection of Christ, and the assurance of His abiding presence among them, the apostles no longer feared death, or the religious leaders, who threatened them. They had not only courage to pursue the cause of Christ, but also, hope for life eternal with Christ in heaven (John 14:1-3; 11:25-26; Luke 18:29). Indeed, the resurrection brought transformation in the lives of the followers of Christ and they remained bonded together in one spirit, "*constantly praying along with the women and Mary the mother of Jesus, and with His brothers*" (Acts 1:14).

"How about Paul?" Without the resurrection, there would have been 'Saul of Tarsus'(Acts 9:11), but no "Paul, the apostle to the Gentiles"(Acts 26: 16-18). As you may remember, Paul was not one of the followers of Christ. After Pentecost, Saul obtained permission from the High Priest to go to Damascus to arrest and cast into prison any disciples of Jesus he might lay hands on in the cities and towns. On the way, he encountered Jesus in a vision and fell to the ground. He was converted, and commissioned with the anointing of the Holy Spirit as an Apostle to the Gentiles. Thus, Paul boldly began to proclaim the Good News of Jesus Christ throughout the Gentile world, becoming the defender of the faith, which he once sought to destroy (Acts 9:4-6, 11-12, 26: 16-18). All this transformation took place, because Jesus truly rose again from the dead, and is seated at the right hand of God, ever living to make intercession for all, who believe in Him. When Saul pursued after salvation in Judaism, he failed miserably, for *"without me"*, Jesus says, *"you can do nothing"* (John 15:5). But, with Him as your Teacher, Guide and Strength, you are a winner, because, *"I,"* says the Lord, *"will never leave you, nor forsake you"* (Hebrew 13: 5).

If you, too, have failed in your walk with Christ, your family obligations, or your job, I counsel you to gather up courage and, in humility, repent as Peter did, and turn to Jesus. Do not give up or quit your divinely appointed position. "*Draw near to God, and He will draw near to you*" (James 4:8), because He is much closer to you than you can think or imagine. Even if, like Paul, you had persecuted a number of Christians previously, it is still not too late for you to turn to the Lord for forgiveness (1 John 1: 9). Remember, the chief business of the Lord, which He was anointed to accomplish here on earth was, and still is, *"To preach the gospel to the poor; to heal the brokenhearted, to preach deliverance to the captives and recovery of sight to the blind, to set at liberty them that are bruised"* (Luke 4:18)

Right now, Christ is calling you, (especially those of you who, like Peter, are facing all kinds of difficult situations and temptations in your lives): saying:

> *Come to me, all you who are weary and burdened, and I will give you rest. Take my yoke upon you and learn from me, for I am gentle and humble in heart, and you will find rest for your souls. For my yoke is easy and my burden is light.* (Matthew 11:28-30).

Dear reader, in case you consider yourself too sinful to come to Jesus, then, listen to His promise to all who respond to His call, *"whoever comes to me I will never drive away"* (John 6:37). Therefore, do not hesitate to yield yourself into His open arms, for He stands right where you are to receive you as a newborn child in the kingdom of God. I believe it was in the light of this encouraging message of Christ to all believers, especially, in times of crisis, that the Hebrew writer was inspired to pen the following:

> *Since the children have flesh and blood, He too shared in their humanity so that by his death he might destroy him who holds the power of death-that is, the Devil—and free those who all their lives were held in slavery by their fear of death . . .. Because he himself suffered when he was tempted, He is able to help those who are being tempted.* (Hebrew 2: 14-15,18).

Thus, being always conscious of the fact that Jesus has overcome every temptation, suffering and death, Christians have assurance of salvation, hope and courage to pursue their daily lives, working diligently in whatever category of employment or situation they find themselves. They know assuredly that Christ will bless and reward them accordingly, and that their good works in Christ will not be in vain. It was with similar motivation that the Apostle Paul wrote to the Corinthian Church, *"Therefore, my dear brothers (and sisters), stand firm. Let nothing move you. Always give yourselves fully to the work of the Lord, because you know that your labour in the Lord is not in vain"* (1 Corinthians15:58; Ephesians 6: 8*).*

The question is, "How can we stand firm and unmovable in Christ?" "What was the power that sustained Peter and the rest of the apostles to accomplish the task their Master entrusted to them?" In answer to these questions, I am reminded of Jesus' final instructions to His disciples before ascending into heaven. Jesus was fully aware that His disciples could not carry out the Great Commission (Matt. 28:19-20) He had entrusted into their hands, until they receive divine power. *"I am going to send you what my Father had promised,"* He said, *"but stay in the city until you have been clothed with power from on high"*(Luke 24:49).

At this point, let us turn to the next chapter to discuss further how the disciples were empowered with the Spirit to accomplish their Master's business.

CHAPTER SEVENTEEN

EMPOWERMENT BY THE HOLY SPIRIT

The work of the Holy Spirit in our lives as Christians will be taken very seriously, if we understand Who the Spirit is, and the importance of His role in our lives.

Who is the Holy Spirit?

He is God. He is the third Person of the Trinity, co-equal with God, the Father and God, the Son, and is worshipped together with the Godhead. He is the Christian's source of power to live a consistent lifestyle of love and obedience, which reflects the glory of God. The work of the apostles was made possible by the power of the Holy Spirit, whom Jesus Christ promised. Among His final words just before leaving them for His place on high, Jesus reiterated His promise, saying, "*You will receive power when the Holy Spirit comes on you; and you will be my witnesses in Jerusalem, and in all Judea and Samaria, and to the ends of the earth*" (Acts 2:8). This promise was duly fulfilled on the day of Pentecost, as Luke reported:

> *When the day of Pentecost came, they were all together in one place. Suddenly a sound like the blowing of a violent wind came from heaven and*

> *filled the whole house where they were sitting. They saw what seemed to be tongues of fire that separated and came to rest on each of them. All of them were filled with the Holy Spirit and began to speak in other tongues as the Spirit enabled them* (Acts 2:1-4).

The Holy Spirit is for all Believers in Christ

There is a number of people in various Churches, who hold the view that the Holy Spirit is God's special gift to special people in leadership position in the Church. They base their argument on the way in which God's Spirit came upon people, who were called into the Prophetic ministry in the Old Testament period (e.g. 1 Samuel 3:10-14; Isaiah 6:1-8; Jeremiah 1:5). It is quite true that in the Old Testament era, the Holy Spirit equipped some people for special service to God, yet, God had plans to make His gift of the Spirit available to all people. This is evidenced in the prophecy of Joel:

> *And afterward, I will pour out my Spirit on all people. Your sons and daughters will prophesy, your old men will dream dreams, your young men will see visions. Even on my servants, both men and women, I will pour out my Spirit in those days...And everyone Who calls on the name of the Lord will be saved* (Joel 2: 28-29, 32; Acts 2:17, 21).

The obvious question to ask here is, "how do we receive the Holy Spirit?" The answer will NOT be found in the calling upon other gods or ancestral spirits through libation, but from Peter's anointed message to the large audience who listened to him on the day of Pentecost, as follows:

> *Repent and be baptized everyone of you, in the name of Jesus Christ for the forgiveness of your sins. And you will receive the gift of the Holy Spirit. The promise is for you and your children and for all who are far off—for all whom the Lord our God will call* (Acts 2:38-39).

The Scriptures bear witness that after Peter's sermon, as many as three thousand converts were added to the company of believers in Jerusalem. Thus, we can confidently say that Pentecost marked the birthday of the Church in Jerusalem. As the Church began to expand, the exclusiveness of the Jews as the elect of God began to break down, giving way to God's universalism, because it pleased God to give the Holy Spirit to the gentile believers, as declared in Peter's message to Cornelius:

> *I now realize how true it is that God does not show favoritism but accepts men (and women) from every nation who fear him and do what is right.*
>
> *While Peter was still speaking these words, the Holy Spirit came on all who heard the message. The circumcised believers who had come with Peter were astonished that the gift of the Holy Spirit had been poured out even on the Gentiles. For they heard them speaking in tongues and praising God. Then Peter said, 'Can anyone keep these people from being baptized with water? They have received the Holy Spirit just as we have'.*
>
> *So he ordered that they be baptized in the name of Jesus Christ* (Acts 10:34-35, 44-48).

Cornelius and his household were thus incorporated into the universal Church much to the displeasure of the circumcised believers in Jerusalem (see Acts 11:1-3). However, Peter's response to their objection clearly pointed out to them that *"this is the Lord's doing, and it is marvelous in our eyes". "Therefore, what God has joined together, let no man separate"* (Psalms 118:23; Matthew 19:6). Thus, the work of God continues unabated, and no one can stop it until all His purposes are fulfilled.

Since God is just, and there is no partiality in Him, His gift to humanity, namely, Jesus Christ, Holy Spirit, salvation, the church, including all other gifts of the Holy Spirit (ref. I Corinthians 12:4-11; Romans 12: 6-8; Ephesians 4:11-13) are truly meant for all believers, regardless of race, color, rank or gender. This is affirmed by Scripture:

> *You are all children of God through faith in Christ Jesus, for all of you who were baptized into Christ have clothed yourselves with Christ. There is neither Jew nor Greek, slave nor free, male nor female, for you are all one in Christ Jesus. If you belong to Christ, then you are Abraham's seed, and heirs according to the promise* (Galatians 3:26-29).

It is the work of the Holy Spirit to bring men and women together with our children into one fellowship or family under the headship of Jesus Christ. This cannot be achieved by any other god or ancestral spirit or human power or wisdom, except the Spirit of God.

The Work of the Holy Spirit

The kingdom of God that was preached by Jesus Christ is universally present and dynamically active through the Holy Spirit. Hence, before Peter (under the guidance of the Holy Spirit-Acts 10:10-15) could reach the house of Cornelius, the Holy Spirit had already prepared the entire household to receive the Good News.

The Spirit functions in the Church in various forms such as preaching, healing, worship and sacraments. Nevertheless, I have come to realize through God's revelation that the Spirit appears incognito in secular structures. The Holy Spirit—the presence of God active in time and space, was poured out on the believers at Pentecost, creating the body of Christ—the Church. Simultaneously, the Spirit was poured forth on the world—on "all flesh" (Joel 2:28) to draw all persons to Christ and to the Church (Acts 2:17-21). Hence, before an individual's encounter with Christ through the preaching of the Gospel, the Spirit functions in the person unconsciously, speaking through personal needs, hungers, and questions. John Wesley calls this *"Prevenient Grace"*— the gracious, active work of God through His Spirit to move a sinner toward Christ for salvation. In other words, God takes the initiative to bring lost humanity to Himself through the work of His Holy Spirit (John 3; Romans 5: 8).

The Fruit of the Spirit

One of the major works of the Holy Spirit in the believer, is to transform him into the image of Christ, so that such a person will no longer exhibit the sinful lifestyle, which is characteristic of the old nature, but will begin to bear the fruit of the Spirit, which Paul speaks about in Galatians 5:22, "*But the fruit of the Spirit is love, joy, peace, patience, kindness, goodness, faithfulness, gentleness and self-control.*"

Paul emphasizes that, "*Those who belong to Christ Jesus have crucified the sinful nature with its passions and desires*" (Galatians 5:24). Thus, he could state further to the Corinthians, "*if anyone is in Christ, he is a new creation; the old has gone, the new has come*" (2 Corinthians 5:17). Therefore, the best criterion by which to identify a true Christian from a none-Christian is to look at his/her lifestyle. Hence, Jesus stated, "*By their fruit, you will recognize them*" (Matthew 7:15). Let us take an example in the life of a young girl of 13, who lived with her single mother in a certain community. She did not respect her Mom. She would not make her bed or clean her room, nor do the dishes after meals. Her school performance was poor, because she would not stay home to do her homework. Her mother nearly gave up on her.

However, during one summer, her mother succeeded in persuading her to attend a Summer Camp. She agreed to go, because some of her mates were going, and she thought it would be just fun to join them. But the camp was no place for fun. The morning began with Bible story and devotion, with each participant learning one memory verse each day. Every activity was under the control and discipline of the Camp Leaders (a School Chaplain and Youth Leader). By the way, this was a Christian Camp organized by a Church Group.

When the camp was over, the 13-year old wayward girl, was never the same again. Why? What happened? She told her mom that everyone at the Camp was nice and kind to her, especially their Leaders. "*So I began to hate my bad habits;*" she confessed to her mom, "*and I told my Chaplain to help me change for the better. He prayed with me to receive Jesus into my life. That prayer was answered, and Jesus changed my life. Mom, 'am a new person!*"

She concluded her testimony in a loud voice, and her mom could see light shining in her eyes as bright as the rays of the sun, coupled with unspeakable joy and peace in her heart. Isn't that wonderful? Yes, it is, indeed! This young girl is now a new creation in Christ, bearing the fruit of the Spirit. Praise the Lord! Hallelujah!!

CHAPTER EIGHTEEN

NEW LIFE FOR ALL WHO BELIEVE IN CHRIST

With the Good News of the mighty working of the Holy Spirit in the world, there is hope for new life for all who sincerely turn to Jesus Christ for salvation. For though Christ died for the forgiveness of our sins, without the work of the Holy Spirit there would have been no transformation of life for believers. Furthermore, there would have been no hope for change from evil to goodness and from sin to righteousness. Let us refresh our minds with a few biblical examples.

Case Stories of People who came to Jesus

Case 1:

In His discourse with the Samaritan woman by the well, Jesus hinted on the New Life, which those who come to Him would receive, *"Everyone who drinks this water will be thirsty again. Whoever drinks the water I give him will never thirst. Indeed, the water I give him will become in him a spring of water welling up to eternal life"* (John. 4:13). Those who are familiar with this story will remember that on hearing Jesus talk about this special water, the Samaritan woman asked, *"Sir, give me this water so that I won't get thirsty and have to keep coming here to draw water"* (John

4:15). Finally, when Jesus knew just how much she wanted to see the Promised Messiah, He revealed Himself to her, saying: *"I, who speak to you am he"* (John 4:26).

Upon this thrilling, face-to-face-encounter with Jesus Christ, the Messiah, the woman ran to Samaria, testifying to all and sundry her experience with Jesus. Her testimony led to the conversion of many Samaritans, who gratefully invited Jesus to be their guest Then, those who believed said to the woman: *"We no longer believe just because of what you said; now we have heard for ourselves, and we know that this man really is the Savior of the world"* (John 4:42). It is very important to observe here that though traditionally, Jews have nothing to do with Samaritans, yet Jesus broke down traditional barriers and accepted their invitation and stayed among them for two days. What was the outcome of His two-day stay with them? It is written: *"And because of His words many more became believers"* (John. 4:41). By believing in Jesus Christ, the Samaritan woman was saved. Through her testimony, other Samaritans were also saved; and by inviting Jesus to Samaria, they opened the way for numerous Samaritans to become believers. It began with one person, then a group, and finally, the city or community.

It has dawned on me rather sadly, that many people have heard the Good News, but did not believe in Jesus. By rejecting Jesus on religious, racial or traditional grounds, they are lost together with their families, and a whole community of people.

Due to tradition, no Jew, particularly, a religious Leader, such as a Teacher or Scribe, or any Pharisee, would have even bothered to speak with the Samaritan woman at the well in the first place; let alone to live among them for a while. Nevertheless, Jesus obliged, in order that many lost souls in Samaria might have new life through faith in Him. Jesus did not allow the tradition of His time to hinder His divinely-appointed task, namely, "to seek and to save what was lost" (Luke 19:10). As David Egner observed: "He crossed all kinds of traditional barriers to talk with tax-collectors, sinners, non-Jews, people of mixed races, the poor as well as the rich. He came to identify with each of us, and to pay the price for all our sins" (David Egner, *Our Daily Bread, "The Underbird*", Monday, October 27, 2003).

I consider this evangelistic strategy of Christ worthy of emulation by all soul-winners. There are well-meaning pastors and evangelists out there, seeking to win sinners for Christ, but they find it difficult, and at times impossible, to share the Good News with some ethnic groups of people, because of prejudice or color of their skin. That is unfortunate, and uncharacteristic of Christ, who crossed barriers of race, religion, rank, gender, riches or poverty, with the Good News of the Kingdom of God. He had only one aim, "*To seek and to save the lost; and that you might have life and have it more abundantly*" (John 10:10).

As soul-winners, we need to humble ourselves and learn to follow our Master and His strategy for drawing sinners into the Kingdom, if we claim to be His true disciples.

Case 2:

Another interesting story about New Life in Jesus is recorded in Luke 19:1-10. This has to do with a man called Zacchaeus, who climbed a tree in order to have a clear view of Jesus, because of the crowd. Moreover, he was short in stature; and Jesus was going to pass that way on His journey to Jerusalem. We are also told that Zacchaeus was a chief tax-collector and was wealthy. Many of the Jews did not like tax collectors, because they were employed by the Roman Government to exact tax from their fellow Jews.

However, when Jesus reached the tree, He looked up, and ordered Zacchaeus to come down from the tree, saying, *"Zacchaeus, come down immediately. I must stay at your house today"* (Luke 19:5). Zacchaeus came down at once and welcomed Jesus gladly. As they headed home, the crowd began to murmur, *"He has gone to be the guest of a sinner"* (Luke 10:7). Knowing the reason for their murmuring, Zacchaeus stood up and said to the Lord, "*Look, Lord! Here and now I give half of my possessions to the poor, and if I have cheated anybody out of anything, I will pay back four times the amount*" (Luke 19:5). Jesus then said to him, *"Today salvation has come to this house, because this man, too, is a son of Abraham. For the Son of Man came to seek and to save what was lost)* (Luke. 19:9-10). Yes! Indeed, Jesus knew what He was about and would not in the least be deterred by criticism from His opponents, each of whom was equally as sinful as Zacchaeus, who has humbly repented and publicly confessed his sin of extortion. To him also, Jesus declared His acceptance of him as a child of God by virtue of his faith in Him. Zacchaeus captured the essence of the moment and made a decision to commit his life and all to Christ. He also refused to be discouraged by his enemies, who sought only his downfall and not his salvation in Christ. He did not depend on his wealth or allow pride to hinder his decision to accept Jesus as his Lord and Savior when the hour struck. He simply received Christ into his heart, when he heard Him knocking at the door of his heart.

What about you, my friend? Have you received Jesus into your heart as your personal Savior and Lord of your life? There are a lot of people who hear the Good News, yet allow riches, pride, criticisms, spouses, relatives, friends, or enemies, to prevent them from coming to Christ. Zacchaeus, like the Samaritan woman, seized the opportunity without delay. As the saying goes: "Opportunity comes, but once." With that in mind, Zacchaeus ceased the opportunity to meet his Savior, when He chanced to pass his way, regardless of his own sinfulness or opposition from his enemies, or critics.

Case 3.

A third vivid example of one who broke through all ranks of opposition to get to Jesus was the case of blind Bartimaeus recorded in Mark 10:46-52 (see also Mtt.20-29; Luke18: 35-43). Mark informs us that as Jesus was leaving Jericho to continue His journey to Jerusalem, followed by a large crowd, blind Bartimaeus was sitting by the roadside begging. But, when he heard that it was Jesus of Nazareth, he began to shout: *"Jesus, Son of David, have mercy on me!"* Even though it is recorded that, *"many rebuked him and told him to be quiet,"* blind Bartimaeus wouldn't let go his chance for healing, so he kept on shouting 'all the more', *"Son of David, have mercy on me!"* (Mark 10:48).

On hearing his cry, Jesus stopped and said, *"Call him."* , then throwing his cloak aside, he jumped to his feet and came to Jesus. "What do you want me to do for you?" (Mark 10:51), Jesus asked him. The blind man said to Him, *"I want to see."* To the surprise of everybody, including His disciples, Jesus said to him, *"Go your way, your faith has made you well"* (Mark 10: 52). Instantly Bartimaeus received his sight and followed Jesus on the way.

Like the individuals in the two previous stories, Bartimaeus did not allow himself to be overcome by the opposing forces he faced in his life, namely, the rebuke from the crowd, his personal weakness—his blindness, which made it difficult for him to find his way to Christ, and his robe (cloak) that got in his way. Bartimaeus rose above all these hindrances and cried out to Jesus for the healing he very much needed. He believed that apart from Jesus, no other person would be able to heal him. And he was right.

Secondly, he sensed that Jesus might not pass that way again. Therefore, he determined to press forward with courage to obtain what he needed from the Lord. Surely, he was not denied his request. In this story and many others, Jesus fulfilled His promise: *"He who comes to me, I will in no wise cast out"* (John 6:37).

Many individuals like Bartimaeus had failed to come to Jesus to be saved or healed or delivered from a particular situation, because they gave in to certain stumbling blocks that came their way. It is important for us to remember that nothing can be achieved without effort. As someone has said, "Life is war." Similarly, we must struggle hard to let go our own self-pride, turn deaf ears to criticisms from our enemies, including the devil, who always seeks our downfall and destruction. Then, with a humble acknowledgment of our need of a Savior, we must humbly, yet courageously, turn to the Lord Jesus Christ for deliverance from our sinful condition. We come to Jesus, just as we are, armed with only one assurance, that our Lord will never, never, turn anybody away from Him.

See how beautifully Christina Georgina Rossetti, the hymnist, writes about this:

None other Lamb, no other Name,
None other hope in heaven or earth or sea,
None other hiding place from guilt and shame,
None beside Thee.

My faith burns low, my hope burns low;
Only my heart's desire cries out in me,
By the deep thunder of its wants and woe,
Cries out to Thee.

Lord Thou art life, though I be dead;
Love's fire Thou art, however cold I be:
Nor heaven have I, nor place to lay my head,
Nor home, but Thee.
(M.H.B. 94: verses 1-3).

Before going any further from where you are at the moment, you may find it beneficial to lay down the book, and ponder for a while about your life and God's love for you. Count today as your day of salvation, if you have not already given your life to the Lord Jesus. If you are a Christian, taking a moment to rededicate your life afresh to the Lord would yield greater blessings upon your life and family than not doing anything about this anointed message of salvation. This enables us as believers to look to the future with hope. We shall discuss this subject fully in the next chapter.

CHAPTER NINETEEN

THE CHRISTIAN HOPE

Before dealing with the subject, *"the Christian Hope"*, let us firstly discuss what *"Hope"* is in the ordinary sense of the word.

What is Hope?

Generally speaking, this is a question that several people tend to ask. According to the Dictionary of the New Century Version of the Holy Bible, *"Hope"* in the general sense may be defined as *"looking forward to something you really expect to happen"*, p. 1537. Thus, in its common usage, we often put less emphasis on the "expectation" component of hope. For instance, one may say: *"I wish my College Team wins the championship this year, but I have been wishing that for the past five years"*. Thus, we still look forward to a desired end, yet we don't stake our lives on whether or not it happens, because the thing hoped for is uncertain at best. In other words, being human as we are, we do not have the power or absolute control to enable us change or prevent the daily events or circumstances that come our way. As a matter of fact, hope always carries the idea of *"looking forward to the desirable"*, but with remote possibility, as in the following example: *"I hope my husband wins $25,000.00 from the game of 'Wheel of Fortune'* to-*night, but I am aware that his chances of winning are less than his chances of* *receiving a surprised visit from his mom this weekend."* In practical experience, we realize that our hope always tends to be feeble and desperate. The simple reason for this tendency is that the basis of our hope is so flimsy that it cannot stand the test of time, stress, or strain that comes our way to cause a change in our situation.

As an ordinary human society, therefore, we may be likened to those Paul describes in Ephesians 2: 12, who are *"separated from Christ"* and *consequently "without hope . . . and without God in the world."* In other words, real hope is a divine virtue, which we can receive from no one else, except from God through faith in Jesus Christ. Now, let us examine the type of hope that we can have in Christ.

The Christian Hope:

Hope in the Biblical or Christian point of view is quite different. In the Scriptures, *hope* is a certainty—a confident expectation of what God will do in the future, based on His past faithfulness and promises. It is certain because of who God is—namely, God is faithful, and His Word is trustworthy. God is a reliable reason/source for our hope. For instance, it was on the basis of God's own integrity and ability that God made the promise to bless Abraham and give him many descendants (See Genesis 12:1-3, 22:16-18; Hebrews 6:13-15).

Abraham and his wife Sarah were long past their natural, child-bearing years, yet their hope in God's promise was not wishful thinking, but a confident trust in the One who could deliver. Biblical/Christian hope, is therefore, hope in God and His promises, even though we have not yet seen the complete fulfillment of the promises. This kind of hope is solid and dependable- *"an anchor for the soul, sure and strong"* (Hebrews 6:19). To the Jews exiled in Babylon, for example, God's promise of hope came to through the prophet Jeremiah, saying, *"I know the plans I have for you, plans to prosper you and not to harm you, plans to give you hope and a future"* (Jeremiah 29: 11).

Indeed, this is a kind of hope on which we can stake our lives right from the very beginning. The people of God have been a people of hope. Thus, the Holy Bible, is God's message of hope for a hopeless world. All who trust in the Lord and cast their hope on Him will not be ashamed or disappointed.

For example, beginning from God's promise of a descendant of Adam and Eve, who would crush the head of the serpent (Genesis 3:15), to the promise of the land of Canaan to Abraham's descendants (Genesis 12:7), to the promise of descendants of David who would rule for ever (1 Chronicles 17:11-14), to the promise of Jesus' return (1 Thessalonians 4:16; Revelation 22:7, 12:20), the people of God have believed God and waited in hope for the day of fulfillment.

It is important to note that those who first received the promises did not see their fulfillment (Hebrews 11:39), however, their willingness to walk by God's promise, not their circumstances, as Jesus said, *blessed are those who have not seen and yet have believed*" (John 20: 29 b). It is a vivid example and inspiration to us in the latter days of the dispensation of the Holy Spirit to persevere in hope, as declared in the following Scripture:

> *Therefore, since we are surrounded by such a great cloud of witnesses, let us throw off everything that hinders and the sin that so easily entangles, and let us run with perseverance the race marked out for us. Let us fix our eyes on Jesus, the author and perfecter of our faith, who for the joy set before Him endured the cross, scorning its shame, and sat down at the right hand of the throne of God. Consider Him who endured such opposition from sinful men, so that you will not grow weary and lose heart* (Hebrews 12:1-3).

Now, someone may raise the question: "How can we practise living in hope in our daily lives?" For a detailed discussion on this question, let us turn to the next chapter.

CHAPTER TWENTY

LIVING IN HOPE AS FAITHFUL DISCIPLES OF CHRIST

In what way does Biblical/Christian hope help us to live as faithful followers of Christ in our time? The Psalmist in Ps. 39:7, helps us to understand that to hope in God is to make God the object of our hope; it means placing our trust in His promises and His ability to fulfill them. This will, among other things, include:

i. Trusting God to raise us from the dead and to give us eternal life (Acts 23:6; 1 Corinthians15: 19; Titus 1:2);
ii. Trusting God to grant us a share in His glory (Romans 5:1-5);
iii. Trusting God to redeem all of creation from ruin (Romans 8:18-25).

This trust in God is not passive. It is demonstrated in a life of perseverance and faithful obedience to God (Hebrew 12:1-3). Trust in God will lead us to act on His Word (Matthew 7:21). Our hope in Him surely means that we take His commands seriously, becoming doers of His Word and not hearers only to deceive ourselves (James

1: 22). In order to keep our hope unmovable in Christ, we must be deeply rooted, built up and established in the Holy Scriptures, by means of which God revealed Himself, and also spoke to the Prophets. The Prophets, in turn, proclaimed the Word to God's people, reminding them of God's covenant relationship and of His commandments. By means of that constant reminder, and the reading and studying of the Torah, the people of Israel, though not all, managed through the help of the Holy Spirit, to keep their identity as a people of God. It is the responsibility of every parent to teach their children the Scriptures, as follows:

> *Hear, O Israel: The Lord our God, the Lord is one. Love the Lord your God with all your heart and with all your soul and with all your strength. These commandments that I give you today are to be upon your hearts. Impress them on your children. Talk about them when you sit at home and when you walk along the road, when you lie down and when you get up. Tie them as symbols on your hands and bind them on your foreheads. Write them on the door frames of your houses and on your gates* (Deuteronomy 6:4-9).

Reading through the above passage carefully, we observe a unique method recommended by the Priestly writer as to how the Scriptures should be taught to our children. That is, from the rising of the sun to the setting of the same, and in whatever situation we find ourselves—whether we are at home or outside the home, we should be alert with the Word of God.

Jesus Taught the Religious Leaders the Holy Scriptures

Careful study of the Gospels will reveal that Jesus knew the Old Testament Scriptures and often quoted them to His critics to support His claim or action. For example, in His temptation by Satan in the wilderness, Jesus used the Holy Scriptures as the only weapon to defeat His tempter. On another occasion, one of the experts in the law (i.e., a lawyer) tested Him, saying: *"Teacher, which is the greatest commandment in the Law?"* In answer, Jesus rightly quoted the Deuteronomy 6:4f., as mentioned in the above passage, *"Love the Lord your God with all your heart and with all your soul and with all your mind. This is the first and greatest commandment. And the second is like it: Love your neighbor as yourself. All the Law and the Prophets hang on these two commandments*" (Matthew 22:37-40).

When the lawyer demanded further to know *"Who is my neighbor?"* Jesus narrated the now popular story in the Bible, *"The Good Samaritan"* (Luke 10: 30-36). Then He asked the questioner to identify who was real neighbor to the wounded man. He replied, "*The one who had mercy on him.*" Jesus finally, told him, "*Go and do likewise*" (Luke 10:37). In His response to the Lawyer, Jesus summed up what life is all about here in terms of love relationship toward God, toward our neighbour, and to ourselves. You cannot transmit love to someone, unless you have personally tasted the love of God first for yourself. Then from that loving perspective, you can practise the same love relationship toward your neighbor. Rebecca Manly Pippert wrote: *"Our sociology reveals our theology. The way we treat others reveals what we think God is like. The way we treat others is critical. People will understand as much of the love of God as they see in our lives. The first Bible people will read will be your life."*

For instance, I recently listened to a powerful testimony of a man, who became converted as a result of the prayers and the exemplary life of his Christian wife. When they first married, according to the man's testimony, both of them were not Christians, but later on, his wife gave her life to Christ. That was when, what they now describe as *"spiritual mismatch in marriage,"* began to disturb their previously *"happy"* marriage. He testified that whenever his wife went to Church, he stayed at home or hanged out with friends. However, his wife loved him unconditionally, always exercising a lot of compassion, patience, gentleness, restraint, and forgiveness, toward him for his wrong doings. He called his marriage "a spiritual miss-match." But his wife pinned her trust in God's promise as declared in Ezekiel, and constantly interceded for her husband, hoping that one day, he would yield to the love of God revealed in Christ Jesus our Lord, who died for our sins. Here is God's promise as Ezekiel prophesized:

> *I will cleanse you from all your impurities and from all your idols. I will give you a new heart and put a new spirit in you; I will remove from you your heart of stone and give you a heart of flesh. And I will put my Spirit in you and move you to follow my decrees and be careful to keep my laws* (Ezekiel 36:25-27).

Finally, the husband, too, an accredited journalist, became converted and answered God's call to the ministry. Today, both husband and wife are Conference Speakers, experienced Marriage Counselors, and authors on various Christian topics.

Rebecca continued, *"We are called, therefore, to mirror the love of God—a love that is so extravagant that we must never keep it to ourselves. We must spread it around. It is not a mushy love, all sentiment and no action. Jesus' love drove him deeply into the lives of people. He cared for their wholeness. When he went out into a day he did not ask himself, 'Is this my social action day or do I give them the salvation message?' Jesus cared for people as he found them. So must we care for their wholeness—spiritual, social, psychological, you name it."* Concluding, Rebecca stated, *"our love for God, others and ourselves, and all the actions that the law entails, mirrors what the law is all about and what it is preparing us for. We do not try to prove our own righteousness by obeying the Law as some of the Pharisees tried to do. Rather we accept the law's verdict on us: we are sinners. Moreover, we acknowledge that only when we live 'according to the Spirit' can we fulfill the law's righteous requirements. By living in Christ's Spirit, we joyfully submit to God's law, because it tells us what is pleasing to God, what the things of the Spirit are and what it means to walk in the Spirit"* (Rebecca Manley Pippert, *Out of the Saltshaker*, p. 76-77).

Realizing that Jesus had given the right answer, the questioner had nothing more to say, but to agree with Him. On many occasions, the religious leaders came to test Jesus with questions concerning the Law or the Scriptures in terms of the Sabbath or marriage and divorce. There was no way in which Jesus could make them understand His ministry other than teaching or reminding them of the very Scriptures, namely, the Law. Law in this context refers not only to the Ten Commandments, but the whole of God's moral law in the Old Testament, which the people of God, especially, the Pharisees hold dearly (John 5: 39).

The Question About Resurrection

Let us take another example in the case of the Sadducees, who did not believe in the doctrine of resurrection. They came to Jesus with a question, saying:

> *Teacher, Moses told us that if a man dies without having children, his brother must marry the widow and have children for him. Now there were seven brothers among us. The first married and died, and since he had no children, he left his wife to his brother. The same thing happened to the second and third brother, right on down to the seventh. Finally, the woman died. Now then, at the resurrection, whose wife will she be of the seven, since all of them were married to her? (Matthew 22: 24-28).*

Again, using the Scriptures, Jesus easily outwitted them with an answer, which proved their ignorance. He said:

> *You are in error because you do not know the Scriptures or the power of God. At the resurrection people will neither marry nor be given in marriage, they will be like the angels in heaven. But about the resurrection of the dead, have you not read what God said to you, "I am the God of Abraham, the God of Isaac, and the God of Jacob"? He is not the God of the dead, but of the living* (Matthew 22: 29-32).

Living By the Word Of God

These are, but a few of many examples of the use of Scriptures by Jesus in answer to many tricky questions that were put to Him by His critics, namely, the Pharisees and the Sadducees. Without knowing God's Word or the Holy Scriptures, we shall not know the character and holiness of God, who made us in His own image. And without knowing God through the study of His Word, we shall NOT be able to even know or value ourselves as human beings, worthy of moral conduct. Without moral judgment, we would find ourselves living like beasts, and dying like beasts. As humans made in God's image, we are to measure our lives by the moral standard or principles laid down by God in the Holy Scriptures for guidance in our daily conduct. Just as carpenters or masons use plumb line to check whether a wall being erected is square with the floor, even so God's word gauges our lives in accordance with God's principles to find out how we are doing.

For instance, when Israel backslid, and turned away from following God's commandments, God's word came to the Prophet Amos, in a vision in which Amos saw a straight wall and the Lord standing by it with a plumb line. Since Israel's conduct did not match with God's Word, they suffered severe judgment from God. Commenting on God's judgment on Israel, Dave Egner of RBC Ministries had this to say:

> *As followers of Jesus Christ, we have a plumb line by which we can evaluate our lives. It is the word of God with its principles and commands. When faced with moral choices, we see what the Scriptures teach. When we follow the Lord's directives, we need not fear what His plumb line will reveal in our lives. (Our Daily Bread*, Dec. 17, 2002*).*

It follows, therefore, that knowing the Scriptures and living by them, is the wisest thing we can do to enjoy real peace and happiness in this life through Christ. For, it is *"in your light that we see light",* says the Psalmist (Psalm 36:9). He knows for certain that this is God's world, and humans cannot live and work successfully in this world without God's guidance from the Holy Scriptures; otherwise, all our efforts end in total defeat. King David wrote from the experience of his walk with the Lord:

> *Your word is a lamp to my feet and a light for my*

> *path. I have taken an oath and confirmed it, and I will follow your righteous laws. I have suffered much; preserve my life, O Lord, according to your word.. . . The wicked have set a snare for me, but I have not strayed from your precepts. Your statutes are my heritage forever; they are the joy of my heart* (Psalms 119:105-107 & 110-111).

To David, therefore, God's word is very precious; indeed, it is *"more precious than thousands of silver and gold"* (Psalm 119:72). Thus, David made his desire for God's Word his first priority; and pinned his hope and trust in the Scriptures. David never made a move or went to battle without first consulting the prophet for God's counsel or guidance, because he knew that victory was impossible, except God was with him. With God, David could say, "All the nations surrounded me, but in the name of the LORD I cut them off….I was pushed back and about to fall, but the LORD helped me. The LORD is my strength and my song; He has become my salvation (Psalms 118: 10, 13). Consequently, David never lost a battle (1 Samuel 30:3-8; 2 Samuel 5:17-21). If the Head of every nation, tribe and family throughout the world, particularly, in Africa, like King David, would seek the Lord and love His Word more than anything else, there would be fulfillment of peoples' hopes and aspirations—spiritually, psychologically, and materially.

With the Lord as the Shepherd, Guide, Wisdom, and Strength of our Leaders, all of us as a people under God, would surely succeed and prosper in whatever we set our mind to do, regardless of the problems that may come our way. "For, with God, all things are possible" (Mark 10:27). However, someone may ask: "How will God make all things possible for me?" Well, here is how God may work in your life: For instance, regardless of your rank in your family or community, the Bible declares: *"If you believe in Christ with all of your heart, and confess with your mouth that God raised Him from the dead, then you will be saved"* (Romans 10:9).

At that very moment, the Lord takes His rightful place in your heart by means of His Holy Spirit to enable you to submit to His teachings as prescribed in the Holy Scriptures, as King David experienced. Henceforth, the Lord takes over your life, to *"guide you in the path of righteousness for His name's sake"* (Psalms 23:3). The Holy Scriptures underscore the truth that *"righteousness exalts a nation, but sin is a disgrace to any people"* (Proverbs 14:34). It follows, therefore, that any country, whose people live righteously in obedience to God, will be blessed with peace and prosperity, while a country living in sin or disobedience to God will inevitably find no peace, but disturbance, poverty, disaster and death.

For instance, as a result of Israel's disobedience to God's commandments, God made *"the sun go down at noon and darken the earth in broad daylight,... "religious feasts into mourning, and your singing into weeping"* (Amos 8: 9-10). On the other hand, obedience to God comes with God's promise of providence, as Prophet Isaiah declared to Israel: *"If you are willing and obedient, you will eat the best from the land"* (Isaiah 1:19). That means, by faith, you have made the Lord God, Almighty, who lives in you with fullness of love, goodness, and mercy, not only your Savior, but also your Provider, Shepherd, and the Source of all your needs, as He was to King David. Thus, you can humbly and confidently say with David, *"The Lord is my Shepherd; I shall not want...He guides me in the path of righteousness, for His name's sake. . . .Goodness and mercy shall follow me all the days of my life, and I will dwell in the house of the Lord forever* " (Psalm 23:1, 6). This is not to suggest here that we as believers are able to please God or fulfill the Law's demands on us. *"We in the twentieth century,"* says Rebecca Pippert, *"tend to neglect God's Law too much. But we must not abandon the law as having meaning for the people of the Old Testament . . . . Our love for God, others and ourselves, and all the actions that the relationship entails, mirrors what the law is all about and what it is preparing us for. We do not try to prove our own righteousness by obeying the law, as some Pharisees tried to do. Rather we accept the law's verdict on us: we are sinners. We are what we are by the grace of God, because God's love is unconditional" (Ibid. p.77).*

CHAPTER TWENTY-ONE

THE BENEFITS OF KNOWING THE HOLY SCRIPTURES

At this juncture, I consider it appropriate to share with you some of the benefits that we can derive from a serious study of the Holy Scriptures. This is of prime importance because from our human experience, we know that we cannot have a close relationship with a person unless we really know the character of that person; neither shall any two people in their right mind enter into a contract unless they can trust each other. Jesus said, *"You diligently study the Scriptures because ...by them you possess eternal life. These are the Scriptures that testify about me"* (John 5: 39). Thus, by studying the Scriptures, we get to know the Lord in an intimate way and are richly blessed. Now, Let us explore some of the benefits we can derive from studying the Scriptures.

The Word Leads to Success and Prosperity

After the death of Moses, the man of God, the mantle of leadership of the people of Israel fell on the shoulders of young Joshua, the son of Nun. Naturally, Joshua felt quite inadequate for this great task entrusted into his hands. But God promised to be with Joshua as much as He was with Moses, and added the following injunction:

> *Be strong and very courageous. Be careful to obey*

> *all the Law My servant Moses gave you; do not turn from it to the right or to the left, that you may be successful wherever you go. Do not let this book of the Law depart from your mouth; meditate on it day and night, so that you may be careful to do everything written in it. Then you will be prosperous and successful* (Joshua 1:7-8).

Before going any further, I want to make it clear here that God's promise of "*success*" and "*prosperity*" is not merely material prosperity, but embraces spiritual and physical well-being in terms of the quality of life, that bears the fruit of love, "*righteousness, peace and joy in the fullness of the Holy Spiri*t" (Romans 14: 17), and reaches out to others in need, so that God is glorified in all things. That is to say, so long as the people of Israel under Joshua remain obedient, God *"will neither fail nor forsake"* them (Hebrews 13:5), but will meet in abundance "*every need* (of theirs) *according to His riches in glory by Christ Jesus*" (Philippians 4:19). It stands for total well-being/wholeness of life. Take, for instance, John's prayer for his fellow believers: "*Beloved, I wish above all things that thou mayest prosper and be in heath, even as thy soul prospereth*" *(3 John 1: 2, KJV).* Commenting on this, Charles Stanley wrote:

> *The prayer of John was that the people would prosper in all things—their material, social, natural, financial, outer lives—just as they would prosper in their personal health and their spiritual lives. The prosperity he desired for them covered their entire lives. It was prosperity that might be described as "wholeness in action"*
> *(Charles Stanley, Success God's Way, pp. 14-15).*

Now, let's return to Joshua. In saying to Joshua, *"then you will be prosprous and successful,*" God deisired the prosperity of His people to embrace every aspect of their lives, if they lived in obedience to His Word. Inspired by the Spirit of God, and under His guidance, Joshua took courage and led the Israelites victoriously to the Promised Land, crossing the great Jordan River with the Ark of God going ahead of the people of Israel. As the Lord empowered Moses to cross the Red Sea, even so did He see young Joshua through the Jordan. He overcame every obstacle, and won all their battles, including the great walled city of Jericho, for the "*commander of the Lord's army*" was with him (Joshua 5:15). The Lord promised to be with him for victory, and He did, because the Lord is faithful.

Joshua did not rely on his military expertise or experience acquired over the years from serving under Moses, but depended completely on the Lord through obedience to God's Word. Joshua understood clearly that without obedience to the Commandments of the Lord, he could do nothing. Hence, he made the Word of the Lord his Guiding Light and Principle, Strength and Salvation, Refuge and Defence, Wisdom, and his All in All; and the Lord never failed him or forsook him. Similarly, all and sundry, who take God's Word seriously and obey Him, will never be disappointed, because, God, who spoke the heavens and the earth into being by the Word of His mouth, is faithful and will always keep His promise to all who obey Him. On the other hand, if we choose our own way, we encounter defeat, and sometimes disaster.

Neglecting the Word Results in Defeat

After Israel's overwhelming victory over Jericho, they had to attack Ai, a much smaller country than Jericho. However, instead of seeking counsel from the Lord, Joshua, the Leader of the Israelites, took advice from the spies, who had spied the land of Ai. They said to Joshua,, "*Not all the people will have to go against Ai. Send two or three thousand men and do not weary all the people, for only a few men are there*" (Joshua 7:3). Joshua complied, and sent three thousand of his men, "*but they were routed by the men of Ai,*" says the Scripture, "*who killed about thirty-six of them. They chased the Israelites from the city gate...and struck them down on the slopes*" (Joshua 7:4-5). Why was Israel defeated and thirty-six of them killed? I can think of two main reasons. Firstly, Joshua did not seek counsel from God as expected of him as a leader of the people of God.

Secondly, Achan had sinned against God's commandment by stealing some of the devoted things and hiding them in his tent. When Achan was found out, he and his entire family were stoned to death, according to the Scriptures (Deuteronomy 17:2-7). "*For the wages of sin is death*" (Romans 6:23). In this episode, we see the proof of God's faithfulness to His Word: "*It is not by might nor by power, but by my Spirit*" (Zecheriah 4:6), for the Lord says, "*Without me you can do nothing*" (John 15:5).

As leaders and individual followers of Christ, we must learn a great lesson from Israel's mistake and seek God's mighty power and guidance in all our endeavors in order to win the battle of life. This is imperative because we have learnt that human effort alone is no match against the forces that assail us on our upward journey to heaven. Now, let us take a cue from Jesus' example.

Jesus Defeated Satan with the Word of God:

In His encounter with Satan in the wilderness, Jesus used the Scriptures to defeat him. Let us take the second temptation, for instance: here, the Devil led Jesus to the peak of the temple and said to Him:

> *"If you are the Son of God, throw yourself down from here. For it is written, He will command his angels concerning you to guard you carefully; they will lift you up in their hands, so that you will not strike your foot against a stone." Jesus answered him, "It says: 'Do not put the Lord your God to the test'* " (Luke 4: 8-12).

It is interesting to observe here that Satan also knows the Scriptures, and so he could quote them to Jesus. Doesn't that warn you and me to take the Holy writ more seriously than ever before, and to master how to apply it accordingly to our daily lives, especially, in times of temptation? You see, my friend, if Satan dared to tempt Jesus, the Son of God, and wanted to trick Him to misapply God's word to His life, surely will he come after us, even in our moment of serious prayer and worship to tempt us. Ignorance of the

Scriptures will inevitably lead to defeat by the Devil, who, as Peter says, "*prowls around like a roaring lion, looking for someone to devour*" (1 Peter 5:8b). Our only sure hope for victory lies in our meditating and memorizing the Scriptures as our weapon to guard ourselves against our arch-enemy, Satan.

The Key to Victorious Christian Life

Christ's victory over Satan did not happen automatically, but through prayer and fasting, and the right application of the Word of God. It is the greatest weapon that God has provided for every Christian. We must learn to keep and use it in our battle against our own sinful inclination and the Devil. This is how the writer of Hebrews describes the Word of God.

> *For the word of God is living and active. Sharper than any double-edged sword, It penetrates even to dividing soul and spirit, joints and marrow; it judges the thoughts and attitudes of the heart. Nothing in all creation is hidden from God's sight. Everything is uncovered and laid bare before the eyes of him to whom we must give account* (Hebrews 4:12).

Hence, mastering God's Word and using it rightly in every circumstance or situation in which we find ourselves is the key to victorious Christian life in this world of sin and woe. In his second Epistle to young Timothy 3: 16-17, Paul explains to him how the Scriptures are able to equip believers to become useful citizens in the community; as follows, "*All Scripture is God-breathed and is useful for teaching, rebuking, correcting and training in righteousness, so that the man of God may be thoroughly equipped for every good work.*" It is clear from the passage that believers are the best people to be hired, because we are hard working, honest and trustworthy. A few years ago, I worked as a cashier at C.V.S. (Customer, Value, Service), which is one of the biggest pharmaceutical stores in the Washington Metropolitan area. Once a week we received a consignment of goods, which needed to be unloaded from a truck. The manager would leave me alone at the cash register to handle the customers, while he and the rest of my colleagues would unload the goods from the truck. One day, when he was asked why he let me alone to serve the customers, he replied, "Because John is able to handle the customers and the register better than any of you." I guess my colleagues naturally were not happy with his response, but they knew that what he said was true. This continued till I left the store for another job in a Medical Office, where I was put in charge of Medical Records. My success as a cashier or Office Clerk depended on God's Word upon which I meditated early each morning before going to work. It enabled me to get on well, not only with my fellow workers, but also customers, some of whom were troublesome. But with patience and gentleness, through the working of the Holy Spirit, I was able to handle every situation to the glory of God, and for the blessing of C.V.S. and the community, which I served.

The Word Equips us for Spiritual warfare

The benefits derived from equipping ourselves with God's Word are seen not only in our encounter with difficult situations, but particularly in spiritual warfare. Satan, our arch-enemy, sometimes attacks us in our unguarded moments. Our victory over him depends solely on how we can apply the Word against him.

Paul explains it further in this way:

> *For though we live in the world, we do not wage war as the world does. The weapons we fight with are not the weapons of the world. On the contrary, they have divine power to demolish strongholds. We demolish arguments and every pretension that sets itself up against the knowledge of God, and we take captive every thought to make it obedient to Christ* (2 Corinthains 10: 3-5).

Someone may ask: "Why are 'our weapons not the weapons of this world'?" The reason is simple: here is why:

> *For our struggle is not against flesh and blood, but*

> *against the rulers, against the authorities, against the powers of this dark world and against the spiritual forces of evil in the heavenly realms. Therefore, put on the full armor of God, so that when the day of evil comes, you may be able to stand your ground* (Ephesians 6:12-13).

What is this "full armor of God" that we need to put on to ensure victory over Satan?

Let us look for the answer to this question in the next chapter, where we can discuss the subject in detail in the light of Paul's letter to the Ephesians, chapter 6:10-18.

CHAPTER TWENTY-TWO

TAKE WITH YOU "THE FULL ARMOR OF GOD"

(Ephesians 6: 11)

From his observance of the Roman soldier, who guarded him while in prison in Rome, St. Paul prescribes for believers a set of powerful weapons, described as ***"The full armor of God"***, listed in Eph. 6:11-18, as follows:

"The Belt of Truth"(Ephesians 6:14)

Knowing that Satan and his group of demons use deceit and tricks to gain dominion over humans, the Holy Spirit revealed to Paul that our first weapon of defense should always be to speak the truth. Under no circumstances must we, as followers of Christ, Who is the Truth, distort or misrepresent the truth, regardless of whatever advantage we might gain by so doing; lest we become victims of the devil, "*for he is a liar,*" says Jesus, "*and the father of lies*" (John 8:44). Speaking the truth, therefore, keeps us abiding in Christ; and with Christ, "*we are more than conquerors ....*" (Romans 8:37).

"The Breastplate of Righteousness" (Ephesians 6:14b)

Since Satan lives and thrives in sin, any sin in our lives makes us vulnerable to demonic influence. Though we have received the righteousness of Christ (imputed righteousness-II Cor. 5:21), we must continually determine to hold on to our protection of holy living by the power of God. It means daily submission of ourselves entirely to the control of the Holy Spirit in thought, word, and deed.

"The Shoe of The Gospel Of Peace" (Ephesians 6:15)

Holding fast to the Good News that, *"we have peace with God through our Lord Jesus Christ,"* we can stand firm against any satanic maneuvers. This emphasizes, once again, the importance of getting grip of the Scriptures, especially, the Gospels and applying them to our daily walk at home, or work place. For instance, if a soldier loses his shoes on the battle field, he becomes immobile, and unable to stand and fight against the enemy. Without shoes, he cannot run either; therefore, he inevitably falls victim to the enemy. Just as the shoes of a soldier protect his feet from being wounded, so that he can move about with his weapon to fight the enemy till he overcomes him, so do "the shoes of the Gospel of peace" worn by the Christian shield him from the attacks of Satan, and enables him to go everywhere in the security of his shoes, sharing the Good News with others that Christ might save them from sin and dominion of Satan.

With your shoes on, therefore, you have "authority to trample on snakes and scorpions and overcome all the power of the enemy; and nothing will harm you" (Luke 10: 19). As it is written: *"How beautiful are the feet of those who bring good news"* (Romans 10:15).

"The Shield of Faith" (Eph. 6: 16)

Paul goes on further to teach us that in order to quench the fiery darts of the enemy, we must believe wholeheartedly whatever God's Word says about our life. That is to say, we must not doubt the Holy Scriptures. We should take God by His Word, stand by it, depend on it, and faithfully apply it to our daily life, for, according to James, *"Faith without works is dead"* (James 2:26). What is a shield? In this context, a shield is a bulletproof steel plate won by a Roman soldier to protect mainly his chest (that is, his heart) from being hit or wounded, if shot at on the chest by an enemy.

Similarly, a Christian who holds fast to his/her faith will

strongly resist the devil in all his temptations or attacks, not allowing any force or circumstance to overcome his/her faith in the Lord. This is the kind of faith that John describes as *"victory that overcomes the world"*, and that is, *"Only he/she who believes that Jesus Christ is the Son of God*" (I John. 5: 4-5). It is the unflinching faith of a person, who knows without an iota of doubt that his God, has power to deliver, no matter what the circumstances surrounding you. Just believe that our God is able.

A typical example of this kind of faith was demonstrated by the three friends of Daniel, who defied the King's orders to bow down to the image in Babylon. They declared:

> *O Nebuchadnezzar, we do not need to defend ourselves before you in this matter. If we are throne into the blazing furnace, the God we serve is able to save us from it, and he will rescue us from your hand, O king. But even if he does not, we want you to know, O king, that we will not serve your gods or worship the image of gold you have set up.* (Daniel 3: 16b-18).

Surely, the God of Shadrach, Meshach and Abednego was, indeed, able to deliver them from the blazing furnace. Their miraculous deliverance proved the overarching nature of the power of God over the kingdom of men. With this experience, king Nebuchadnezzar made a new decree in favor of the kingdom of God of the three faithful friends, and *"promoted them in the province of Babylon*" (Daniel 3:28-30). Thus, with strong faith in Christ, we, too, will overcome our adversary.

"The Helmet of Salvation" (Ephesians 6:17)

This has to do with the confidence that there is coming a great celebration of victory in the future, coupled with the *"hope of salvation*" (1 Thessalonians 5:8). In this instance, Paul compares the Word of God to a helmet, which is usually worn to shield the head from anything that might hurt or destroy it. Thus, with the helmet always in the right place, we are kept by the power of God, who has saved us from sin and the dominion of Satan. We must always be conscious of our salvation through the Lord Jesus Christ, which promotes confidence and empowers believers to look to Christ, clinging to His promise, *"Surely, I am with you always, to the very end of the age."* (Matthew 28:20).

"The Sword of the Spirit " (Ephesians 6: 17b)

Knowing the Holy Scriptures (the Word of God) as the sure foundation of our faith, we learn how to use it with authority. The Word of God is our best offensive weapon against the devil. Jesus defeated Satan with the Word of God (Matthew 4:1-11). Supposing Jesus did not know the Scriptures, and so could not use it with authority as He should, Satan would still have been reigning supreme, and we would have continued to be his victims. "But, thanks be to God Who gives us the victory through our Lord Jesus Christ," who has overcome Satan, not only with the Word of God in His temptation in the wilderness, but also, finally, on the Cross at Calvary. "Halellujah!"

However, we must be reminded that Satan has not been bound yet, he is still on the loose, "*roaming about, seeking someone to devour*". Peter therefore warns us to "*resist him firmly in the faith*" (1 Peter 5:8), that is, with the Word of God, used in the name of Jesus Christ. John testifies to the power of the Word, which defeats the enemy when he wrote:

> *Then I heard a loud voice in heaven, saying:*
> *'Now have come the salvation and the power and the kingdom of our God, and the authority of his Christ. For the accuser of our brothers, who accuses them before our God day and night, has been hurled down. They overcame him by the blood of the lamb and by the word of their testimony; they did not love their lives so much as to shrink from death'* (Revelation 12:10b-11).

Remember, dear friend, that there is no other person in heaven or on earth or beneath the earth, who has overcome Satan, except

Jesus Christ, the Son of God. That is why Paul testifies in his epistle to the Philippians the pre-eminence of Jesus as follows:

> *Therefore, God exalted him to the highest place and gave him the name that is above every name, that at the name of Jesus every knee should bow, in heaven and on earth and under the earth, and every tongue confess that Jesus Christ is Lord, to the glory of God the Father* (Philippians. 2:9-11).

After learning to wear the full armor of God to ensure victory over the devil, we must get to know who our enemy is, in order that we may be more serious than we have ever been with our life and stay close to our Master, so that through Him, we too, might have an edge over Satan.

This is very necessary because there are people in various places of this world, who deny the existence of Satan. They contend that it is only an idea in one's mind, and not anything real. Those who hold this view have not as yet encountered the dark side of life. They are still in the Disney world: day-dreaming. But, that should not surprise you, my friend, because, as I speak, there are people of both high and middle-income classes of the world, who do not believe in the existence of God, let alone the reality of the devil. Nevertheless, it is true that God exists; and so does Satan. There are those who believe in the existence of Satan, yet do not know how to face and defeat him on the battlefield.

In the following pages, therefore, we shall discuss the enemy of God and the followers of Christ. We shall find out who he is from the biblical point of view. It is my hope that such knowledge will help readers to draw closer to Christ than ever before, and thus join the faithful soldiers of Christ, who keep watch over the city of God, protecting themselves and the church from Satan through the mighty resources provided for us in the Holy Scriptures.

CHAPTER TWENTY-THREE

KNOW YOUR ENEMY

The greatest enemy of humanity is the Devil, who is also called, *"Satan"* (Job 1:6; Zecheriah 3:2; Matthew 12:26, 16:23; Luke 10:18). He was the cause of the downfall of our first parents, namely, Adam and Eve. He still goes on unabated, '*stealing, killing and destroying*' (John 10:10) precious human beings. His enmity against God and His creation began thousands of years ago in heaven. According to the Scriptures, Satan was originally a precious angel of God. He was known as "*Lucifer, morning star/son of the dawn*" (Isaiah 14:12), with a leadership role among the angelic beings, who worship the Almighty Jehovah day and night in the heavenly realm, crying: *"Holy, holy, holy is the Lord Almighty; the whole earth is full of His glory*" *(Isaiah 6:3).*

The Duty of Angels

Thus, the primary duty of angels is to worship God in heaven and, also to serve as ministering spirits to the people of God/believers, as and when God may command. As it is written in the epistle to the Hebrews: *"Are not all angels ministering spirits sent to serve those who will inherit salvation?"* (Hebrew 1:14). There are several instances in the Bible, where angels were sent by God to minister to human beings at critical times in their lives (e. g. Isaiah 6:1-3; Daniel 6:21; Revelation 4:6-8; Acts 12: 7-10).

Another vivid example of deliverance through ministration of angels can be seen in the story of the Prophet Elijah. During the three and a half years of drought in the land of Israel, an angel was sent by God to minister to him (1 Kings 19:5-7). Then, there is also an interesting, dramatic story about Jacob and his wrestling with an angel of God, (Genesis 32: 24-29). Then, also, we are familiar with the wonderful story of Mary, to whom the angel, Gabriel brought the Good News of the miraculous conception and birth of Jesus (Luke 1:26-38).

Now, let us go to the book of Acts, where we read about the deliverance of Peter and John from prison; Philip was guided to meet and preach to the Ethiopian Eunuch; and finally, Peter was miraculously released from prison at midnight—all these and many more were accomplished by angels, sent by God to minister to His faithful servants in times of special need (Acts 5:19-20, 8:26f, 12:6-10). Since God is no respecter of persons, it does mean that the care He provided through angels for His servants of old, He offers similar care to us who serve him today in various ways according to His purpose.

Lucifer's Rebellion in Heaven
(Ezekiel 28: 14-7; Revelation 12: 1-12)

The Scriptures inform us that on one occasion, Lucifer and one third (1/3) of the angels rebelled against God, and as a result, they were cast down from heaven, because there was found no place for them. Though the scriptures originally refer to the king of Tire, the descriptions go beyond an earthly monarch to Lucifer, as follows:

> *You were the model of perfection, full of wisdom and perfect in beauty, you were in Eden, the Garden of God; you were blameless in your ways till wickedness was found in you. You were anointed as a guardian cherub, for so I ordained you. Your heart became proud on account of your beauty and you corrupted your wisdom because of your splendour. So I threw you to the earth.. . . You have come to a horrible end and will be no more* (Ezekiel 28:12b-13a, 14-15, 17, 19).

Thus, Lucifer no longer was called "son of the dawn" or "morning star", but Satan, "adversary of God, and lord of evil in Judaism and Christianity. He is full of extreme cruelty and wickedness/viciousness" (Webster's New Collegiate Dictionary). He is called by several names in the Scriptures, as for instance: *the serpent* (Genesis 3:1); *the thief, the prince of this world* (John 10:10, 14: 30); *the great dragon, the ancient serpent, the devil/Satan, the accuser* (Revelation 12:9-10). The Akans of Ghana, including the Gas and others call him 'Abonsam'or 'Sasambonsam'. Satan and those angels who teamed up with him in his act of rebellion made a bad decision on that day. By rejecting their divinely appointed position and purpose in heaven, they eternally forfeited their honour and purpose for which they were created. They had not the opportunity to repent of their sin of rebellion. It was obvious that pride made it impossible for Satan to repent. As a result, hell was created for all the bunch of demonic spirits, masterminded by Satan. Now, let us look at some of their demonic activities and learn how to resist them.

Activities of Satan and Evil Spirits:

As we have learned from the Bible, Paul speaks of Satan and his team of demons as *"the rulers, the powers of this dark world"* (Ephesians 6: 12). That means, they operate in darkness so that they will not be seen by anybody, because their deeds are evil and wicked. John echoed the same message when he said, *"Light has come into the world, but men loved darkness instead of light because their deeds were evil. Everyone who does evil hates the light, and will not come into the light for fear that his deeds will be exposed"* (John 3:19-20).

Thus, Peter counsels believers to be ware of the Devil, *"your adversary . . . a roaring lion, seeking someone to devour*" (1 Peter. 5:8). Here, Peter points out the cunning manner in which the Devil operates; in his anger, he goes about, watching and waiting, only to attack anyone, who happens to come his way. It was to keep all dwellers on earth, especially believers, on the alert against the attacks of the devil that a voice from heaven sounded the following warning through John, saying:

> *But woe to the earth and the sea, because the devil has gone down to you! He is filled with fury because he knows that his time is short.. . . Then the dragon was enraged at the woman and went off to make war against the rest of her offspring-those who obey God's commandments and hold to the testimony of Jesus.* (Revelation 12:12b-17)

This reminds me of the story of a teenaged girl, who was possessed by a spirit on her father's farm on the very day that she came of age (i.e., when she reached puberty). After several months of torments by the spirit, the girl became so seriously ill that she was hospitalized for many days. During one of my early morning visitations to patients in the hospital, her mother told me about her daughter's condition. Realizing that *"this kind cannot come out except by prayer and fasting"* (Mark 9:29), I devoted the following day to this assignment, fasting and interceding for this young girl. Then, towards evening, I visited her at the hospital. After about half an hour of intensive prayer of deliverance by the power of the Holy Spirit in the mighty name of the Lord Jesus Christ, the young girl was set free from the evil spirit that had victimized her for more than six months.

My friend, without Christ living in you as your Savior and Lord, you do not have power over Satan and his bunch of demonic forces. And if you are a believer, are you so fully committed to your Christian faith that you are filled with the Holy Spirit, wearing "the whole armour of God?" We need to remind ourselves that it is only Christ, who has defeated the devil in His encounter with him during His earthly ministry. Then, finally, He defeated him completely on the Cross (Colossians 2:13-15). Therefore, without Christ, no one can *"escape from the trap of the devil, who has taken them (humans) captive to do his will"* (2 Timothy 2:26b).

Therefore, I seriously counsel you to yield yourself to Jesus Christ, whom to know is eternal life, and perfect freedom. The hour of decision is now! Tomorrow may be too late! Please, read further on to know much more about the works of evil spirits.

They Slander God and Believers:

With Satan as their leader, demons create doubt in the minds of believers concerning the character of God as Satan did to Eve in the Garden of Eden (Gen. 3:1-5), as well as Job and others (Job 1:9-11; Acts 5:3, 26:18; 2 Corinthians 12:7, Revelation 12: 10-12). It takes a man of God, filled with the Holy Spirit, to discern the cunning voice of the devil, who whispers into our ears, only to deceive us or get us to disobey God.

Have you not at one time, or the other, heard a voice instructing you to retaliate after someone has insulted or mistreated you? That forceful voice agitating you to hurl insults in retaliation is surely Satan's voice. It is usually contrary to God's Word. That is why it is very important for every true child of God to study and equip himself with the Scriptures. There is no other way by which we can know God's Word, let alone to use it against the enemy. Jesus said, "*My sheep hear my voice, and they follow me*." If we sincerely study, meditate, and keep God's Word, the Holy Spirit will always help and guide us to hear and obey the voice of the Lord, but reject Satan's deceitful voice.

They Plant Evil Thoughts in the Minds of People

It was Satan, who moved King David to take census of the people of Israel at a time when it was not appropriate in the sight of God. Doubtlessly, David was motivated by nothing, but pride to boost his ego; and to prove what a great leader/King he has been since his enthronement (1 Chronicles 21: 1). That pride was exactly what caused the downfall of Lucifer, and he always wants to tempt people in high positions with pride, so that they will fall just as he did. For instance, he caused Judas, the treasurer of the ministry of Jesus Christ, the Son of God, not only to harbour thoughts that gradually, but steadily led to his betrayal of Jesus, and worse still, to his suicide (Luke. 22:3; John. 13:2, 6:70).

There is a great lesson that Christian leaders, especially, Ministers, have to learn from what happened to Judas. Sometimes, we become so much engrossed in the ministry, serving the needs of our members, attending meetings here and there, that we have no time to minister to our own spiritual and physical needs and those of our families; thus, leaving a gap for the enemy to enter and attack the family, and the church.

That is the chief reason why Jesus cautioned His followers: *"Watch and pray, so that you do not fall into temptation"* (Matthew 26:46).

They Ill-Influence National Leaders

In one of His engagements with His disciples, Jesus speaks about the devil, saying: *"The prince of this world is coming. He has no hold on me"* (John. 14:30). Yes, indeed! The devil "has no hold on" Jesus, because Jesus, though fully man, He is also fully God. Thus, unlike any of us, Jesus was not conceived by the seed of man, but by the power of the Holy Spirit (Luke 1:26-38). Therefore, since He that is in Jesus (God-the Holy Spirit) is greater than he (the devil), who is in the world, Jesus overcame the devil in all his temptations he brought in His way directly or indirectly during His earthly ministry (Matthew 4:1-11; Colossians 2:1-15).

The Devil Blinds the Minds of Unbelievers

Writing to the Corinthian church, Paul also refers to one of the activities of Satan as follows: *the "god of this age has blinded the minds of unbelievers, so that they cannot see the light of the gospel of the glory of Christ, who is the image of God*" (2 Corinthians 4:4). This, as well as other references clearly suggest to you and me that Satan has the power to influence any pagan king, Head of State, or someone in authority, to commit acts of wickedness, such as torturing to death or killing by firing squad all who dare to oppose his policies. Some national leaders in Africa and other parts of the world are guilty of such diabolical acts in their attempts to pursue their own political agenda. Adolf Hitler of Germany, for instance, killed thousands of Jews in a gas chamber, Idi Amin, former President of Uganda, gunned down many of his opponents, as well as other wicked leaders, who got rid of their opponents out of hatred for them and not for the love and progress of their countries.

Another fitting example is the case of Haman, whose hatred for Modecai's refusal to bow to him, developed into hatred for the whole Jewish race in the kingdom of Ahasuerus of Persia, and his determination to annihilate them completely from the face of the earth (Esther 3:6). But, in the end, by God's intervention through the prayers of Queen Esther and the Jews, Haman, the enemy of the Jews, was hung on the gallows he had prepared for his enemy, Mordecai (Esther 8:9-10). As it is written, "If a man digs a pit, he will fall into it; if a man rolls a stone, it will roll back on him" (Proverbs 26:27).

In other words, "*God cannot be mocked,*" says Paul. "*A man reaps what he sows. The one who sows to please his sinful nature, from that nature will reap destruction; the one who sows to please the Spirit* (that is, God), *from the Spirit will reap eternal life*" (Galatians 6:7). What are we of this generation sowing, and what do we expect to reap in return? This is a question each reader must ponder over carefully, and honestly answer for oneself. Surely, Haman's attempt to destroy the Jews could be likened to the work of the Antichrist (Revelation 13:2, 4), and all who work for the devil and try to hinder God's work in this world. King Saul of Israel, under the influence of an evil spirit, twice threw a sword at David, intending to "pin him to the wall", but David smartly eluded him in both incidents (1 Samuel 18:10-12). However, Saul and his son Jonathan both died in Israel's battle against the Philistines at Mount Gilboa (2 Samuel 1:4).

There is another instance where Satan used "a lying spirit" to lead King Ahab to his death (1 Kings 22:20-23, 37-38). He also assigned a demonic spirit to control the king of Persia (Daniel 10:10-21). It is a prophecy recorded by John that through evil spirits, Satan will finally *"gather kings of the whole world for the battle of Armageddon"*(Revelation 16:13-14, 16). Now, having known these concrete examples of the havoc that Satan and his demonic allies can cause among humanity, we must ask the next question: *"How can we overcome him?"* Honestly speaking, I regret to say that there is no human being, who is able to face the devil and overcome him, except the Lord, Jesus Christ.

If Satan succeeded in deceiving Adam and Eve, and thereby created death among humanity through their disobedience to God, it is no wonder that he is called, *"the prince of this world"*(John. 14:30), and *"the ruler of the kingdom of the air, the spirit who is now at work in those who are disobedient"* (Ephesians 2:2). Since the fall of Adam and Eve, the first representatives of the human race, humanity abdicated their God-given authority and privilege as overseers/stewards of God's creation (Genesis 1:27f.). However, by God's gracious intervention, there is Good News, as Professor Conn puts it: "The tree of Eden became the tree of Calvary". That is only part of the Good News. Let us be reminded that as Haman perished in the gallows in his own home, so shall Satan be cast and destroyed in the lake of fire prepared for him and his angels, as well as all, who, like Haman, follow his wicked plans. The rest of the matter is that Jesus "*was raised* (from the dead) *on the third day in accordance with the Scriptures*" (1 Corinthians 15:4). By His resurrection, "*Jesus has abolished death and brought immortality to light through the gospel*" (2 Timothy 1:10); HALLELUJAH!! AMEN!! !

Gordon Lindsay connects Christ's victory over Satan with His prayer and fasting in the wilderness and declares:

> *As Adam and Eve's disobedience by eating the forbidden fruit was the original cause of man's losing his God-given dominion in the Garden of Eden, so Christ's fasting forty days and nights in the wilderness, there overcoming the fiercest onslaughts of the enemy, made possible the restoration of man's dominion. (Gordon Lindsey, Prayer and Fasting: The Master Key to the Impossible, Ohiseyi Press Ltd. Ibadan, 1990, P. 1).*

This then leads us to the answer to the question: "How can we resist and overcome Satan and his demonic forces?" The answer comes from Jesus' response to His disciples when they wanted to know why they were not able to cast out a demon from a young boy, whose father approached them for help. They said to Jesus, "*Why couldn't we drive him out?*" Jesus replied: "*This kind can come forth by nothing, but by prayer and fasting*" (Mark 9:28-29-A.V./K.J.V.). In the other translations of the Bible, such as NIV, the word "fasting" is omitted. Nevertheless, having experienced the benefits of fasting personally, I strongly recommend it to mature believers, who can practice it as a discipline to their prayer life. Since Jesus Christ, the Son of God, and the apostles, found it necessary to fast and pray in the pursuit of their faith, and fulfillment of their ministries, we cannot do otherwise. It is only by so doing that we, too, can really be faithful stewards of the legacy entrusted to our charge.

CHAPTER TWENTY-FOUR

HOW TO RESIST SATAN

I want to begin with the sound counsel offered to all believers by James, the brother of Jesus, and presiding elder of the first Christian Council of the Church in Jerusalem. He stated, *"Therefore submit to God. Resist the devil and he will flee from you"* (James 4:7). That is to say, we should have the desire to do God's will, plus humility to obey or submit to Him. It implies counting yourselves as dead to sin but alive to God in Christ Jesus. *"Therefore, do not let sin reign in your mortal body so that you obey its evil desires"* (Romans 6:11-12). We must refuse to yield to the devil's tricks or temptations, in the name of the Lord Jesus Christ by the power of the Holy Spirit. The way to go about this task of resisting the devil is PRAYER. "More things are wrought by prayer than this world dreams of", as written by Alfred Tennyson several ages ago-is true to this day and age.

The importance of prayer was underscored by Jesus in His statement to the merchants, who had made the temple a market place, "Is it not written: *'My house shall be called a House of Prayer for all nations? But you have made it a den of robbers'"* (Mark 12:17). In saying this, Jesus rebuked the Leaders of the temple worship for the following reasons:

- They turned the house of God into a market place.

- They cheated on the worshippers who came to exchange their money for offering or a lamb for sacrifice.
- They hindered *"all (the other) nations"*, from coming to the temple to worship and pray to God.

Jesus exemplified the essence of prayer during His ministry, in that He would often withdraw Himself into a solitary place, after a busy day's work, in order to pray to God, His Father in heaven. Mark wrote, *"Very early in the morning, while it was still dark, Jesus got up, left the house and went off to a solitary place, where he prayed"* (Mark 1:35). Having observed prayer as an integral part of Jesus' ministry, the disciples also came to Jesus with their request: "Lord, teach us to pray" (Luke. 11:1). Accordingly, Jesus taught His followers what is commonly known as 'the Lord's Prayer' (Luke 11:2ff & Matthew 6:6-9).

It is important to be reminded at this crucial point of this book that we are NOT told to pray to any ancestor or god/goddess, because the dead have no power to help the living here on earth, except the Lord, the living God alone. God declares: *"I am the Lord, and there is no other"* (Isaiah 45:18d). Let us now begin by understanding what prayer is all about, for the sake of those who may not be familiar with this subject. They may ask the question:

What is Prayer?

Prayer is audible or inaudible expression of our heart's concerns to God. Here is what the hymn writer James Montgomery, says about prayer:

Prayer is the soul's sincere desire,
Uttered or unexpressed,
The motion of a hidden fire
That trembles in the breast.

Prayer is the burden of a sigh,
The falling of a tear,
The upward glancing of an eye
When none but God is near.

Prayer is the simplest form of speech
That infant lips can try;
Prayer the sublimest strains that reach
The majesty on high.

Prayer is the contrite sinner's voice
Returning from his ways,
While angels in their songs rejoice,
And cry: Behold he prays!

Prayer is the Christian's vital breath,
The Christian's native air,
His watchword at the gates of death;
He enters heaven with prayer.
(M.H.B. 533 verses 1-5 by James Montgomery, 1771-1854).

Knowing that *"God is spirit,"* and that no one else, apart from God can meet our various needs-whether spiritual, physical or emotional—and that PRAYER is the only means by which we (humans) can communicate with God, we must readily respond to God's gracious invitation to come to Him with our problems: "Call upon me", He says, "in the day of trouble; I will deliver you, and you will honour me"(Psalms 50:15). Again, in the gospel of Matthew, Jesus gently invites all people to come, irrespective of rank, race, colour or gender: *"Come to me, all you who are weary and burdened, and I will give you rest"* (Matthew 11:28).

Prayer is, therefore, a *privilege*, as well as the responsibility of every true child of God. It is a privilege, because we are dealing with a God, who is "the King, the Lord Almighty", who is holy, and too pure to look upon sin. Even the angels in heaven cannot look upon God; they have to cover their faces to praise His holiness and majesty, *"Holy, holy, holy is the Lord Almighty; the whole earth is full of His glory"* (Isaiah 6:3).

In spite of His holiness, God bids us—sinful humans— to come to Him with all our concerns. Thus, prayer is like coming to our loving father/mother, who is willing to receive and listen to us unconditionally, regardless of the size of our need.

On the other hand, prayer can be regarded as a *responsibility of every believer* in obedient response to the call of God (to duty). Listen to this, for example, "*If my people, who are called by my name will humble themselves and pray and seek my face and turn from their wicked ways, then will I hear from heaven and will forgive their sin and will heal their land"* (2 Chronicles 7:14). We cannot, but simply obey God's call to duty, because He has told us to pray. It is thus, evident that the purpose of prayer is to determine God's will in a matter/situation, and to pray for its fulfillment. As Christians, we must welcome the act of prayer as both privilege and responsibility to co-operate with the Triune God in the creative work of our fellow human beings.

The following are several examples of the call on believers to pray, "*As for me, far be it from me that I should sin against the Lord by failing to pray for you. And I will teach you the Way that is good and right"* (1 Samuel 12:23). 1 Timothy 2: 1-2 *also states that, "I urge, then, first of all, that requests, prayers, Intercession and thanksgiving be made for everyone—for kings and all those in authority, that we may live peaceful and quiet lives in all godliness and holiness,"* while Ephesians 6:18-19 states:

> *And pray in the Spirit on all occasions with all kinds of prayers and requests. With this in mind, be alert and always keep on praying for all the saints. Pray also for me, that whenever I open my mouth, words may be given me so that I will fearlessly make known the mystery of the gospel . . .*

Furthermore, Matthew 26:41 states, "*Watch and pray so that you will not fall into temptation. The spirit is willing, but the body is weak"*. All these referencess emphasize the point that the victories of faithful Saints recorded in the Holy Scriptures came *about "Not by might nor by power, but by my Spirit, says the Lord of Hosts,"* through the constant act of prayer in which they invested much of their precious time, life and ministry. As they waited patiently upon the Lord in prayer, God never disappointed them. For the Scripture declares:

"Call to me and I will answer you and tell you great and unsearchable things you do not know" (Jeremiah 33:3). *The assurance we have from Paul is this: "the one who calls you is faithful and he will do it"* (1 Thessalonians 5:24). Counting on God's faithfulness to His promises, and also knowing how much prayer can accomplish, Paul, therefore, urges all believers to pray at all times: *"Pray without ceasing"* (1 Thessalonians. 5:17).

Prayer is a Priority and Discipline

As indicated earlier in the above passage, a careful study of the life and ministry of Jesus will show that PRAYER had priority in Jesus' life not only over physical rest, but also over social life, as well as even over food. Prayer was, indeed, the primary communication link between Jesus and His Father. The same must be true for us, if we are truly His disciples. It is written as follows:, *"After he had dismissed them He went up on a mountainside by himself to pray*" (Matthew 14:23*). "One of those days Jesus went out to a mountainside to pray, and spent the night praying to God"* (Luke 6:12).

Can you imagine Jesus, the Holy Son of God, holding all-night prayer all by Himself on a mountain? Yet, He did it in order to be in tune with His Father, and to receive wisdom, power, and direction necessary to accomplish His divine mission. And He got what He needed. That is the way our Master went, and we, the servants, must follow His trail, which alone can lead us to victory and glory in His name. The Church must organize prayer vigil occasionally to meet the needs of the members.

Prayer is a Ministry unto God

The biblical concept of the priesthood of all believers qualifies every Christian to be called "a priest unto the Lord". Hence, we must always aim at ministering to the Lord before ministering to people. As children of God, we must not fail to minister to God through the acts of praise and worship, and to commune with Him through prayer and meditation, in the name of Jesus Christ, our Lord.

This priestly duty is bestowed upon us not by virtue of our own righteousness, but by virtue of the blood of Jesus, which has justified us, making us righteous so that we might enter the Holy of Holies boldly, yet with humility and confidence into the very presence of God. Peter wrote, "*But you are a chosen people, a royal priesthood, a holy nation, a people belonging to God, that you may declare the praises of him who called you out of darkness into his wonderful light*" (1 Peter 2:9). In an earlier verse he wrote that, "*As you come to him, the Living Stone . . . . You also, like living stones, are being built into a spiritual house to be a holy priesthood, offering spiritual sacrifices acceptable to God through Jesus Christ*" (1 Peter 2:5). Proverbs 15:8 also states that, '*The Lord detests the sacrifice of the wicked, But the prayer of the upright pleases him.*"

Hence, as the people of God, we must always see it as our necessary duty, as well as privilege to minister to our God, and so to receive power, wisdom and direction before going out to minister to the world with its problems and temptations.

Prayer is a Unique Communication with God

This is when we come to spend time with the Lord, because we love Him. Here, our conversation reaches down to the deep recesses of our hearts, and our prayers turn into heart-to-heart dialogue with our heavenly Father. For, as "God made known His ways to Moses," His servant, and His wonderful "deeds to the people of Israel," (Ps. 103:7), so does He desire to do through God, the Holy Spirit, for those who are committed to His service in our time.

> *The Lord would speak to Moses face to face, as a man speaks with his friend. Then Moses would return to the camp, but his young aide Joshua, son of Nun, did not leave the tent. Moses said to the Lord, "You have been telling me, Lead these people, but you have not let me know whom you will send with me. You have said, 'I know you by name and you have found favour with me.' If you are pleased with*

> *me, teach me your ways so I may know you and continue to find favor with you. Remember that this nation is your people. The Lord replied, "My presence will go with you, and I will give you rest"* (Exodus 33:11-14).

Thanks to God that by these, and many other ways, Moses, Israel's great intercessor, pleaded on their behalf in the presence of the Lord, and helped to deliver his people from many afflictions, which would otherwise have fallen on them in the wilderness.

Whether you are somebody in authority or not, Black or White, rich or poor, man or woman, it is important to know that as a Christian, your prayer can bring deliverance through faith in Christ. All the forces of evil that have crippled many Africans and Whites alike will lose their grip through the effectual prayer of believers in the matchless name of Jesus Christ. For "*the Son of God appeared to destroy the works of the devil*" (1 John. 3: 8).

Prayer Opens our Spiritual Eyes

It is encouraging news to know that through the act of prayer, the Lord graciously makes it possible for believers to see things in the spiritual realm that we cannot see or know in any other way. Here are a few examples to stimulate your thirst for prayers:

- *"Sacrifice thank offering to God, fulfill your vow to the Most High; and call upon me in the day of trouble; I will deliver you, and you will honour me"* (Psalms 50:14-15).
- *"Don't be afraid, the Prophet answered. Those who are with us are more than those who are with them. And Elisha prayed, "O, Lord open his eyes so he may see". Then the Lord opened the servant's eyes, and he looked and saw the hills full of horses and chariots of fire all around Elisha"* (2 Kings 6:16-17).

The Bible describes demonic forces as "*the powers of this dark world*" (Ephesians 6:12), and it is by means of prayer that the Lord graciously enables believers to see what is hidden from the natural sight; and empowers us to overcome them. Thus Joseph Scriven exclaimed:

O what a privilege we have in Jesus
All our sins and grief to bear!
What a privilege to carry
everything to God in prayer!
O what peace we often forfeit
O what needless pain we bear,
all because we do not carry
everything to God in prayer!
(M. H. B. 538 V. 1, by Joseph Medlicott Scriven, 1820-86).

Prayer Makes a Way for God's Will on Earth

What a powerful thought it is for believers to know that the entire powers of heaven wait for the church militant (that is, all believers on earth, namely the universal church) to pray for wonders to happen.

Teaching His disciples how to pray, Jesus said, among other things, *"Thy will be done on earth as it is in heaven"* (Matthew 6:10). He further assured them: *I tell you the truth, whatever you bind on earth will be bound in heaven, and whatever you loose on earth will be loosed in heaven. Again, I tell you that if two of you on earth agree on anything you ask for, it will be done for you by my Father in heaven. For where two or three come together in my name, there am I with them* (Matthew 18:18-20).

What Jesus means here obviously is that God, by His divine purpose, has somehow limited His activities on earth. However, He graciously waits to respond to the prayers of His children. I am thrilled here by the remembrance of John's vision of the twenty-four elders, who fall prostrate before the Lamb, holding *"golden bowls of incense, which are the prayers of the saints"*(Revelation 5:8).

E. Stanley Jones had this to say about prayers of believers, "We align ourselves with the purpose and power of God, and He is able to do things through us that He could not do otherwise." That means that God has delegated to believers a measure of His divine authority to be exercised through prayer, and so by calling on Him, we move, as it were, God's "victorious right hand" to work mightily on behalf of His people. From time immemorial, God has always sought for a man, an intercessor-who would passionately plead for the people, so that His perfect will and purpose might be done on earth as in heaven. The following is a fitting example in the history of Israel, which occurred during the days of the Prophet Ezekiel:

> *I looked for a man among them who would build up the wall and stand before me in the gap on behalf of the land so that I would not have to destroy it, but I found none. So I will pour out my wrath on them and consume them with my fiery anger, bringing down on their own heads all they have done, declares the Sovereign Lord* (Ezekiel 22:30-31).

Isaiah 62:6-7 also states that, "I *have posted watchmen on your walls, O Jerusalem; they will never be silent day or night. You who call on the Lord, give yourselves no rest, and give Him no rest till He establishes Jerusalem and makes her the praise of the earth.*"

In the two passages quoted above, we observe in the first instance, that lack of an intercessor, would result in the destruction of Israel. Whereas, in the second case, prayer-warriors would keep watch and pray without ceasing, until the purpose of God was fulfilled in Jerusalem, which would cause everyone to praise the Lord. May I remind you, dear friend, that the intercessors are not told to call on other gods or pour libation to Israel's ancestors; that would not bring victory and honour to Jerusalem, but disaster and disgrace. And that is exactly what is going on in most parts of the world today, especially in Africa. Therefore, if we really want to experience spiritual freedom and economic prosperity in the land, then we must have intercessors, who will call on God day and night, and give God no rest, till He establishes Africa "*and makes her a praise on the earth*".

Prayer Enables Believers to Receive Revelation

As we continue to walk closely with God in prayer and obedience to Him, He will reveal to us through the in-dwelling Holy Spirit what He wants us to pray for, pointing to a specific problem in the family or in a situation. In His permissive will, God allows us to see what He sees, in order that we may act (i.e. through prayer and action) to bring a change for the better. There is, however, a caution here that we need to observe and that is, as intercessors, we must carefully guard against divulging secrets that are made known to us through prayer. We must seek God's clear guidance and be obedient as to when and how to share the revelation with the person or people concerned. For instance, while praying (this happened about fifteen years ago), the Lord revealed to me that an acquaintance of mine was dead and a grave was being dug for him. How must I break such news to him or even his wife? What made it further difficult was the fact that the man in question was fit and well, going about his business as usual.

After praying for wisdom and guidance, I was told to go and share the gospel with him, and to lead him to come to saving faith in Jesus Christ, using specifically John 5:24, *"I tell you the truth, whoever hears my word and believes him who sent me has eternal life and will not be condemned; he has crossed over from death to life"*. Without delay, I visited this man in the evening of that very day I received guidance from the Lord. I did exactly as I was told, without mentioning anything about the vision. A few days after my visit, I went back as a follow-up exercise. The wife told me he had to leave suddenly for his village near Kumasi, because some soldiers had been sent by the then AFRC regime of Ghana to arrest him. Why? Only God knows the answer. But, whatever the reason might be, he got the hint and left the city before the soldiers arrived. Those were the days when almost every well-to-do-person in Ghana was suspected of ill-gotten money and was charged with corruption by the previous regime of the Armed Forces Revolutionary Council (AFRC). One could be arrested, taken to army barracks to be interrogated/beaten, imprisoned or killed, depending on the result of the probe.

It was not until I heard of his story that I really understood the revelation I had on him. Surely, the Lord knew what was to befall him, and He graciously delivered him from imminent death. He indeed, *"crossed from death to life"*, because he believed in Jesus Christ as his Savior and Lord. I thank God for making me a vessel through whom His message of salvation could reach that man, at the right time, lest he would have died according to the revelation. Here are some passages to confirm this truth about revelation through prayer:

> *Then Joshua tore his clothes and fell facedown to the ground before the ark of the Lord (obviously praying for revelation—my insertion), and remaining there till evening. And Joshua said, "Ah Sovereign Lord, why did you ever bring this people across the Jordan to deliver us into the hands of the Amorites to destroy us? . . . The Canaanites and the other people of the country will hear about this and they will surround us and wipe out our name from the earth. What then will you do for your own great name?*
>
> *The Lord said to Joshua, "Stand up! What are you doing down on your face? Israel has sinned, they have violated my covenant, which I commanded them to keep. They have taken some of the devoted things . . . That is why the Israelites cannot stand against their enemies* (Joshua 7:6-7, 9-12).

In this passage, we find Joshua, the successor of Moses, perplexed and sorrow-stricken, prostrated before the Lord in prayer from morning till evening hour. Then the Lord revealed to him the cause of their defeat by their enemies. Achan had stolen some of the devoted things (namely, a piece of silver, a robe and a bar of gold) and hidden them in his tent.

To purge Israel of this sin, and to get them back on track, holy, and consecrated before the presence of God, Achan was brought out from his tribe and together with his household, was stoned to death and burned with fire. That done, they were cleansed, and fully empowered by God to defeat their enemies.

The following passage describes Jesus praising God for the revelation to His disciples:

> *At that time Jesus, full of joy through the Holy Spirit, said, "I praise you, Father, Lord of heaven and earth, because you have hidden these things from the wise and learned, and revealed them to little children. Yes, Father, for this was your good pleasure. All things have been committed to me by my Father. No one knows who the Son is except the Father, and no one knows who the Father is except the Son and those to whom the Son chooses to reveal Him (Luke 10:21-22).*

Paul, too, shares his experience of revelation:

> *To keep me from becoming conceited because of these surpassingly great revelations, there was given me a thorn in my flesh, a messenger of Satan, to torment me. Three times I pleaded with the Lord to take it away from me. But he said to me, "My grace is sufficient for you, for my power is made perfect in weakness." Therefore, I will boast all the more gladly about my weaknesses, so that Christ's power may rest on me.* (2 Corinthians 12: 7-9)

What we need to note here is that, like the apostle Paul, whenever we are going through any hard situation, we should not hesitate to take it to the Lord in prayer in order to know His mind or revelation about it. With God's revelation, we will be able to bear our yoke, knowing that the grace of God is sufficient to see us through.

It is very important to note here that no earthly being, ancestor, or god, has the power to deliver us from pain or suffering, except the Lord. "When our hearts are filled with pain," says McCasland, "it is good to call on God in prayer—morning, noon, and night."

Prayer Must Be in Accordance with God's Word

In order for our prayers to achieve fruitful results or answers, we must learn to pray in accordance with what God has said in the Holy Scriptures. We must speak forth His Word in faith, not by special formula or in vain repetitions, "*like pagans, because they think they will be heard because of their many words*" (Matthew 6:7). The Word of the Lord is "*Spirit and life*," it is also "*like fire and like a hammer that breaks a rock in pieces*" (John 6:63; Jeremiah 23:29). Therefore, if it is spoken in faith through the power of the Holy Spirit, it goes forth with anointing to perform what is intended. The following examples may be helpful.

> *As the snow and the rain come down from heaven, and do not return to it without watering the earth and making it bud and flourish, so that it yields seed for the sower and bread for the eater, so is my word that goes out from my mouth: It will not return to me empty, but will accomplish what I desire and achieve the purpose for which I sent it* (Isaiah 55:10-11).

Peter observed the result of Jesus' Words and said to Him,

> *"Rabbi, the fig tree you cursed has withered!" "Have faith in God," Jesus answered. "I tell you the truth, if anyone says to this mountain, Go, throw yourself into the sea, and does not doubt in his heart but believes that what he says will happen, it will be done for him. Therefore, I tell you, whatever you ask for in prayer, believe that you have received it, and it will be yours* (Mark 11:21 - 24).

Hebrews 11:6 states that, "*And without faith it is impossible to please God, because anyone who comes to Him must believe that He exists and that He rewards those who earnestly seek him.*" As you might have already noted earlier in the examples of Christ and the apostles, the key to the greatest resistance that leads to victory over our enemy—the Devil, is PRAYER and FASTING.

The regular, normal prayer will NOT DO IT, unless it is ignited with FASTING, as the Lord advised His followers. Now, let us read on to see the key role that prayer and fasting play in the lives of Christian warriors.

CHAPTER TWENTY-FIVE

PRAYER AND FASTING

Let us begin by reminding ourselves once again of what Jesus said to His disciples, "*This kind can come forth by nothing, but by prayer and fasting*"(Mark 9:28-29 from KJV).

The scriptures are pregnant with evidence as to what powerful effect prayer and fasting have on every human situation; even to the point of pulling down strongholds and completely destroying the works of Satan. No military force or the power of atomic bomb can do this, except the Spirit of the Living God (Zechariah 4: 6). The example of Moses as a leader of the people of Israel may set the pace at this point:

When the Israelites were rebellious against God in the wilderness, they came under the judgment of God, and He declared, *"I have seen these people", the Lord said to Moses, "They are a stiff necked people. Now, leave me alone so that my anger may burn against them and that I may destroy them. Then I will make you into a great nation"* (Exodus 32:9-10).

Moved with sympathy and compassion for his people, Moses went into prayer and fasting for forty days and nights, pleading their case before God at Mount Sinai. (Exodus 34:28). In his prayer, Moses pleaded for three things: firstly, that Israel might receive divine forgiveness; secondly, that he (Moses) might have a vision of God's glory; and thirdly, that God's presence might accompany them on their journey to the Promised Land.

In the end, God granted the prayer of Moses and made a covenant with him. When he came down from the mountain, his face shone with such a glow of God that the people of Israel could not look upon him. Moses had to cover his face with a veil. (Exodus 34:35)

Thus the forty days of prayer and fasting by Moses resulted in the breaking of the powers of darkness and the moving of God's compassion for the restoration of Israel. Let me assure you that the God who gave Moses the break-through has not changed. *"He is the same yesterday, today, and for ever"* (Hebrew 13: 8). Therefore, if you are the head of a nation, community, Church, family, or business, facing insurmountable problems, follow the example of Moses. "*God is love*," and "*cares for you*" (1 John 4:8; 1 Peter 5:7). He will surely answer your prayers for the blessing of your people, and for a testimony to His faithfulness, and to the glory of His Holy name.

Jesus is Our Best Example

Now, let us move on further to the New Testament, where Jesus Christ, the Son of God, exemplified the significance of prayer and fasting for a successful ministry when He went through it for forty days and nights in the wilderness, resulting in His victory over Satan. (Luke 4:1-12; Matthew 4: 1-11)

We often think of prayer as preparation for the battle, but Christ has shown us that it is the battle itself. Prayer together with fasting was the heart of His ministry. Where was it that Jesus' sweat was like great drops of blood? It was not in Pilate's hall, nor on His way to Golgotha. It was right there—in the center of Gethsemane, where He cried to His Father in prayer as it is written in the Scriptures. There Jesus *"offered up prayers and supplications, with vehement cries and tears to God who was able to save Him from death"* (Hebrews 5:7).

When the test finally came, Jesus walked up to the cross at Calvary with courage, and *"there disarmed the principalities and powers and made a public example of them, triumphing over them by the cross"* (Colossians 2: 15). That victory was the result of much prayer and fasting.

Gordon Lindsay, in page one of his book, *Prayer and Fasting: The Master Key to the Impossible*, summed up the essence of Christ's prayer and fasting in the wilderness as follows:

> *As Adam and Eve's disobedience by eating the forbidden fruit was original cause of man's losing his God-given dominion in the Garden of Eden, so Christ's fasting forty days and nights in the wilderness, there overcoming the fiercest onslaughts of the enemy, made possible the restoration of man's dominion.*

It is indeed, my ardent, constant prayer that the religious and political leaders of Africa in general, as well as those of Ghana, in particular, will do their best to follow the good examples of Jesus and the holy men and women of God. We have to team up together to fast and pray, in order to experience the power of God that will usher in spiritual, political, as well as economic freedom, which God has promised to those who obey Him (Deuteronomy 28: 1-14).

Hence, King David prayed thus, "*You are the God who performs miracles; you display your power among the peoples. With your mighty arm you redeemed your people" (*Psalms 77:14). Following the good example of the Lord, the early church took prayer and fasting very seriously. Hence, the elders of the church at Antioch prayed and fasted before commissioning Paul and Barnabas for the missionary work in the Gentile world (Acts 13: 1-3).

How did Paul and Barnabas fare in their missionary work; was it a failure or success? Under the guidance and anointing power of the Holy Spirit, they definitely carried out a successful mission to the glory of God. Though they encountered problems and opposition from Jews and non-Jews, they were able to overcome every obstacle by the supernatural power of the Holy Spirit at work in them. What happened in Cyprus is a typical example of the prevailing power of God in their mission as Luke reports:

> *They traveled through the whole island until they reached Paphos. There they met a Jewish sorcerer*

> *and false prophet named Bar-Jesus, who was an attendant of the proconsul, Sergius Paulus. The proconsul, an intelligent man, sent for Barnabas and Saul because he wanted to hear the word of God. But Elymas, the sorcerer, opposed them and tried to turn the proconsul from the faith* (Acts 13:6-8).

Luke added the following :

> *Then Saul, who was also called Paul, filled with the Holy Spirit, looked straight at Elymas and said, "You are a child of the devil and enemy of everything that is right! You are full of all kinds of deceit and trickery. Will you ever stop perverting the right ways of the Lord? Now the hand of the Lord is against you. You are going to be blind, and for a time you will be unable to see the light of the sun. Immediately, mist and darkness came over him, and he groped about, seeking someone to lead him by the hand. When the proconsul saw what had happened, he believed, for he was amazed at the teaching about the Lord* (Acts 13: 9 - 12).

It is important for us to remember that Paul and his companion, Barnabas, had been fasting and praying before they set off for their missionary work. Being filled with the Holy Spirit, they were able to overcome the devil, who opposed them through Elymas, the sorcerer. For, as Jesus has warned us: *"This kind can come forth by nothing, except by prayer and fasting"* (Mark 9:29—KJV).

Prayer and Fasting by the Household/Local Church

Besides individual efforts at prayer and fasting, a whole household led by a parent may engage in it for a worthy cause. Or it could be undertaken by the entire members of a church under the leadership of the Pastor. In either case, there should be a particular purpose, which shall be a blessing to the participants, and a glory to God. For instance, if a member of the family or church is in a serious condition of illness, the entire group may enter into prayer and fasting on behalf of the sick person. Intercessory prayers are necessary for victory over the enemy as noted in the previous passages: Here, James encourages believers to pray in times of trouble or sickness:

> *Is any one of you in trouble? He should pray. Is any one happy? Let him sing songs of praise. Is any one of you sick? Let him call the elders of the church to pray over him and anoint him with oil in the name of the Lord. And the prayer offered in faith will raise him up. If he has sinned, he will be forgiven. Therefore confess your sins to each other and pray for each other so that you may be healed. The prayer of a righteous man is powerful and effective.* (James 5:13-16)

Members of Calvary Redeeming Methodist Church, for instance, occasionally engage in a week of prayer and fasting as a necessary prelude for the annual revival, as well as other times such as the Passion Week preceding Easter Sunday or Church Anniversary, as the occasion may demand. Recently, we set aside a week to pray and fast in preparation for our outreach program ear-marked for the year, 2003. Sincere prayer and fasting, as we saw in the examples of our Lord and the apostles, yields much power for a successful ministry. Besides church programs, I personally engage in prayer and fasting when I have a preaching appointment or coun-seling and deliverance session with someone with demonic oppres-sion. For example, I asked a female member of the church to join me in prayer and fasting for three days before facing the task of exorcising a demon from her seven-year-old step-son. When I went into prayer together with the mother, by the grace of God, the young boy was set free in the mighty name of Jesus Christ.

If a member of the family or congregation has a medical or physical condition, which makes it unhealthy or impossible for him/her to do fasting, the one concerned should not be discouraged from praying, for the Bible entreats Christians to "*pray without ceasing*" (1 Thessalonians. 5: 17).

That is the duty of all true believers.

I want to encourage you seriously to start today, praying and fasting earnestly to God in the name of His Son, Jesus Christ. Remember to confess your sin first, and then forgive anyone who might have offended you. Then ask the Lord to forgive and cleanse you from every hidden/secret sin known to Him, because before Him, no secret can be hidden. If you do this with a sincere heart, I guarantee you will, sooner or later, reap fruitful results of blessings for yourself and your entire family.

Fasting acceptable to God

Though there is no gainsaying the fact that prayer and fasting can achieve great results, it must not be taken as a magic wand that automatically performs wonders at any time for one's own self-glorification. God frowns upon such prayers, even if we fast for many days. A situation very relevant to our discussion here occurred in the days of the prophet Isaiah, through whom God's Word came to the Jews in the land of Judah. They were highly religious Jews, who had fasted and prayed constantly to God, yet their prayers seemed to have fallen on deaf ears. Listen to how God describes their fasting, their complaint and God's final answer in the following passage:

> *For day after day they seek Me out; they seem eager to know My ways, as if they were a nation that does what is right and has not forsaken the commands of its God. They ask Me for just decisions . . .. Why have we fasted, they say, and you have not seen it? Why have we humbled ourselves, and you have not noticed? Yet on the day of your fasting, you do as you please and exploit all your workers. Your fasting ends in quarreling and strife, and in striking each other with wicked fists. You cannot fast as you do today and expect your voice to be heard on high. Is this the kind of fasting I have chosen.? . . . Is not this the kind of fasting I have chosen: To lose the chains*

> *of injustice and untie the cords of the yoke, to set the oppressed free and break every yoke? Is not to share your food with the young and to provide the poor wanderer with shelter—where you see the naked, to clothe him, and not to turn away from your own blood? Then you will call, and the Lord will answer; You will cry for help, and He will say: Here am I* (Isaiah 58: 2-5, 6-7, 9).

This passage teaches us the biblical principle that "*God is holy, and we must be holy*" (1 Peter 1:16).

For that reason, we cannot live in disobedience to God's Word and expect Him to have any regard to our fasting and prayers. For instance, praying and fasting for answers to particular problems, while cheating your spouse or an employee in business circles is an abomination before God. As a people of God, perhaps, we need to be reminded that God is a God of truth, and that nothing is hidden before Him. Thus, we all as human beings ("made in God's image") stand naked before His-all-seeing eyes, because God is omnipresent, as well as omniscient as declared in the Scriptures (Psalms. 139: 1-5, 7-12; Proverbs 15:3).

It is only as we deal truthfully and honestly with one another, and worship God in Spirit and truth, shall we have access to His throne through Jesus Christ, our Lord. Then, our prayers will be answered accordingly. Let us do a little self-examination as we ponder over these soul-searching questions:

- *i. Where do we stand in our relationship with God?*
- *ii. How is our relationship with our household, and friends? If we are truly reconciled with God, and our neighbours, our prayers will not be hindered (Psalms 66:18; Matthew 5:23).*

I must, however, sound another caution here that prayer is not necessarily a means by which believers persuade God to grant us our requests, but rather a way to receive His grace to fulfill His will in our lives. Vernon Grounds put it this way: "Prayer isn't the way to get God to do what we want. It's an expression of our trust in His power, wisdom, and grace. No matter what we ask God to do for us, we are to have the attitude of Jesus, who said, *'Nevertheless, not as I will, but as You will'"* (Matthew 26:39). The key to answers to prayers is found in the words of Jesus to His disciples in John 15:7, *"If you remain in me and my words remain in you, ask whatever you wish, and it will be given you."* In other words, if we keep His Words, His Spirit in us will guide us to pray aright, and our prayers shall be answered. It does assure all believers that God answers prayers. Paul puts it this way, *"He who did not spare His own Son, but gave Him up for us all–how will He not also, along with Him, graciously give us all things?"* (Romans 8:32).

Therefore, we need always to remember that God, our Father in heaven loves us so much that He will not deny His children anything that is best for our lives, because after all, we are His, and He is ours, and so whether we live or die, we belong to Him (Romans 14:8).

That thought should definitely cause us to depend on God through Jesus Christ, our Savior, and not on ancestors or gods, spirits or angels. For "*Without me*," Jesus says, "*you can do nothing*." Now, let us turn to the following section for the subject of Hindrances to Prayer.

Hindrances to prayer (with or without Fasting)

Now, having spent much time talking about prayer and fasting, it is important at this juncture to look at ways in which our prayers could be hindered. One of the essential elements of prayer is the spiritual condition in which we find ourselves in the presence of God, because that can be a stumbling block to our prayers, regardless of our fasting. The Psalmist wrote, "*If I had cherished sin in my heart, the Lord would not have listened; but God has surely listened and heard my voice in prayer. Praise be to God, who has not rejected my prayer or withheld His love from me!"* (Psalms 66:18-20).

Since I have already dealt with the subject, SIN, I do not intend to write any further about it at this point. However, I must add that it is always necessary to examine ourselves in the light of the Scriptures and to be sensitive to the voice of the Holy Spirit. This will help us to make sure that we "have clean hands and a pure heart"(Psalms 24:4).

The following are common hindrances, which should be noted, and confessed, if any, before embarking on the holy path of prayer and fasting:

- *Bitterness of heart (1 Peter 3:7, Matthew 5: 23)*
- *Unforgiving spirit (Mark 11:25)*
- *Unconfessed sin (1 John 1:8)*
- *Doubt (James 1:6-7)*
- *Inconsistency (Luke 18:1-8)*
- *Lack of determination (Luke 18:1-8)*

King David's classic prayer of confession after his sin against Bathsheba and murder of her husband, Uriah, recorded in Psalm 51, may serve as a good example of a truly penitent heart. In his confession, David acknowledged his sin, and prayed to forsake it completely. He prayed to be totally cleansed from it. He justified God for judging him on account of his sin, and pleaded for renewal. He trusted in God's everlasting love, and asked for restoration, so that he might once, again, rejoice in God's salvation. David promises to tell others about God's righteousness, and teach sinners about the ways of God. Finally, David declares his willingness to *"offer a sacrifice of thanksgiving and a whole burnt-offering"* acceptable to God.

Commenting on this passage, Rev. Dr. John MacCarthur, pointed out that any true prayer of confession before the Lord must follow David's classic example. The next chapter will discuss how to offer prayer as a substitute for libation.

CHAPTER TWENTY-SIX

PRAYER AS SUBSTITUTE FOR LIBATION

Having studied how to pray and fast, we are now in a better position to replace the usual libation with a ritual acceptable in the sight of God. We are to pray to the Living God, our Creator, and Father in heaven, "*who richly provides us with everything for our enjoyment*" (1 Timothy 6: 17), in the name of Jesus Christ, and by the power of the Holy Spirit. One may ask: "How must we do this? The following is a suggested pattern:

Drumming, Singing and Dancing

As usual with every Ghanaian festival, the function may be preceded with drumming, singing and dancing. The initial part may be drumming alone, calling attention to the great day, and inviting all and sundry to come down to the festival through the beating of the drum: *"This is the day the Lord has made, let us rejoice and be glad in it"* (Psalm 118: 24).

This may be followed with Akan lyrics, which lift the name of God, offering Him praises, honour and adoration for His greatness and majesty. We must thank the Almighty God for His love and care in providing us with food, shelter, health and family and community, as well as every other need. This first part may take about an hour, after which the rest of the program may continue as follows:

- An ordained Minister or an Elder of any recognized denomination in the community or city may be invited by the Paramount chief/King to offer prayers to God in the name of Jesus, on behalf of the chief, clan or the people.
- In his prayer, he must mention the names of the founding fathers and ancestors of the community, thanking God for their great and virtuous lives, and achievements worthy of emulation by posterity.
- He must also give thanks to God, for their families and the gift of children they brought forth; for "*children are an heritage of the Lord, the fruit of the womb is His reward*" (Psalms 127:3).
- Pray for God's forgiveness for sins of commission and omission. And ask for the cleansing power of the blood of the Lamb of God to purify the people and make every one spotlessly pure in the presence of God.
- Pray for protection, brotherly love, and wisdom for sound judgment, good governance, and prosperity for the chief and his elders, and for all families and people of the land (both at home and abroad), including strangers among you, that all may dwell in safety and in the fear of God.
- Finally, commit the future of the community and the nation to the Lord, thanking Him for all that is past, and trusting Him for all that is to come.
- The King/Paramount Chief takes his oath of allegiance and addresses the audience.
- Conclusion: The function may come to an end with final drumming and dancing. This is the time for Nana (the King/Chief) and the Queen to have the honour of taking the floor, dancing to the applause of the audience. The elders could join them on the floor.
- After "Nananom" (the Chief and his elders) have retired from the floor, the rest may continue till the end of the function.

- Dismissal with Prayer: Since the function was started with prayer, it must also end with prayer, thanking God for a successful festival, and committing the days ahead to His fatherly care.

Then, the people disperse to their various homes, pondering over some of the issues the Chief raised in his address. Since the Chief, his elders, and the entire community have been entrusted to God in prayer, all must put their faith to work by living in accordance with God's Word, trusting that '*the Lord is with you always to the end of the world*' (Matthew 28:20). As Pastors, kings, elders, and all people in authority, begin to seek the face of God to do His will, God will surely begin to fulfill for us His rich promises, declared in the following passage:

> *If you fully obey the Lord your God, and carefully follow all His commands I give you today, the Lord your God will set you high above all the nations on earth. You will be blessed in the city and blessed in the country. The fruit of your womb will be blessed, and the crops and the young of your livestock—the calves of your herds and the lambs of your flocks. Your basket and your kneading trough will be blessed. You will be blessed when you come in and blessed when you go out.* (Deuteronomy 28:1, 3-6).

Just as we humans will not entrust our treasure to our disobedient and careless son, so God, who is holy and righteous, will "*not give dogs what is sacred or throw His pearls to pigs*" (Matthew 7: 6). On the other hand, we are quite willing as parents to entrust our precious goods to our sons and daughters when we know they are mature and trustworthy.

The story of the Canaanite woman in Matthew's Gospel brings home the point I am trying to make at this stage. It is recorded in Matthew's Gospel that Jesus withdrew to the region belonging to Tyre and Sidon, apparently to get away from a busy schedule for a little rest.

Then a Canaanite woman approached Jesus, "*crying out, 'Lord, Son of David, have mercy on me! My daughter is suffering terribly from demon possession*' (Matthew 15:22). Though Jesus did not answer her immediately, the woman kept on crying after Him.

Finally Jesus said to her, "I was sent only to the lost sheep of Israel". The woman came and knelt before him pleading, "Lord, help me!" Then Jesus made a statement, which was to test the faith of this woman:

> *"It is not right to take the children's bread and toss it to their dogs." "Yes, Lord," says the woman, "but even the dogs eat the crumbs that fall from their masters' table." Then Jesus answered, "Woman, you have great faith! Your request is granted." And her daughter was healed at that very hour* (Matthew 15:22-28).

This story of Jesus' encounter with the woman of Canaan illustrates the inclusive nature of Christ's ministry. It expands beyond racial and cultural boundaries with grace and compassion, meeting the needs of all, who are truly seeking the Lord. *"Whoever comes to me"*, says Jesus, *"I will never drive away"* (John 6:37). For He has also said, *"Ask and it will be given to you; seek and you will find; knock and the door will be opened to you"* (Matthew 7:7).

Therefore, with these promises from the Lord, we must look to the future with high hopes, trusting in the providential care of God, whose "*goodness and mercy*" endure forever. Hence, I am quite optimistic about the future, that God has something better for the world, particularly, Africa, if we set our hearts to do His will through the power of His Holy Spirit, which He gives freely to all who believe in Him. Let us now turn to the next chapter for detailed discussion on this crucial subject.

CHAPTER TWENTY-SEVEN

AFRICANS SHALL RISE AND SHINE

The concluding chapter of this book focuses on the not-too-far-distant glorious future of Africa. In the book of Isaiah chapter 60: 1-3, it is written:

> *Arise, shine, for your light has come, and the glory of the Lord rises upon you. See, darkness covers the earth and thick darkness is over the peoples, but the Lord rises upon you and His glory appears over you. Nations will come to your light, and Kings to the brightness of your dawn.*

This prophecy of Isaiah originally pointed to the coming of Christ—the Messianic age of the nation of Israel. It points forward to the period of the Lord Jesus Christ, who will establish the New Covenant through His ministry, death, resurrection, ascension, and the pouring of the Holy Spirit "upon all flesh" (that is, all believers in Christ—Jews and Gentiles, Black and White, Asian and Brown, and all alike).

In applying the same message to ourselves in our present situation, I am fully convinced that the Lord has already showered what Ezekiel calls "showers of blessing" (Ezekiel 34: 26) upon Africa, in order that we might turn from every act of darkness to His marvelous light, and put on the new life of righteousness through faith in Jesus Christ. Surely, this is not our own doing, but "*the Lord's doing, and it is marvelous in our eyes*" (Psalms 118:23).

Yes! I believe strongly that the Lord expects us to be revitalized by the power of the Holy Spirit and to occupy our rightful place in every sphere of human endeavor, namely, political arena, science and technology, education, commerce and industry. Gone were the days when we allowed ourselves and the land to be exploited. In the words of the great apostle, Paul, we are exhorted: *"Wake up, O sleeper, rise from the dead, and Christ will shine on you"* (Ephesians 5:14).

This passage reminds me of a wonderful Art work calved out of bronze by an experienced sculptor, depicting the map of Africa, with an African male rising up from his slumber. It points to the future with hope for a better life for Africa. I have the conviction that it does further refer to all peoples of African descent, who, for one reason or the other, have migrated from their native countries and homes in pursuit of fortune in other parts of the world.

The vision is a reminder of a similar message Jeremiah received from Jehovah concerning the Jews enslaved in Babylon. God revealed to His servant that his fellow Jews would return to Jerusalem to rebuild their nation after seventy years of bondage. Here is part of the encouraging message Jeremiah sent to the Jews in Babylon:

> *This is what the Lord Almighty, the God of Israel, says to all those I carried into exile from Jerusalem to Babylon. "Build houses and settle down; plant gardens and eat what they produce. Marry and have sons and daughters; Find wives for your sons and give your daughters in marriage . . .. Also, seek the peace and prosperity of the city to which I have carried you into exile. Pray to the Lord for it, because if it prospers, you too will prosper. This is what the Lords says: "When seventy years are completed for Babylon, I will come to you and fulfill*

> *my gracious promise to bring you back to this place. For I know the plans I have for you, declares the Lord. Plans to prosper you and not to harm you, plans to give you hope and a future* (Jeremiah 29: 4-7, 10-11).

By this vision, the Lord graciously assured me that just as the Jews, led by Nehemiah and Ezra, returned home to rebuild their country, Israel, so shall people from Africa return for the reconstruction of their native lands, parts of which had lane unproductive for years. One may ask a legitimate question: "When and how is God going to cause Africans to rise and shine? This is a two-fold question:

i. "When will this happen?"

My answer is that God's light has already begun to shine upon the Continent of Africa; and a good number of Africans have responded to God's call, and are fulfilling their divinely-appointed roles in various ways or ministries throughout the world. Let us begin with a few examples from the Bible. From the records of the Holy Scriptures, Africans have been used in accordance with God's plan of Salvation for humankind from the beginning. When God called Abraham, he left his country and came to Bethel and pitched his tent, with Bethel on the West. There, we are told, " *he built an altar to the Lord and called on the name of the Lord*" (Genesis 12:8). But it is recorded that as he continued his journey toward south, he encountered severe famine. Guess where God directed him to go for sustenance—it was Egypt in North Africa. Here in Egypt, Abraham and his nephew, Lot became so wealthy in terms of oxen, sheep, silver and gold that when they returned to Bethel, "*the land could not support them while they stayed together*" (Genesis 13:6). Consequently, they had to part company, and Lot chose to settle in the Jordan toward the east, close to the land of Sodom and Gomorrah while Abraham lived in the land of Canaan (Genesis 13:11-12).

Several years later, when a similar serious famine hit Jacob and his family, they took refuge in Egypt, where his son Joseph, by divine providence, had been prepared to supply them all their needs in abundance. It was in Egypt in Africa that Jacob and his household of 70 people grew into the nation of Israel. This is how Mosy Madugba of Nigeria puts it:

> *It is right to say that Africa played a significant role in the formation of Israel in the sense that the Israel that you see today was incubated in Africa. This shows that God has a covenant of preservation, a covenant of supply with that continent . . .. Africans have always been used by divine election to run the last leg of the relay race in God's plan. When you come to the New Testament and consider the life of Jesus, as soon as He was born, the enemy came after Him. Satan wanted to snuff life out of Him, and God said to the earthly father, "take Him away. I have a place where I keep and nurture my people, take him to Africa". Thus Jesus was taken to Africa. (Mosy U. Madugba, Africa's Time of Recovery, p. 43-45).*

It is interesting to see how God, in His sovereign will, uses various people from generation to generation to fulfill His divine purpose. Thus, beginning from Abraham, the father of our faith, right up to Jesus Christ—the Promised Messiah, Africa had been a safe haven for "all the agents of redemption whom God used" (Ibid.).

Right now there are several African scholars being used to fulfill God's plan for freedom, peace, and justice in the world. A good example to cite here is His Excellency, Honorable Kofi Annan, the Ghanaian who is the Secretary General of the United Nations. He has been serving as efficiently as any of his predecessors in such an honourable position. Then also, we have Professor Albert Wright, who is the Co-Coordinator of the Task Force on Water and Sanitation for the United Nations Millenium Development Project established by Kofi Annan. He is also the Chairman of the Africa Water Task Force, a member of the Technical Committee of the Global Water Partnership, and consultant in several developing countries on urban sanitation policies. The importance of his work to Africa's development cannot be over emphasized.

Another Christian brother worthy of mention here is Dr. George Bonney, who is resident in Rockville, Maryland. He is professor in Statistics and Genetics at the National Human Genom Center of the College of Medicine at the Howard University in Washington, D.C. Dr. Bonney, is a Conference Speaker, and is widely used in the service of the community by teaming up with medical specialists to advise people on how to avoid certain hereditary or infectious diseases, such as Hiv/Aids, High Blood Pressure, etc. Those who need treatment, but have no Medical Insurance, receive necessary guidance in securing manageable Insurance that will meet their needs.

It will excite you further to know what God is doing for Ghana through Mr. Horace Dei, who feels commissioned by the Lord to undertake development projects, captioned *"Science Saves Lives"* at Akwapem Mampong in the Eastern section of Ghana. Mr. Dei and his team of generous, devoted Christians, have the vision to feed the young people of the land with both academic and biblical knowledge. They have learned from the Scriptures that academic ahievement and material prosperity without spiritual insight or divine wisdom, that is, without God, leads to pride, and pride leads to destruction (Proverbs 11: 2a; 16: 18). Hence, the team has established a computer Science school, Hershey Carpentry Center, cafetaria, Home Science Center, as well as Science Resource Center, where Bible knowledge is basic education. They also believe that if people are poor and hungry, they find it difficult, if not impossible, to heed the gospel. Therefore, they aim at giving what they call *"soft loans"* to those who want to start farming or any type of business to make them self-supporting. Mr. Dei, who is a stounch member of the Emory United Methodist Church in Washington, D. C. , solicites financial donations from generous individuals, and private companies, such as Hershey, for the funding of this wonderful project. He hopes to extend it to the other regions in due course.

Among Ghanaian pastors being used in several ways in the development of Ghana are Revds. Kwabena and Christiana Darko, a married couple, and co-pastures of *"Oasis of Love Ministries"* at Ahodwo, a suburb of Kumasi in the Ashanti Region of Ghana. Besides their vibrant church, which is teeming with members, they have also established a beautiful school from kindergartin to Junior Secondary School (JSS) to cater for the youth in the rural areas. His school helps to reduce the influx of students from the hinterland seeking admission to schools in the cities. In addition to his pastoral and other responsibilities, Rev. Darko makes time for his thriving paultry business, which has become so successful that entreprenuers from across Africa come to consult him about the techniques of success in business. Again, Rev. Darko is one of the National Executives of the Full Gospel Men's Fellowship, Ghana Chapter, and among a selected- few religious leaders, who advise President Kufuor on religeous policies. Whenever needed, he accompanies the President on his international tours.

My friends, it is good news to know, as evidenced in the previous passages, that the Omnipresent God, in His misterious way, is using His people not only from within, but also outside Ghana/Africa to fulfill His divine purpose for Ghana, in particular, and African, in general, and the world at large. At this juncture, I want to add to the list of God's kingdom-builders another servant of God, in the person of Rev. Seth Asare, Senior Pastor of the Newton United Methodist Church in Boston, Massachusetts, U. S. A. Every year, he leads a Mission Team to undertake various development projects in much needed areas of the country. Last year's Mission Team, which included Pastor Ruth, Dick, Julie Merriam, Dr. John Ogren, Donna Fish and others, was warmly welcomed at the Kotoka International Airport, Accra by Rt. Rev. Kow Egyir, then Bishop of the Sekondi Diocese of the Methodist Church, Ghana. Viable projects carried out by the team were Evangelistic activities in Churches, including a Vacation Bible School, completion of a chapel at Azani Village near Busua, located a few miles from the Atlantic Coast, and the completion of a School-wing to the Chapel, began by Mission 2002.

The following is part of their Church Mission Report:

> *Dr. John treated many hundreds of patients over one day period! Each patient got a free examination*

and was then given a prescription for medicine or else diagnosis to see a specialist. Money for the purchase of medicine was provided by the team ahead of time. Many had eye problems, including one boy with a large tumor.

The team has received a land from the Chief of Azani to start a palm oil processing plant in Azani. As a sign of their commitment to the project, the Bishop held a ground-breaking ceremony at the site.

In March, 2004, Rev. Dr. Asare teamed up with the Most Rev. Dr. Robert Aboagye-Mensah, Presiding Bishop of the Methodist Conference, Ghana, for a massive Evangelistic Campaign that won hundreds of souls for Christ.

The last, but not the least to be mentioned here among the great helping hands towards Ghana's betterment is Thomas Oduro Kwarteng who is busily engaged in a multi-medical industry, fitted with all kinds of computerized machinery for development projects in Ghana.

With these few examples as instruments, which God has prepared for His use in Ghana, Africa, and other places, let us move on to the second part of the question.

ii. "How is God going to do this?"

In answering this question, I am reminded of what Jehovah did for Israel as we read from the Holy Scriptures. For instance, before God sent Moses to Egypt to deliver the Jews from bondage, He had prepared Moses for forty years in the wilderness (Exodus 3-4); before calling Moses to rest from his office as a leader of God's people, God had prepared young Joshua to take up the role of leadership from his master Moses (Joshua 1: 1-9); before they reached the border of Jericho, God had sent ahead His captain to direct Joshua as to what to do to capture the city of Jericho (Joshua 5: 13-6: 20); and before the spies set foot in the city, God had already prepared a harlot by name Rahab, who received the spies into her home (Joshua 2: 1-24), feeding them with all the information they needed for the overthrow of Jericho.

Truly, fellow believers, as we have seen in the Bible, God does not work in a vaccum. Though God is all-powerful, and *"with God all things are possible*", yet in His divine wisdom and economy, He desires often to use human beings, regardless of rank, gender, or weakness, to achieve His purpose in this world. This simply proves that God does not send out anyone to do anything in His name, without His grace and power to fulfill the same for His glory and the blessing of the people concerned. What God requires each of us to do is to *"trust Him with all your heart and lean not on your own understanding; in all your ways acknowledge Him, and He will make your paths straight*" (Proverbs 3: 5-6). For it is when we have nothing, but God alone to lean on that He is willing to prove Himself mighty on our behalf and to work His miracles in our lives. Then, the world will know assuredly that we serve a mighty, living God, whose *"eyes range throughout the earth to strengthen those whose hearts are fully committed to Him*" (2 Chronicles 16: 9).

Read further the following powerful statement made by Bishop T.D. Jakes that had since strengthened my faith in the Lord, and boosted my confidence in what the Lord can do with a believer. He said: *"Never be intimidated by your dreams. It does not need to look like it will come true in order for it to come true. Because we believe, worship and pray to God Almighty, who'is able to do exceeding abundantly above all that we can ask or think, according to His power that is at work in us*' (Ephesians 3:20), *through His Son, Jesus Christ, our Lord.*" Bishop Jakes, one of the dynamic African American preachers of our time, was speaking to a large audience at a telecast Church service on one occasion in January 2003. Bishop T.D. Jakes further stated, among other things (paraphrased as follows):

> *The gold, the diamond, the bauxite, the manganese and timber are not in the United States or Europe or Asia, but in Africa. Yet many African countries live in poverty due to corruption, which has eaten into the very fabric of the continent. Nevertheless, if Africans would turn their hearts toward God, God*

> *would bring about a changed life, which would lead to righteousness, peace and prosperity, according to God's power that is at work within them.*

This is, indeed, a confirmation of my faith in what Jehovah God can do with a people who put their trust in Him. It gladdens my heart and propels me to go on in the line of ministry the Lord has graciously entrusted to me by the inspiration of His Holy Spirit in the name of Jesus Christ, our Lord. I strongly believe that God is at work in various individuals, fulfilling His purpose in diverse ways throughout the world.

In his book, *Africa's Time of Recovery* (pp. 41-42), Rev. Mosy U. Madugba has this to say about Africa:

> *The African continent has the largest reserve of mineral resources. It is the richest continent in the whole world, and God intentionally made it so for a purpose, so that at the appropriate time, Africa can help to preserve the world in times of need. If it is physically the richest continent in the world, the physical is a reflection of the manifestation of the spiritual. That means it also has the potential to be the continent with the richest spiritual content in the world.*

It is interesting to read how with profound spiritual insight, Madugba reminds his readers of the famine in the days of Abraham and how "he was led by divine providence to go nowhere else but Africa," where *"he was blessed with wealth in the form of oxen, sheep, servants, both male and female, all manner of treasure in gold and silver"(*Ibid). Thus, according to Madugba, *"God had made a preparation for Africa to be His treasure house,"* in order that out of this treasure, God might provide or fulfill both the physical and spiritual needs of the people of the world. This may sound like a fairy tale to the skeptics, yet it is true. "For With God all things are possible" (Mark 10: 27).

iii. Africa as a Place of Refuge For God's People

Critical study of the Bible from Genesis to the New Testament will show how God, by His divine providence and wisdom, has made Africa to be safe haven for His chosen people. Again, Madugba writes:

> *It was in Africa that all agents of redemption whom God used were preserved from Abraham right up to Jesus Christ. As a newborn infant He was preserved from untimely death in Africa. Abraham was preserved physically on earth in Africa from untimely death through famine. Jacob too was preserved there; and Jesus Himself was preserved in Africa. It is evident by these that God has a covenant and of course a partnership with Africa. God does not forget covenants. Oh! He is a great covenant keeper and He has chosen in this season to remember Africa (P. 46).*

I am very much encouraged by what both Bishop Jakes and Madugba have said about Africa, because I share similar vision and hope for my fellow Africans. Moreover, part of Bishop Jakes' message that lifts my aspirations higher than I can ever describe here was what he said about Joseph, the dreamer, who was hated by his senior siblings. Though his jealous brothers sold him into slavery and was later imprisoned, yet by divine intervention, Joseph was released from prison to become the Prime Minister, next in authority to Pharaoh, King of Egypt. By implication, the same God, who lifted up Joseph from prison to the position of Prime Minister in a foreign land, to deliver the Egyptians and his father's house from famine and death, will likewise deliver His precious sons and daughters of Africa from Satanic powers and the evil life of selfishness, corruption, and poverty in the land.

My question is: "Is anything too hard for God?" No! "*With God, nothing is impossible*" (Jeremiah 32:27; Luke 18:27). As God inspired Nehemiah and Ezra to motivate their fellow Jews to rise up for spiritual renewal and the reconstruction of the walls and the city of Jerusalem, so will the Almighty God, "*. . . the King eternal, immortal, invisible, the only wise God*" (1 Timothy 1:17), raise converted, committed, and anointed leaders of Africa (some of whom may still be living abroad; they will come home in God's time with divine zeal) to rally their people together for spiritual, political, economic, and social reformation in the entire continent of Africa. I believe this will begin with Ghana, where the light is already shining bright to lead the way.

At that time and age, Africa shall have Spirit-filled men and women of all walks of life—attorneys, academicians, teachers, university/college graduates, and middle-class workers. It will include God-fearing, traditional kings and political leaders, who are strong in the Lord, who will seek to live and govern by the BOOK (the Holy Bible). They will spread forth the fruit of the Spirit through word and deed wherever they may be in order to maintain love, peace, justice and unity in the land.

According to the records of Missionary Agency run by Madugba and his colleagues in Nigeria, the greatest number of missionaries on the surface of the earth is in Africa, seriously engaged in the spread of the Gospel. This truth is reaffirmed by another African writer, Jean-Marc Ela from the Cameroon, as follows:

> *Nowadays, when the majority of Christians are no longer in the West but in the Third World, is it time for us Africans to reclaim the gospel, and bring our disinherited peoples face to face with it? For in the words of Paul V1, we face critical situations where "bold transformations"* and "urgent reforms should be undertaken without delay" (Ela, Jean-Marc, My Faith as an African, p. 115).

Yes, indeed, Pastors, as well as committed lay-leaders must not only be more prayerful, but also move out beyond their local congregations and take the Bible to homes and villages and by-ways so that all and sundry in Africa and beyond might hear the Good News. For "*bold transformations*" and "*urgent reforms should be undertaken without delay,*" says Pope Paul VI.

Jean-Marc Ela made further observation on the shift of the center of Christianity:

> *Christianity has endured for a long time, maintaining its Greco-Latin heritage within the context of a society fashioned by Western models. Today the Church must examine that entire experience, recognizing that it has lost its cultural monopoly as well as the theological systems that seemed to guarantee it. A new age is beginning that gives great importance to non-Western Churches, and Africa plays a decisive role in this migration of the Church to the Southern hemisphere. While the loss of China has been felt as a heavy blow to the history of missions, Paul VI did not hesitate to declare that Africa is "the new homeland of Christ* (Ibid. p. 116).

Thus, it is evident that my fellow believers like Ela, Madugba, and Pope VI, see eye-to-eye with me that with the present concentration of the gospel on Africa, God is surely preparing men and women of Africa to raise up an army of the Lord, set on fire for war against Satan and every form of false religion that seems to deceive the people from following the true Way of salvation in Jesus Christ. Ela concluded his observations as follows:

> *The center of gravity of Christianity continues to shift. It is possible that the black continent will become a real prize for the church. The one hundred and fifty million Christians in Africa today are significant resource on the religious map of the world and for the vitality of the Christian faith (Jean-Marc Ela, My Faith as an African*, p.115-6).

It follows, therefore, that God will call believers to be rulers and people in authority, who shall use the natural resources of the land, not for their own selfish ends, as some selfish politicians and kings had done in the past, but for the progress and betterment of the people as a whole. For, these new brand of leaders, know for certain that sooner or later, they will stand before the Judgment Seat of the Supreme Judge, Jesus Christ, *"the King of Kings, and Lord of Lords"* (1 Timothy 6:15), to render to Him the account of their stewardship.

The African Enterprise

It is encouraging to know that since 1961, "African Enterprise", an interdenominational ministry, made of seasoned evangelists and pastors, has been preaching the Gospel in the cities in partnership with local Churches. Under the directorship of Malcolm Graham (U.S.) and David Richardson (Canada), trained African evangelists are presently engaged in various Christian activities in ten cities in Africa.

I was greatly touched by the following report from Michael Cassidy of the "African Enterprise":

> *I want to encourage you as you pray about your response this month to our ministry, to seriously consider the incredible Training Programs undertaken by my colleagues around Africa. The measurement of their efforts undoubtedly comes in the feedback we receive from participants. For instance, Ms Margaret Shomolo, Director of Research in the Provincial Government, South Africa, said: "It has been one of the most enriching courses I have attended. I am going back home a new person with a much better understanding of myself, my strengths and weaknesses (Michael Cassidy, African Enterprise, August, 2003).*

Then Johannes Roseldome of the Salvation Army commented:

> *I have grown spiritually especially in the area of leadership and feel equipped and well prepared to go back and share with all those that are under my leadership and also train officers and others to be*

> *better leaders for the Kingdom* (Michael Cassidy, *African Enterprise*, August, 2003).

This is so encouraging and very much appreciated by those who attend and discover for themselves what leadership in Africa is all about.

Some of the topics tackled by our facilitators (trainers) are *'Calling and Preparation into Leadership', 'Dealing with temptation and failure in Leadership', and 'Abandoning Power—Grace and Humility in Leadership'*. These Training Programs are wonderful opportunities for African leaders to grow in integrity and ability. Michael concludes this report with a plea: *"Won't you stand with us in these worthy endeavours?"* Having read about the good work being done by Cassidy and his colleagues, all lovers of Christ must endeavour to contribute generously in money and kind to support such a worthy ministry in Africa by these dedicated people of God.

As the Lord has graciously revealed in this vision, the greatest problem facing Africa is not poverty, but misappropriation of the resources of the land by selfish individuals in high positions of authority. Why do they behave like this? Because they do not know Christ, and the devil has lured them into believing a lie that they can make it without God; just as he did to Adam and Eve (Genesis 3: 1-7). Therefore, the good work being done by various missionary agents sponsored by other denominations around the world, incuding religious bodies such as the World Methodist Council of Churches, All Africa Conference of Churches headed by Professor K. A. Dickson, past Presiding Bishop of the Methodist Church, Ghana, World Vision, Africa House of Prayer, the Scripture Union, African Enterprise, in collaboration with local Churches, cannot be overemphasized. There are still other missions and individual evangelists engaged in spreading the Good News for the total liberation of the continent of Africa, yet lack of space will not permit me to list all of them here. However, there is assurance that their work will never go unrewarded by the Master, who has called them into His ministry. Therefore, we must all contribute our quota by word and deed to make Africa completely free from the dominion of Satanic forces to serve the living God, and thus usher the entire continent and the rest of the world into the status of peace, righteousness, success and prosperity destined for humanity by the goodness and mercy of God through Jesus Christ.

Whatever our station in life as individuals, we need to order our lives daily in the fear and obedience of the Lord, looking to no other Master, but the Savior and Lord, "*Jesus Christ, the Author and Perfecter of our faith, who for the joy set before Him endured the cross, scorning its shame, and sat down at the right hand of the throne of God*" (Hebrews 12:2), "*and is also interceding for us*" (Romans 8: 34). Hence, King David speaks concerning the Lord: "*He leads me in the path of righteousness for His name's sake*" (Psalms 23:3).

At this juncture, one may ask the question: "Where in Africa is God's light moving in a special way to achieve the divine goal for Africa and the world at large? Rev. Madugba mentioned three countries, namely, South Africa, Nigeria, and Ghana, as unique places in Africa, where spiritual revival has begun, and the mighty work of God is manifested, effecting visible changes in religious, social, political, and economic life of the people. Let us now turn to the next chapter to discuss the case of Ghana in more detail.

CHAPTER TWENTY-EIGHT

GHANA – AS THE STAR OF AFRICA

In 1983, while serving as a pastor of the Bethel Methodist Church at Samreboi, in the interior of the Western Region of Ghana, I had a dream in which I saw a bright star coming down from heaven and settling on Ghana. Its brightness and beauty attracted many people, not only from Africa, but also from other parts of the world. Not long after that dream, I was visited by Mr. Feih, then National Director of the Boys Brigade of the Presbyterian Church of Ghana, who was on a trip to Enchie, near the border of Cote d' Ivoire in West Africa. In our conversation, I shared my dream with Brother Feih. To my surprise, he told me that he had had a similar dream a few weeks prior to embarking on his regional trip. We both rejoiced greatly, believing strongly that God was about to do something great in Ghana, and that He would pour His Spirit upon the nation in a special way, to bring about a great revival in the lives of believers. We believed further that through such a revival, God would draw into His kingdom many people from within and outside of the continent of Africa. Hallelujah!

The dream reminded us of the prophecy of Isaiah which he declared as follows:

The people walking in darkness have seen a great

> *light; on those living in the land of the shadow of death a light has dawned. You have enlarged the nation and increased their joy; they rejoice before you as people rejoice at the harvest, as men rejoice when dividing the plunder.....For to us a child is born, to us a son is given, and the government will be on his shoulders* (Isaiah 9:1-3, 6).

Brother Feih and I rejoiced greatly about this prophecy, believing that as God graciously brought His Son, Jesus Christ in the fulfillment of His Word for the salvation of *"the lost sheep of Israel,"* so will He do for Ghana and Africa as a whole. For we, indeed, stand in need of great deliverance, which can come from no one else, but God alone. Here, I see the relevance of a profound, prophetic statement of hope for Africa uttered in a sermon by the then Presiding Bishop of the Batimore-Washington Conference of the United Methodist Church, Bishop Felton May, as follows: *"GOD HAS A **NEW AFRICA**."* We have realized that the first letters of this statement stand for GHANA: **G=GOD, H=HAS, A=A, N=NEW, A=AFRICA.** Thus, GHANA becomes the acronym for ***"GOD HAS A NEW AFRICA,"*** and that simulteneously symbolizes a new name for Ghana by virtue of the fire of revival that God has begun in the nation, which is to impact the rest of Africa in particular, and the world in general. This is GHANA'S NEW NAME: *"GOD HAS A NEW AFRICA*." This gracious work of God should not be a surprise to people, because God had done it before in Israel. God gave Israel a new name after delivering them from exile in Babylon to reflect the new life of righteousness He had purposed to begin in the reminant of Israel through the new covenant relationship (Isaiah 62: 2-4). That was messianic prohecy pointing forward to what Christ would do in the Church. What a profound insight from the lips of Bishop Felton May! In his sermon, the Bishop was referring to the mighty work of God being done in Africa, which is now the focal point of evangelization, and where many souls are turning today to the saving faith in Jesus Christ, our Lord. Praise the Lord ! Hallelujah!!!

Therefore, empowered by the mighty working of the Holy

Spirit, Ghana, (by the grace of God), shall become Africa's Bethleham, which shall champion the great fire of revival in Africa, delivering multititudes of people out of the power of darkness into the marvelous light of the kingdom of God through faith in Jesus Christ. Perhaps, you may ask, *"How can you be certain about this?"* Because God has said so, and *"He who promised is faithful and He will do it*" (1 Thessalonians 5: 24). I am hopeful about this, because of the previous prohecies which the Lord had graciously fulfilled in the lives of His people, and in my ministry since 1968. Thus, we can pluck our faith in God and, like Jeremiah, proclaim: *"For His compassions never fail. They are new every morning. Great is your faithfulness*" towards all who trust in you for salvation (Lamentations 3: 22-3).

Examples of Fulfilled Prophecies

From 1978 through 81, three American evangelists, who were invited as key-speakers to the Pastors' Conference in Kumasi Technical Institute, organized annually by Ghana Evangelism Committee, had predicted that there would be religious revival in Ghana within the following five years. Rev. John Bassaw and I were among the many pastors and lay preachers, including evangelists, who attended these annual Conferences, for the edification of our ministries. We took those prophetic messages very seriously, desiring to be part of such a religious awakening in the country.

Today, as I speak, that prediction has come true. My three visits to Ghana in 1992, 1999 and recently in 2002, have given me the privilege to see the mighty work being done by the Lord through anointed Ministers of the Gospel, Evangelists, Prophets, and Lay/Local Preachers. The fact that a number of places, previously used as movie theaters/cinema halls, have now been turned into places of worship is a clear evidence of the many converts the Lord is drawing into the Church. The reverse is taking place in England, where some church buildings have been converted to play-houses, and restaurants. In Ghana there is a change in the life-style of the people, turning from darkness to light, and from the things of this world to the things of God; and from the temporal to eternal issues of life. *We can say with David, "The Lord's right hand is lifted high;*

the Lord's right hand has done mighty things" (Psalm 118: 16).

For instance, the Odeon cinema hall in Ashanti Newtown, a popular suburb of Kumasi, which was usually full of movie-lovers, especially on weekends, is now a temple of God, where believers meet together to hear the Gospel and worship the Living God. I am speaking from a personal experience here, because this was the place, where my senior brothers and I used to watch movies during weekends, before we became converted. You can imagine my surprise when I saw for the first time this most popular movie theater in Kumasi turned into a place of worship. Can you believe this? We can exclaim with the Psalmist, surely, "*The Lord has done this, and it is marvelous in our eyes....Give thanks to the Lord, for He is good; His love endures for ever" (Psalms 118: 23, 29).*

Today, brother Joseph and I are ministers of the Anglican and Methodist Churches respectively; while the elder one, Daniel (after whom I come), an Accountant, is a Lay Preacher and a chorister at the Bantama Methodist Church, Kumasi. Our only sister, Agnes, who comes after me, is married to the Rt. Rev. John Harvey Ewusi, Bishop of the Sekondi Diocese of the Methodist Church, Ghana. Indeed, the Lord is faithful, and has confirmed His Word.

As I write this book, the Spirit of the Living God is moving mightily upon the soul of the nation of Ghana, converting as many people as may hear and respond to His "still, small voice," (1 Kings. 19: 12 from KJV). The Lord is still speaking to the hearts of individuals and calling them through the various anointed preachers of the Word of God. He may be calling you, too, whoever you are, seeking to come into your life. At this point, perhaps, you may be asking, "How do I become a child of God or a Christian?"

How to Pray to Become a Christian

At this point, if you sincerely desire to be born into the family of God, I want to encourage you to do so, because it is not too late for you to be part of the universal Church of God. Just take a moment to pray sincerely to God (silently or audibly) for salvation in the privacy of your room or hotel, wherever you may be at this hour. But do it now! Let nothing stop you from praying the following prayer to receive Jesus into your life today. You will be glad you did.

O God, I acknowledge the truth that I am a sinner, and I repent of all my sins. I believe that You love me, and that You sent Your only Son, Jesus Christ, to die on the cross to save me from the penalty of all my sins. I believe that Jesus rose again from the dead and lives for evermore. O triumphant Jesus, I humbly invite You now to come into my heart to be my Lord and Savior for the rest of my life. Thank you, my Lord, for accepting me right now as Your child into Your kingdom for Your name's sake. Amen!

If you have sincerely offered this prayer to the Lord, then believe that your sins are forgiven, and that you are now a child of God. (Isaiah 1:18-19; 53: 4-6; Mark 1:14-15; John 1:12: Acts 16:31; Revelation 3:19-20).

Many of the Youth Flock to Church

Nowadays, a considerable number of our youth, including many adults, no longer spend their money and time at the movies or dance halls. Where do we find them? We see them in churches, retreats, camp meetings, crusades, revivals and conferences, listening to the Good News of Jesus Christ, and various teachings on Christian Life. They have no longer anytime to fool around. Why? Because, Jesus has certainly done something new in their lives. They have found a New Home in the House of the Lord. As lost sheep, who have been found by their Shepherd, they love to hear His voice, and to follow Him.

Like David, they are glad when it is said to them: *"Let us go into the house of the Lord"* (Psalms 122: 1). You will find a gifted number of the youth, who are specialists on the organ, guitar or trumpet, among the Church Choir, Choral Group or Praise and Worship team. Whatever part they are gifted to play, they do so with joy and enthusiasm, leading the congregation to *"worship the Lord in the beauty of holiness"* (Psalms 96: 9).

During my visit to Ghana in August 2002, I had the privilege to organize a seven-day crusade in the evenings (from 7.00-9:30) at the

Good Shepherd Methodist Church at Tanokrom, near Takoradi. Each evening, the place was packed to its fullest capacity. The Choral Group that led us in praise and worship consisted of the youth of the Church, dedicated to the service of God. One can feel the touch of their songs, because they sing with heart and soul. These were the same young people—the cream of Ghanaian society—who, until recently, were found loitering about at restaurants, parks, beer-bars, and dance halls. Thanks to *"the Good Shepherd"* (John 10:11), who has graciously saved His lost sheep and gently led them in various ways into the fold of His Church, which is His body. They now hear His voice and follow Him. Hallelujah! I can hear almost every African Christian, saying together with Isaiah, *"Surely, God is my salvation; I will trust and not be afraid. The Lord, the Lord, is my strength and my song; He has become my salvation"* (Isaiah 12:2). Yes, indeed, our salvation as individuals and as a people of this world, lies not in the hands of our politicians, but in Jehovah, the immutable God, who is ever faithful to His covenant.

Obviously, I believe that experience has taught all of us, Africans in general, and Ghanaians in particular, as well as other political leaders, chiefs, queens, and people in authority, that without God, we humans cannot make it. As I speak, forty-six years of independence and reliance on our human ability, wisdom, political ideology and power, did not bring Ghana real political and economic freedom, and material prosperity we had expected. I think we have sunk into this low economic position so that we might learn never to trust in ourselves or lean upon human flesh again, but on the victorious, everlasting arm of God.

Traditionalists Preach "Sankofa"

At this time of religious awakening, it is sickening to hear traditionalists trying to convince ignorant members of the society to go back to pagan, ancestral practices, which we have discarded since the dawn of Christianity—some six centuries ago. That was when our ancestors worshipped idols made of wood, clay, or stone, to which they offered sacrifices of sheep, goat, rooster, etc. hoping to obtain their favor and protection against enemies, illness or untimely death. But, could any of these idols of wood, clay or stone rise up to offer any help to our ancestors in time of need? No! Not in the least.

Formerly, whenever a Ghanaian chief died, for example, innocent servants, slaves, strangers, were beheaded and buried with the chief on the false belief that they would serve the dead king/chief in the under-world. However, we know for certain that none of these beliefs is true, and that no god/idol fetish priest/priestess/diviner has power to save anybody. If they did, they would have saved our fathers and the whole of Africa from sin, poverty, slavery, demonic influences, illness and death. They would have ushered Africans into new life, peace, success, and prosperity here and now. But, none of these things happened. Such false prophets and entire household stand in dire need of deliverance from Satan's domination. Hence, the Scriptures declare, *"Ignorant are those who carry about idols of wood, who pray to gods that cannot save. And there is no God apart from me, a righteous God and a Savior; there is none but me. Turn to me and be saved, all you ends of the earth, for I am God and there is no other"* (Isa. 45: 20b -21c, 22). Gyekye, therefore, sounds the following strong warning to all proponents of *"Sankofa"* (return for it): *"a return to the past must be guided by critical examination."*

Caution: Do Not Look Back

Since we have come thus far, by the grace of God, and have known the Truth, which has set us free from those vain idols which previously entangled and victimized us, why should we go back to mess up ourselves with traditions or cultural practices (e. g. libation, belief in other gods, etc.)? These religious practices did not lead our ancestors to salvation, prosperity or success in life. Why should we be made to return to the unprofitable idolatry, which we have discarded? A dog, for instance, will return to its vomit; and a pig will also go back to wallow in the mud, regardless of how clean its owner might have bathed it. But, we are neither dogs nor pigs to return to our vomit or mud, after we have been cleansed by the precious blood of Jesus Christ through the Baptism of the Holy Spirit. Like Paul, we must now *"forget what is behind, and strain toward what is ahead, pressing on toward the goal to win the prize for which God has called us heavenward in Christ Jesus"* (Philippians 3:13-14).

If, as Africans, we acted like pagans in the past, we do not follow that religious belief and life-style or walk in darkness anymore. Paul puts it this way: *"And that is what some of you were. But you were washed, you were sanctified, you were justified in the name of the Lord Jesus Christ and by the Spirit of our Lord."* (1 Corinthians 6:11).

We need to pick up courage through faith in Christ, affirming that the God of our fathers, Abraham, Isaac, and Jacob, who saved them and their descendants, is more than able to sustain us to the end through Jesus Christ. Here is God's promise: *"If you are willing and obedient, you will eat the good of the land; but if you resist and rebel, you will be devoured by the sword. For the mouth of the Lord has spoken"* (Isaiah 1:19-20).

Like the Galatian believers, we ought to jealously guard our God-given salvation and freedom in Christ against traditionalists, or false teachers of Christianity, who want to mislead believers (especially, Ghanaian Christians) into darkness once again. Let us listen to the words of Paul:

> *It is for freedom that Christ has set us free. Stand firm, then, and do not let yourselves be burdened again by a yoke of slavery. I, Paul, tell you that if you let yourselves be circumcised, Christ will be of no value to you at all. Again, I declare to every man who lets himself be circumcised that he is obligated to obey the whole Law. You who are trying to be justified by law have been alienated from Christ; you have fallen away from grace* (Galatians 5:1-4)

What Paul means here is that believers are saved by grace (ref. Eph. 2:8), and not by their good works, the law, or circumcision, because no one can be saved by his own good deeds. Therefore, anyone who turns away from grace to follow the law makes void the grace of God, and is under a curse (Galatians 3:10-11).

To be under a curse is to live in sin and under the bondage of Satan, and subject to eternal condemnation. The Apostle Paul does not want any of his converts to backslide into such a horrible situation; neither do I desire in the least to find any human being, particularly believers, in that situation. Therefore, **WE SHOULD NOT LOOK BACK**, lest we perish as lot's wife (Genesis 19: 26).

Those Who Look Back Are Not Worthy

Let us take an example of a new employee, who keeps talking and making reference to his former job in terms of all the benefits he used to enjoy. Such a worker cannot be productive to his new employer, who has hired him into his business. The reason is that he cannot focus on his present business, while still thinking about his former job with its benefits and friends he has left behind. That will sap his energy, dampen his interest in the new job, and render him incapable of meeting the demands of the job for which he was hired. Guess what his Master will say to him: *"You are fired!"*

The Effect of Looking Back

Talking about **"Looking Back**"reminds me of what Jesus said to a man who desired to follow Him, but pleaded with Jesus, saying: *"but first let me go back and say good-bye to my family." Jesus responded: "No one who puts his hand to the plow and looks back is fit for service in the kingdom of God*" (Luke 9:61-62).

As Christians, 'Looking back' has the effect of diverting our attention or focus from Christ to the things of the world; and can eventually draw us away from following the Lord. Hence, the admonition: "DO NOT LOOK BACK." Let us take a practical example here. While a student in the Middle School and later in Technical Institute, I was respectively a member of both the soccer and athletic teams. I participated in the 440 x 4, and 880 x 4 relays teams for my school. I was a good long-distance runner. My nick-name was "SLOW BUT SURE," because I adopted a slow-but-a-sure style of winning a race. Thus, even though I would start slowly, yet I would increase my pace gradually during the race, and finally, speed up towards the end to win the prize.

I do still remember one of the stern warnings given by our sports master/coach to the athletes was: "Once you start the race, do not look back at the other athletes, who are running closely behind you, trying to overtake you in the race." He explained that whenever you look back, your focus is shifted and, therefore, your speed is inevitably reduced within that limited time. Secondly, as you slow down your speed, your opponent will overtake you. Thirdly, as you look back, you may miss your track, and step into the next track, and be disqualified from the race completely. Fourthly, "looking back" is a sign of the feeling of insecurity, and of fear of losing the race to your opponent. Certainly, you will lose it, because looking back does not remove your fear, but compounds it.

Therefore, in short, spiritually speaking, "looking back" (for the believer) means 'backsliding'. It is failure to stay on course. It means turning away from your trust in God/Christ—the Maker of heaven and earth—to other gods, or anything, to which you give your uttermost attention, love and loyalty, beside the true God. It follows that you are depending on the flesh or what you or the world (with all its wisdom and technology) can enable you to do in order to achieve your goal. James defines "looking-back" as adultery or friendship with the world:

> *You adulterous people, don't you know that friendship with the world is hatred toward God? Anyone who chooses to be a friend of the world becomes an enemy of God. Or do you think Scripture says without reason that the Spirit God caused to live in us envies intensely?* (James 4:4-5)

"Sankofa" can lead to Idolatry (Looking Back)

It follows clearly, as James puts it in the above passage, that going back to traditional religious practice or ancestral worship ('Sankofa') amounts to the sin of idolatry, which provokes the Lord to anger. For instance, in the days of Jeremiah, the idolatrous behavior of Israel so provoked the Lord that God refused to listen to prayers offered on their behalf:

> *Do not pray for this people nor offer any plea or petition for them; do not plead with me, for I will not listen to you. Do you not see what they are doing in the towns of Judah and in the streets of Jerusalem? The children gather wood, the fathers light the fire,*

> *and the women knead the dough and make cakes of bread for the Queen of heaven. They pour out drink offerings to other gods to provoke me to anger. But am I the one they are provoking?, declares the Lord. Are they not rather harming themselves to their own shame?* (Jeremiah 7:16-19)

In order not to provoke God to anger, it behooves every true believer to prayerfully avoid "looking back", or indulging in acts tantamount to idolatry. We must bear in mind that no human or earthly power or wisdom can enable us to achieve our mission. God alone, who has called us individually into His eternal kingdom knows, and has the ultimate, divine plan He wants each of us to follow. Besides, God alone, and no one else, has the power by which we can achieve our individual, divinely-appointed, goals, because *"Unless the Lord builds the house, its builders labor in vain. Unless the Lord watches over the city, the watchmen stand guard in vain"* (Psalms 127:1).

Perhaps, we need to be reminded that the Christian life is like a race that Christ has set before us. As a believer, therefore, you must seriously determine to look straight ahead of you on the track in which you stand, and to get ready to move forward with diligence as your team-mate approaches to hand over the baton to you. Once you get hold of the baton, you have to run as fast as you can without looking back, till you reach the end of the race. Looking forward instead of backwards has a lot of benefits. First of all, looking straight ahead has the advantage of inspiring you to exert your energy on the race set before you. Secondly, it enables you to stay focused on the race so that you do not miss your track. Thirdly, it enables you to sustain your energy, and therefore, gives you the ability to increase your speed in the final round to win the race. Similarly, as fellow believers, we are advised not to look behind in our walk with Christ, but always looking forward, with our eyes *"fixed on Jesus, the author and perfecter of our faith, who for the joy set before Him endured the cross, scorning its shame, and sat down at the right hand of the throne of God"* (Hebrews 12:2).

"Fixing our eyes on Jesus" means casting all our cares on the

Lord. It means depending solely on Him to supply all our needs, physically, emotionally, and spiritually, through the mighty working of the Holy Spirit in us. Just as all the Prophets, and the apostles, had to be filled with the Spirit of God to fulfill the divinely-appointed service, so we who are called of God in these latter days, ought to receive God's anointing power to enable us accomplish our divinely-appointed tasks. For, it is *"Not by might, nor by power, but by my Spirit", says the Lord Almighty"* (Zechariah 4:6).

It Calls For Total Commitment

In order for any group of believers to be Spirit-filled vessels, who are to lift up the name of the Lord in their community, they must be fully committed to God and the task of building and extending His Kingdom in that particular part of the world. One may be fully committed to a job, but may rely on his own ability and plan to accomplish it.

However, biblical commitment involves surrender to God through faith in Christ. It means reliance on God's plan and power for the achievement of that particular goal. For example, Zerubbabel and his team of Jewish leaders, who had returned from exile, firstly, committed themselves to the Lord, and secondly, to the task God had assigned them. None of them, namely, Zerubbabel, Nehemiah, or Ezra, allowed himself to be drawn away from their divinely—appointed task of rebuilding the wall of Jerusalem, the Temple and renewing their covenant relationship with God in accordance with the Holy Scriptures.

Most importantly, they depended on God's power, wisdom and direction through daily prayer and adherence to God's Word in every aspect of the project. Hence, in spite of the constant opposition they encountered from Sanballat and Tobiah (Nehemiah. 2:10), from the beginning to the end, they were able to complete the reconstruction of the walls of Jerusalem and the Temple, because they relied on Jehovah God, and not on themselves. The following is part of Nehemiah's report:

> *So the wall was completed on the twenty-fifth of Elul in fifty-two days. When all our enemies heard about*

> *this, all the surrounding nations were afraid and lost their self-confidence, because they realized that this work had been done with the help of God.* (Nehemiah 6:15-16)

Another typical example, which may encourage you is found in Acts chapter three, where Peter and John healed the lame man at the Beautiful Gate of the Temple in Jerusalem. This miracle drew a large crowd to the apostles, Peter and John. To direct the attention of the crowd to Jesus instead of them, the apostles *began "teaching the people and proclaiming in Jesus the resurrection of the dead"* (Acts 4:2).

But, the religious leaders of the Jews had them arrested and put in jail in Jerusalem. The following morning, they were made to appear before the Sanhedrin (that is, the Supreme Court of the Jews) in Jerusalem and questioned. One would have thought that facing such highly religious authority of the Jews would frighten the apostles into submission. But, Peter' s courageous response to their question stunned them.

> *"By what power or what name did you do this?" Then Peter, filled with the Holy Spirit, said to them: "Rulers and elders of the people! If we are being called to account today for an act of kindness shown to a cripple and are asked how he was healed, then know this, you and all the people of Israel: It is by the name of Jesus Christ of Nazareth, whom you crucified but whom God raised from the dead, that this stands before you healed. He is the 'stone you builders rejected, which has become the capstone.' Salvation is found in no one else, for there is no other name under heaven given to men by which we must be saved"* (Acts 4: 7 - 12).

The Scripture says:

> *When they (i. e., the High Priest, the religious Leaders,*

> *as well as the Lawyers of the Supreme Court) saw the courage of Peter and John and realized that they were unschooled, ordinary men, they were astonished and they took notice that they had been with Jesus* (Acts 4:13).

It is further reported that on their release, after several threats, Peter and John did not relax on their oars, or take things for granted; neither did they claim any victory or glory for themselves for healing the cripple. But they "went back to their own people, and reported all that the chief priests and elders had said to them. When they heard this, they raised their voices together in prayer to God" (Acts 4:24) as follows:

> *Sovereign Lord, you made heaven and the earth and the sea, and everything in them. You spoke by the Holy Spirit through the mouth of your servant, our father David: 'Why do the nations rage and peoples plot in vain? The kings of the earth take their stand and the rulers gather together against the Lord and against His Anointed One.' Indeed, Herod and Pontius Pilate met together with the Gentiles and the people of Israel in this city to conspire against your holy servant Jesus, whom you anointed. They did what your power and will had decided beforehand should happen. Now, Lord, consider their threats and enable your servants to speak your word with great boldness. Stretch out your hand to heal and perform miraculous signs and wonders through the name of your holy servant Jesus* (Acts 4:24-30).

God Answered Their Prayer

It is reported in the Scriptures that, "after they had prayed, the place where they were meeting was shaken. And they were all filled with the Holy Spirit and spoke the word of God boldly" (Acts 4:31).

Now it is significant to note that the result of their prayer, namely, 'the shaking of the ground where they stood' (as I was led to understand) was primarily to break down the walls/barriers of opposition erected by the religious leaders of Jerusalem. Secondly, it was to endue them with power from God for continuous proclamation of the Gospel. Thirdly, it ushered them into a strong bond of unity and love for one another. For up to this time of their Christian journey, there were still areas of weaknesses among them (as the body of Christ), which needed to be addressed and strengthened (See for example, Acts 5:1-11).

As we may recall, Jesus prayed to God for His followers: *"that all of them may be one"* (John 17: 21); and also commanded them to *"Love one another. As I have loved you, so you must love one another. By this all men will know that you are my disciples, if you love one another."* (John 13: 34b -35).

Therefore, the answer to their prayer was a fulfillment of Jesus' high-priestly prayer for *"love and unity"* He had asked for His disciples (John 17: 22-23) in order to get them deeply rooted on the solid foundation, built on the unflinching faith in Jesus Christ, who is *"the Rock"* (1 Corinthians 10: 4) upon which stands the church—the body of Christ. Faith, Love and unity, emanating from *"the bond of the Spirit"* are inseparable virtues for the advancement of the church. God in Christ knew exatly what His followers needed and answered their prayers accordingly. *"All the believers were one in heart and mind" (Acts 4: 32).* For a church without solid faith, love and unity cannot stand, let alone to fight against any division or opposition that might come her way. Thus, their fear and timidity were replaced with faith and boldness, as we read: *"With great power the apostles continued to testify to the resurrection of the Lord Jesus, and much grace was upon them all"* (Acts 4: 33).

Finally, the result was also to give them financial break-through. For example, the rich among them began to have compassion for the needy and gave generously to meet the needs of strangers, and the poor among them, so that none was found wanting, as stated:

> *There were no needy persons among them. For, from time to time those who owed lands or houses sold them, brought the money from the sales and put it at*

> *the apostles' feet, and it was distributed to anyone as he had need. Joseph, a Levite from Cyprus, whom the apostles called Barnabas sold a field he owned and brought the money and put it at the apostles' feet.* (Acts 4:34-36)

The Apostles prayed for power and guidance to fulfill the Great Commission, namely, to preach the Good News to all the nations, beginning in Jerusalem and their prayer was answered because they aimed at seeking *"first the kingdom of God and His righteousness"* (Matthew 6:33), and not their own welfare. Accordingly, the Lord empowered them with the Holy Spirit to enable them fulfill both their spiritual and physical needs as well, as seen in the above passage. We must follow their good example.

Meeting the needs of Believers Today

The needs of many church members today cannot be met, because we do not pray enough. I believe we all need to yield ourselves to God in prayer in order to be renewed in love and unity by the Holy Spirit. The regular routine of worship that we go through every Sunday has become so stale and empty of the Spirit of God that it does not inwardly touch or move majority of worshippers to do any acts of kindness. There are poor people in the Church today, especially in many parts of Africa. Nevertheless, the wealthy among us are blind to their own spiritual needs, let alone those of the poor; because they are either not converted or mere babes in Christ, not knowing how to use their money to glorify God.

When we pray, we do not see any results, because, as James says, "you ask with wrong motives" (James 4:3). It behooves us all, especially, Ministers and Leaders of the Church in Africa, to start now to take both our own private, devotional-life and that of the Church very seriously. There is too much politics, jealousy, self-seeking, and humanism in the Church these days. So "the days are evil" (Eph. 5:16).

Therefore, we have to realize that we cannot make any headway towards growth in membership, love, unity and finances of the Church entrusted to our care, unless we repent of our sins, including the lukewarm attitude we show toward the work of God. There is need to pray for fresh anointing of the Holy Spirit upon our lives, and for the manifestation of our spiritual gifts and fulfillment of our individual ministries.

The ministry is the work of God to which we are called. It is such an awesome responsibility, which is far beyond our human capability. *"Our sufficiency is of God,"* says Paul (2 Cor. 3:5). We know we cannot do it, unless we are empowered by the Lord, who called us. Most certainly, He will do it, if we ask Him, because He is aware of all our weaknesses, and promises never to "fail or forsake" any one who sincerely trusts in Him. In fact, it was the awareness of similar, awesome responsibility of shepherding the flock of Christ that led John and Charles Wesley to pour out their concerns in the following popular, but solemn hymn of the Methodists:

A charge to keep I have,
A God to glorify,
A never-dying soul to save,
And fit it for the sky:

To serve the present age,
My calling to fulfill:
O may it all my powers engage
To do my Master's will!

Arm me with jealous care,
As in thy sight to live;
And O Thy servant, Lord, prepare
A strict account to give!

Help me to watch and pray,
And on Thyself rely,
Assured, if I my trust betray,
I shall forever die.
(M. H. B. 578 by Charles Wesley, 1707-88)

Like the apostles, John and Charles Wesley acknowledged their own inadequacy for the task entrusted to them. Hence, they relied completely upon God through prayer for strength, wisdom, courage, dedication and guidance to fulfill their calling. As a result, they were empowered by Him, who called them to accomplish their ministries of Church Music and preaching as faithful servants (Methodists) respectively, yet with love and unity in Christ. In his brief commentary on James 2:1-9, Dave Egner made the following observation concerning the ministry of Jesus: "He crossed traditional barriers to talk with tax-collectors, sinners, non-Jews, people of mixed races, the poor, as well as the rich. He came to identify with each of us, and to pay the price on the cross for all our sins" (Daily Bread, Monday, October 27, 2003).

We need to follow the good examples of our Lord, and of our predecessors by praying constantly for the fullness of the Holy Spirit. By so doing, we will be strengthened to overcome every obstacle that hinders the forward movement of the kingdom of God, not only in Ghana, but also in Africa, and the world at large.

It Calls For a Team of Prayer Warriors

In this connection, I have my fears that our regular, routine prayers will not bring us the measure of divine strength required to achieve our goal. It is therefore, necessary to set up a team of dedicated, Christian men and women as *"Prayer Warriors",* who will "stand in the gap" (Ezekiel 22:30) day and night, interceding for the progress of the church. I believe there are seriously, committed Christians, who love to pray, and are specially gifted in intercessory prayers in various Churches in Africa and other parts of the world. Notably in Africa, for instance, there is *Africa House of Prayer,* consisting of committed church leaders of various denominations led by Rev. Emeka Ngwampah of Nigeria. They meet at vantage places in Africa, interceding for the redemption of unbelievers from the powers of darkness. Another powerful prayer house is *Linkintercessors International,* with Rev. Gifty Niboi as the Director. As their name implies, they link up with various prayer-warriors, particularly women, of various churches in Africa and Europe, who *wail in prayer* for God to send down His power for the release of all under the bondage of sin in Africa and the rest of the world. The Prayer-Warriors of Calvary Redeeming Methodist Church has teamed up with *Linkintercessors International* in the effort to achieve this laudable goal for the glory of God.

Here in the U. S., great preachers like Billy Graham, John Hagee, Kenneth Copplan, Anthony Hayford, John McArthur, Charles Stanley, T. D. Jakes, Benny Hinn, Tony Evans, Seth Asare, Michael Youssef, Rabby Zacharias, to mention only a few, and other member churches of the Television Broadcasting Network (T.B.N.), as well as other preaching networks of white and black churches, have prayer towers whose unceasing, intercessory prayers keep ministries on fire for the extension of the Kingdom of God beyond the borders of America. These are prayer-giants, whose delight is to pray for themselves and the on-going work of various ministries twenty-four hours a day, with fruitful results, which glorify the name of the Lord. As James puts it, *"The prayer of a righteous man is effective and powerful*" (James 5: 16). All believers have the obligation to join the prayer-force to *"pray without ceasing*" (Matthew 26: 41; Luke 18: 1; 1 Thessalonians 5: 17). Jesus commands us: *"watch and pray so that you do not enter into temptation*" *(Matthew 26: 41).*

In the book of the Prophet Isaiah, God promised to establish a new Israel, which is in reference to the Church of Christ, as His people continued in prayer, as follows:

> *I have posted watchmen on your walls, O Jerusalem; they will never be silent day or night. You who call on the Lord, give your selves no rest, and give Him no rest till He establishes Jerusalem and makes it the praise of the earth. Never again will I give your grain as food for your enemies, and never again will foreigners drink the new wine for which you have toiled; but those who harvest it will eat it and praise the Lord, and those who gather the grapes will drink it in the courts of my sanctuary.* (Isaiah 62:6-9)

This is a clear message of promise of Jehovah God to the penitent, new Israel, under the new Covenant, initiated and made available to all believers by Jesus Christ for the past two thousand years. Today, Israel stands as an Independent, Sovereign nation, manning its own affairs, regardless of the struggle for occupation of certain portions of the land between Palestine and Israel. Nevertheless, with the help of peace-talks, and negotiations led by the United Nations, and encouraged by the U.S. in particular, there is hope for lasting peace for both sides in the end. Much in the same way, believers in Africa can also be renewed by the Lord to fulfill the goals He has set before us, if only we will have devoted Christian men and women as *"Prayer Warriors"*, daily interceding for the spiritual and physical well-being of the nations of this world, with focus on Africa.

It is uplifting to our spirits to read from the previous chapter that through the *"African Enterprise"*, the Lord has already put in place *"a Christian interdenominational, cross-__ cultural ministry of evangelism, reconciliation, leadership training, relief and development*." This missionary team works *"with Church leaders to mobilize their congregations in outreach to Africa's cities."* (African Enterprise, July/August, 2004).

The Prayer Request of African Enterprise

The bottom section of the paper has the following prayer request:

> Please, pray for an African city each day along with praying for an African Enterprise leader or event; and do remember all other missionary agents, as well, working in Africa and other parts of the world.
>
> 1. The Christians in the city, that they not be discouraged, that churches be united and minister with compassion.
> 2. The city government and business leaders, that they surrender their lives to God and lead with integrity.
> 3. The unsaved in the city, that they find salvation in Christ.
> 4. Resources, for the transformation of the cities.

Finally, there is a request to pray for Mr. Gottfried Osei-Mensah, who would be presiding over all *the "International Partnership Board meetings."*

It is required of all of us as believers to be resolved as one people; to commit ourselves unreservedly to joining forces with the prayer-warriors of Africa and to pray constantly to God for the redemption of the total continent of Africa, as well as the rest of the world. We need to pray for the fulfillment of God's purpose in whatever area of service He has placed us. Furthermore, we must be conscious of the truth that, without Christ, all our efforts, as individuals, as well as any other people of any nation, will continue to come to naught. But, the Good News is that with God, we can bring down "*the walls of Jericho*," and sink every mountain into a plain ground, because we have God on our side; and "*with God, all things are possible*."

In this connection, I invite all who read this book to join hands with me in interceding in prayer for every city in the continent of Africa, as well as the leaders, events and projects, as earnestly requested by African Enterprise in the previous pages. It was in pursuance of such requests that Antoine Rutayisire, a representative of African Enterprise, for instance, reports the following:

> *AE seeks to mobilize prayer intercessors and others to pray in concert for important issues here in Rwanda. To this end, we organized a large Prayer Crusade at the Christian Life Assembly Church in Kigali. There were one thousand intercessors, pastors and lay people in attendance. We spent time in prayer for the country and also gave teachings on prayer and our vision for a national prayer network. Our hope is that the teaching will be put into action by those in attendance. These prayer crusades will continue on a monthly basis.*

Nico Nteme of the Republic of Congo, also reports as follows:

> *A Leadership Mission devoted to prayer for our*

> *Nation was held in partnership with a group of women from 8 different Christian women's organizations. About 250 women gathered and 54 committed their lives to Christ." (African Enterprise, July/August, 2003).*

These are encouraging reports, which assure us of the great work that the Good Lord is doing in Africa, and that as believers we must all unite to support the various groups of christian workers/missionaries in these areas with both our constant prayers and finances. Apart from praying regularly along with them, Calvary Redeeming Methodist Church will endeavor to offer them financial assistance as the Lord blesses us. It is hoped that other churches will follow suit, trusting that God will surely bring revival to the continent of Africa, because He had done it before in East Africa.

The East Africa Revival—A Living Example

In his book, ***"Revolutionary Love"*** Bishop Festo Kivengere together with Dorothy Smoker, wrote about an inspiring revival, which occurred in East Africa in the 1930s. It began with two devout Christian friends, Simeoni Nsibambi and Dr. Joe Church. "They found each other by God's 'accident' near Kampala, Uganda, when both were spiritually hungry to desperation. They dropped everything and sat together under a tree on Namirembe Hill, studying the New Testament for days to find more about the Holy Spirit. He found them, and led them to the cross of Christ and to a simple way of accepting its power daily for continuous personal reviving." (Festo Kivengere & Dorothy Smoker, *Revolutionary Love*, 1983, P. 60).

According to the story, when the two friends were ignited by the Spirit for Christ, the flame of revival gradually, but intensely spread to other parts of the land, Schools and Colleges, converting the rich and the poor, teachers and students alike, and uniting them into one body in Christ. For instance, "Teams were going out, invited or not, at their own expense, from Rwanda to Burundi and Tanganyika, from western and central Uganda to other provinces, and to Kenya and Sudan." (Ibid.).

This revival of which Festo himself *"became a part in 1940,"* when he was still a school teacher, was said to have lasted half a century. It is reported that the *African Enterprise* is one of the many fruitful results of that fire that was kindled by the Holy Spirit in the hearts of the two friends.

Undoubtedly, the same God that set ablaze the hearts of those two *"spiritually hungry"* Africans in the 1930s, will do it again in our day, if we, too (whether two or three), like them, will sincerely yield ourselves to God as vessels sanctified for His holy use. Then, He will certainly kindle His fire in our temples, as He did in the past. Will you, my friend, be part of this coming revival, even as Bishop Festo Kivengere became a part when he was a teacher?

In your own capacity, you can do nothing, but if you pray, and cast yourself completely upon God through faith in Christ, He will accept you, fill and use you in ways you can never imagine or think possible. "*For with God all things are possible*" (Luke 18:27).

The South Africa Example — A Ray of Hope

I am very much inclined to believe that the release of Nelson Mandela from South African prison on February 11, 1990, did not happen by chance, but by divine intervention. It was certainly the result of the untiring efforts of thousands of Christians throughout the world, who joined hands with Archbishop Desmond Tutu, to lift up their voices in fervent prayers to God for the release of all incarcerated in South Africa for political reasons. Speaking on behalf of his people to the United Nations Security Council, Bishop Tutu stated, among other things:

> *I speak out of a full heart, for I am about to speak about . . . a land God had richly endowed with the good things of the earth, a land rich in mineral deposits of nearly every kind; a land capable of feeding itself and other other lands on the beleaguererd continent of Africa, a veritable breadbasket; a land that could contribute wonderfully to the material and spiritual development and prosperity of all Africa, and indeed of the whole world.*
>
> *And so we would expect that such a land, verita-*

> *bly flowing with milk and honey, should be the land where peace and harmony and contentment reigned supreme. Alas, the opposite is the case. For my beloved country is wracked by division, by alienation, by animosity, by separation, by injustice, avoidable pain and suffering. It is a deeply fragmented society, ridden by fear and anxiety.*

Nevertheless, with constant prayers and hard work, Archbishop Tutu, together with members of the Executive Committee of the South African Council of Churches, held emergency sessions with Mr. P. W. Botha to find out lasting solutions to the rapidly deteriorating situation. Archbishop Tutu conitnued:

> *As a result of our peace initiative, we did get to meet two cabinet ministers, demonstrating thereby our concern to carry out our call to be ministers of reconciliation and ambassadors of Christ. We deplore all forms of violence, the violence of oppressive and unjust society and the violence of those seeking to overthrow that society; for we believe that violence is not the answer to the crisis of our land.*

In saying so, Archbishop Tutu endorses the point being stressed in this book that "*Unless the Lord builds the house, its builders labour in vain*", (Psalms 127: 1), because "*it is not by might not by power, but my Spirit', says the Lord of hosts*" (Zechariah 4:6).

He concluded as follows: *"We dream of a new society that will be truly nonracial, truly democratic, in which people count because they are created in the image of God. We are committed to work for justice, for peace, and for reconciliation"(Desmond Tutu, Modern History Sourcebook: The Question of South* Africa pp. 1, 4).

Dream Fulfilled: "Free at Last!"

On his release from prison, after 27 years of confinement by the South African apartheid system, Nelson Mandela, the leader of the African National Congress, said, as he walked through those prison gates to enter a car on the other side, *"I felt, even at the age of seventy-one, that my life was beginning anew.....I was a free man for the first time in twenty-seven years."* Surely the dream of Archbishop Tutu, Nelson Mandela, and many others, both in and outside South Africa, had been fulfilled. Then he continued:

"I thank all those in the ANC and the democratic movement who had worked so hard for so long." Standing on the same podium with him was Mrs. Coretta Scott King, the wife of the great freedom fighter Martin Luther King, Jr., who had flown from the US to be part of his welcoming guests. Mandela added, making reference to the King's 'immortal words':

"This is one of the most important moments in the life of our country. I stand here before you with deep pride and joy—pride in the ordinary, humble people of this country. You have shown such a calm, patient determination to reclaim this country as your own, and now the joy that we can loudly proclaim from the rooftops—'FREE AT LAST! FREE AT LAST!'

I stand before you humbled by your courage, with a heart full of love for all of you. I regard it as the highest honor to lead the ANC at this moment in our history. I am your servant.... It is not the individuals that matter, but the collective... This is a time to heal the old wounds and build a new South Africa."

Indeed, after about three centuries of colonial rule, the greatest of all days dawned on the land of South Africa, with bright skies, on the day of inauguration of Nelson Mandela as the President of the Republic of South Africa on May 10, 1990. de Klerk, second Deputy President, was the first to be sworn in, followed by Mr. Thabo Mbeki as the first Deputy President. When it was Mandela's turn, he said, *"I pledge to obey and uphold the Constitution and to devote myself to the well-being of the Republic and its people."* To the assembled guests and watchful world, he said:

> *Today, all of us do, by our presence here...confer glory and hope to our newborn liberty. Out of the experience of an extraordinary human disaster that lasted too long, must be born a society of which all humanity will be proud. We, who were outlaws not*

> *long ago, have today been given the rare privilege to be host to the nations of the world on our own soil. We thank all of our international guests for having come to take possession with the people of our country of what is, after all, a common victory for justice, for peace, for human dignity. We have, at last, achieved our political emancipation. We pledge ourselves to liberate all our people from the continuing bondage of poverty, deprivation, suffering, gender, and other discrimination. Never, never, and never again shall it be that this beautiful land will again experience the oppression of one by another...The sun shall never set on so glorious a human achievement. Let freedom reign. God bless Africa! (Nelson Mandela, Long Walk To Freedom, 1994, pp. 539-541*).

I believe it is the dream of all of us in Africa and all others who desire peace in this world that what happened to our brothers and sisters in South Africa will come true for us, too, in the near future. The God who opens and no one can shut, and shuts and none can open, is still on the throne overseeing His creation to fulfill His purpose on earth.

It may interest you to know that Nelson Mandela was 44 when he was cast into prison for political reasons. He was 71 when he was released and gradually, but steadily and courageously, he rallied his people to ultimate freedom. Finally, when the mandate was given to the ANC to form the Government, Mandela said:

> *I saw my mission as one preaching reconciliation, of binding the wounds of the country, of engendering trust, and confidence. I knew that many people, particularly the minorities, whites, coloureds, and Indians, would be feeling anxious about the future and I wanted them to feel secure. I reminded people again and again that the liberation struggle was not a battle against any one group or colour, but a fight*

> *against a system of repression. At every opportunity, I said all South Africans must now unite and join hands and say we are one country, one nation, one people, marching together into the future*." (*Long Walk To Freedom*, p.115).

Warren Wiersbe wrote: *"What people do with authority is a test of character. Do they use their authority to promote themselves or to help others? Do they glorify themselves or glorify God?" (Be Committed, Doing God's Will Whatever the Cost*, p. 96).

Thus, in spite of the atrocities committed by the apartheid regime against his fellow South Africans, Mandela did not seek revenge, mindful of the written Word of God, *"Vengeance is mine, I will repay,"* says the Lord (Romans 12:19). With that in mind, Mandela sought for reconciliation and unity of all South Africans—Black or White, Indian, or Asian, fully believing that *"With God, all things are possible"* (Mark 10:27).

In order to achieve his aim of reconciling and uniting the people of South Africa, Nelson Mandela appointed Archbishop Desmond Tutu, who retired as Anglican Archbishop of Cape Town, as Chairman of the South African Truth and Reconciliation Committee. The Committee's good work resulted in a measure of peace and unity, which played a large role for the economic and political stability of South Africa under Mandela's leadership.

"Good leaders," says Herb Vander Lugt, *"don't rely on domineering self-assertion-neither at home, nor in church, nor in business. Rather, they balance self-assertiveness (which isn't wrong in itself) with the principle of submitting to one another (Ephesians 5:21). They listen respectfully, admit when they are wrong, show a willingness to change, and mix gentleness with firmness. That's submissive leadership—and it works!"*

Ghana on the Path of Reconciliation

When President John Agyekum Kufuor, leader of the New Patriotic Party (NPP), took office as the Head of the Republic of Ghana four years ago, he was faced with a major decision. He had to make up his mind whether to tow the line of those who wanted retaliation against the members of the former military regime, led by Flt. Lt J. J. Rawlings, for the death of their family members, or to bury the past and follow the path of reconciliation. Being a Christian, Kufuor, like Mandela, chose the latter, namely, reconciliation. He quickly set up a special National Reconciliation Committee, whose objective was to seek to reconcile all factions in the country, and work towards unity, peace and progress of the people, from all walks of life, for the common good of the country.

That was the kind of leadership that Kufuor adopted during the four years of his presidency. Backed by the prayer support of Ghanaian Christians and other religious bodies both within and outside the country, President Kufuor steered the course of peace, unity and economic development of Ghana. Talking of the achievements of the Kufuor government, Mr. Ivor Agyeman-Duah, Minister-Counselor of Public Affairs of the Embassy of Ghana in Washington, D. C., stated, *"There is freedom, unity and peace in the country as compared to the period before he took office. There is growth in the economy, inflation is down, and there are new initiatives by the Government, adding value to raw materials"*, he concluded. With these positive changes in Ghana, the Minister was optimistic that Kufuor would win the forthcoming Presidential elections in December 2004, to enable his government to continue with the good work already in progress.

That is the kind of leadership that I believe, will succeed in Africa, in particular, and the world at large. With hope, we patiently wait, like Mandela, for revival of the people everywhere by the Spirit of the Living God, whose timing is always the best for His people.

Solomon wrote: *"There is a time for everything, and a season for every activity under heaven: a time to be born and a time to die, a time to plant and a time to uproot, a time to kill and a time to heal, a time to tear down and a time to build... He has made everything beautiful in its time"* (Ecclesiastes 3:1-3, 10).

The Lord our God, will graciously bring a great revival upon the land in due season, even as He promised Israel in the days of Ezekiel as follows:

> *....I will take you out of the nations; and I will gather you from all the countries and bring you back into your own land. I will sprinkle clean water on you, and you will be clean; I will cleanse you from all your impurities and from all your idols. I will give you a new heart and put a new spirit in you; I will remove from you your heart of stone and give you a heart of flesh. And I will put my Spirit in you and move you to follow my decrees and be carefull to obey my laws. You will live in the land I gave your forefathers; you will be my people, and I will be your God (Ezekiel 36:24-28).*

In fact, signs of revival are evident in several places of the country. With the conversion of a number of kings and queen-mothers, who are making impact on their subjects, and the opening of new churches in the rural areas of the land, we must acknowldge the moving of the Holy Spirit on the lives of Ghanaians and give praise due to God's name.

Nevertheless, we look forward with joyous anticipation for a much extensive revival, which will affect all and sundry. We are trusting in God and His promises, always determined by His grace to do His will, knowing that *"He gives strength to the weary and increases the power of the weak.*" (Isaiah 40 : 29). Remember that He is faithful. He is never late, and in His own time, He will bring deliverance, freedom and peace, to all who wait for Him. The Psalmist said, *"I am still confident of this: I will see the goodness of the Lord in the land of the living. Wait for the Lord; be strong and take heart and wait for the Lord"* (Psalms 27:13-14*). "For the revelation awaits an appointed time; it speaks of the end and will not prove false. Though it lingers, wait for it; it will certainly come and will not delay"* (Habakkuk 2:3).

When that day dawns on us, when this vision is fulfilled, Africa, as well as the rest of "*the earth will be filled with the knowledge of the glory of the Lord, as the waters cover the sea*" (Habakkuk 2:14).

Then, we shall all, black and white alike, together with our children, say with exclamation: "No one could have done this, except the Lord. *"The Lord has done this, and it is marvelous in our eyes. To Him who sits on the throne and to the Lamb be praise and honour and glory and power for ever and ever"* (Psalm 118: 23; Revelation 5:13).

CONCLUSION

In bringing the writing of this vision to a final conclusion, I want, first of all, to give thanks to the Almighty God for using me as a vessel to reveal this vital message, primarily to my fellow Ghanaians, and to other Africans, as well as, all other people, black or white, male or female, young or old, rich or poor, of this world. Secondly, I wish to remind readers, if I may, that God gave me this message (vision), for the following reasons:

- To confirm the truth that God created all humans equal in His image. That God loves all human beings and does not desire that anyone should die in sin due to ignorance of God's Will, as revealed in the Holy Scriptures.
- To teach us that we cannot save ourselves from the consequences of our sins. This sinful situation was aggravated by the worship of idols and ancestors, which has had adverse consequences on families, communities, nations, and the world at large, particularly, Africa, with Ghana as an example. That this has allowed the Devil to gain foothold on numerous people, Black and White alike, who are used to commit acts of wickedness, murder, terrorism, fear, mistrust and insecurity in the world.

Nevertheless, out of God's merciful kindness toward us, He revealed to me not only the cause of our woes, but also, the Way of deliverance from these evils and *"from the coming wrath"*(Matthew 3:7). That is, to turn away from sin, idolatrous practices, occultism, and Satanism, to saving faith in Jesus Christ, who offered His life as sacrifice for the penalty of our sins on the cross at Calvary (John 3: 16; 1 John 1: 9, 2:1-2).

- That in spite of the woeful condition in which we find ourselves, the Scriptures assure us that if we sincerely repent of our sins and accept Jesus as our Lord and Savior, we will receive God's forgiveness and new life in Christ. The Holy Spirit will set God's eternal seal upon the soul of each of us as the guarantee of our new relationship with God, as the sons and daughters of our Father in heaven (1 John 1:9, 5: 11-12; John 1: 12, 3: 16; 2 Corinthians 6: 14-18).
- That God expects all in positions of authority to realize that they are accountable to God, and must use their authority for the common good. Hence, they are to rely on God for power, wisdom and direction, and will find peace and fulfillment of their goals. Furthermore, as individual Christians, we are to conduct ourselves in a way that our new life of righteousness will impact the life of our entire household and communities at large (ref. Matthew 5:13-16; Acts 16:31). For "*righteousness exalts a nation, but sin is a disgrace to any pepole*" (Proverbs. 14:34).
- That God wants all who have come to know the Truth (that is, Jesus Christ) to share the Good News with their neighbors, for *"All have sinned and fall short of the glory of God"* (Romans

3:23); that sinners must repent and turn to the Lord for salvation while it is day. For *"night is coming when no one can work"* (John 9: 4).

- That human beings—Black or White, whether from the East or West, are not made to be independent of God, irrespective of our economic, scientific and technological advancement. Hence, it is only as we maintain our relationship with God through faith in Jesus Christ, that we are enabled by the power and guidance of the Holy Spirit to achieve our life-long, divinely-appointed goals.
- That there is no other God, beside God, the Creator; neither is there any other Savior, or Mediator between God and humans, except our Lord Jesus Christ. Therefore, we must cling to the truth of God's Word, otherwise, we shall find out in the end, to our utter disappointment, and misery, that all our toils and earthly existence is altogether meaningless—as Solomon regrettably found out in his latter days: *"everything was meaningless"* (Ecclesiastes 2: 11).
- That by all means, the Lord is coming again, soon (when exactly, we do not know), to judge the living and the dead; each one of us will be required to give account of his or her life before the holy, and righteous God (Ecclesiastes 12:14; Revelation 22:12; Romans 14:12).
- That since *"God is no respecter of persons,"* (Acts 10: 34) every individual, black or white, male or female, young or old, has a share in the abundance of His grace and gifts—and all the unlimited resources—to meet life's demands—spiritually, physically and emotionally (Philippians 4:19). For God is the One, *"who richly provides us with everything for our enjoyment"* (1 Timothy 6: 17).

Therefore, everyone is invited: come one, come all; particularly, my fellow Africans, let us together get into the heaven-ward wagon of Jesus Christ, Who is *"the Way, the Truth, and the Life; no one can go to the Father except by Me," He declares* (John 14:6). I believe strongly that this is our time to *"rise and shine,"* because our *"light has come"* (Isaiah 60: 1). No one should lag behind. The Lord graciously saves, heals, and abundantly blesses all who sincerely call on Him. It is soul-refreshing to remember that, to Jesus Christ, God has given "all authority in heaven and on earth" (Matthew 28:18), and that,

> *. . . He is seated on the right hand of God, in the heavenly realms, far above all rule and authority, power and dominion, and every title that can be given, not only in the present age, but also in the one to come. And God has placed all things under His feet and appointed Him to be head over everything for the church, which is His body* (Ephesians 1: 21-22).

The Good News is, if we accept Jesus right now, and are willing to follow Him the rest of our lives, He will assuredly lead us every step of the way to the end by means of His Holy Spirit and hereafter to eternal life in heaven, where the righteous live in peace and glory in the presence of God and His holy angels.

On the other hand, if we reject Jesus as our Savior and Lord, we shall certainly be condemned at the judgment seat of Christ, and finally, be cast out together with Satan into hell, *where "there is eternal fire prepared for the devil and his angels; and where there will be weeping and gnashing of teeth."* (Matthew 25: 41, 8:12b).

The irrefutable and irrevocable truth of the matter is that no religion, in this world, besides Christianity, has solution to the sin problem facing humanity. Furthermore, of all religious founders that ever lived, only Jesus Christ, being the Son of God, conceived by the Holy Spirit, lived a sinless life. Though He was tempted at all points of His life, He never succumbed to sin, (Hebrews 5: 7-10), because He was God in human form, fully God and fully human, God—man (John 1: 1, 14).

Therefore, Jesus was the only perfect man, who could solve the human problem of sin, which, since the time immemorial, had separated humanity from God. That is why Jesus declared: *"I came to seek and to save what was lost" (Luke 19:10)*. By God's providence, He died for the forgiveness of the sins of the world. The Scripture says, *It was now about the sixth hour, and darkness came over the whole land until the ninth hour, for the sun stopped shinning. And the curtain of the temple was torn in two* (Luke 23:44-45).

Commenting further on this statement, Ray C. Stedman asked:

> *Why was this curtain torn in two? Because the Holy of Holies was now to be opened up for the first time to human gaze! And because the Holy of Holies of the human spirit was now to be opened up for the first time to the gaze and habitation of God! When the Son of man died, God ripped the veil wide open. He passed through the Holy place, and penetrated into the Holy of Holies, into the secret of humanity- and the reality of humanity's spirit was unveiled. (Adventuring Through Matthew, Mark, and Luke,* P.44).

Since Jesus, by His sacrificial death on the Cross, has opened the gateway to eternal life for all who believe in Him, the writer to the Hebrews penned the following:

> *Brothers(and sisters), since we have confidence to enter the Most Holy Place by the blood of Jesus, by a new and living way opened for us through the curtain, that is , his body, and since we have a great priest over the house of God, let us draw near to God with a sincere heart in full assurance of faith, . . .* (Hebrews 10:19-22).

"That is where we stand now", Ray declared. It is such a blessing, my friends, to grasp the insight that Ray shares here with us on

the benefits of the work of Christ for humanity as he continues in the following:

> *"The secret of humanity is open to anyone who opens his or her own heart to the Son of Man, the perfect man. He alone has penetrated the depths of human spirit. He alone re-establishes the lost relationship with God that enables us to be what God intended us to be. He alone saves and restores what was lost in the fall of man, in the entrance of sin into the world. He alone can restore the marred, distorted image of God in our lives.*
>
> *All the possibility of a fulfilled humanity is available to anyone in whom the spirit of Christ dwells. All that you deeply want to be in the innermost recesses of your heart, you can be. I'm not talking about your goals in life, such as becoming a millionaire or an Olympic gold medalist. No, I'm talking about the deepest, most inexpressible yearnings of your heart-your desire to be connected to God, to know Him, and be known by Him; your desire to have your life count for something in the eternal scheme of things; your desire to be clean and whole and forgiven. Jesus makes it possible for you to fulfill God's best for you, so that you will be mature and Christ-like, filled with love, forgiveness, wholeness, and good works" (Ibid. P. 45).*

Therefore, everyone, who believes in Jesus Christ, receives from God eternal life here and now, through the transforming power of the Holy Spirit in the name of Jesus. Why? *Because "God made Him who had no sin to be sin for us (human beings), so that in Him we might become the righteousness of God"* (2 Corinthians 5:21).

Surely, in Christ, you will discover, for the first time in your life, the amazing truth, and the assurance (through the work of the Holy Spirit in you) that you are accepted as a son/daughter of God. Besides, since God has no second-class children, you will discover how much He loves and cares equally for all who belong to the family of God. Paul confirms it in the following passage:

> *Praise be to the God and Father of our Lord Jesus Christ, who has blessed us in the heavenly realms with every spiritual blessing in Christ. For He* (God) *chose us in Him* (Christ) *before the creation of the world to be blameless in His sight. In love He predestined us to be adopted as His children through Jesus Christ, in accordance with His pleasure and will—to the praise of His glorious grace, by which He has made us accepted in the Beloved* (Ephesians 1: 4-6).

Paul added, *"Consequently, you are no longer foreigners and aliens, but fellow citizens with God's people and members of God's household*" [i.e. members of God's family] (Ephesians 2:19).

Dear reader, with the above-quoted passages of Scripture, you might now have realized your need to accept Jesus as your Savior and Lord. If not, perhaps, the following simple questions may help you make up your mind before it is too late: "Whom have you decided to follow the rest of your life? Who is your chosen Leader or Master in this life? To whom do you owe allegiance? As a human being made in God's image, regardless of your position in society or family, to whom do you look for love, peace, strength, protection, courage, joy and comfort in your daily life?

David McCasland made this observation:

> *Even when life seems overwhelming, we can cry out to the Lord and find His deliverance from distress. It is not health or wealth, but God's unfailing love that sets us free in every circumstance of life. (Daily Bread, Wednesday, November 28, 2002).*

Friend, the unavoidable question each of us needs to answer is: *Where will I spend eternity? Do I have hope to go to heaven with the Lord after my death or will I be condenmned to hell, because of my rejection of Christ* (John 3:19-20)?

As you prayerfully ponder over these questions as to what answers to give, may I rub in this brief, but precious story by Vernon C. Grounds, to guide your decision-making process:

> *During World War 11, B-17 bombers made long flights from the U.S. mainland to pacific island of Saipan. When they landed there, the planes were met by a jeep bearing the sign: "Follow Me!" That little vehicle guided the giant planes to their assigned places in the parking area.*
>
> *One pilot, who by his own admission was not a religious man, made an insightful comment: "That little jeep with its quaint sign always reminds me of Jesus. He was (a lowly) peasant, but the giant men and women of our time would be lost without His direction.*

Vernon continues:

> *Centuries after our Savior walked the streets and hills of Israel, the world with all its advances still needs His example and instruction. When His ways aren't followed, numerous problems and evils arise in our world—including immorality, crime, and greed. How do we follow Jesus' ways?*

The writer answers the question by reiterating what I had said earlier in my conclusion:

> *First of all, we turn from our sin and entrust our lives to Him as our Savior and Lord. Then we seek His will in His Word each day and put it into practice by the power of the Holy Spirit within us. We learn to deny our selfish desires and give ourselves completely to following Jesus (Mark 8:34-35) (Daily Bread, March 5, 2003).*

It thrills my heart, as I conclude the writing of this vision, to know that God has confirmed His message to me through the story by author, Vernon Grounds, a dedicated man of God, working with the RBC Ministries, in Grand Rapids.

In case you are a little doubtful about the truth of this vision, let me furnish you with a few of many examples of prophecies and visions that God, by grace, and not by any merits of my own, had previously revealed to me and faithfully fulfilled in my ministry.

- ***Wednesday, December 28, 1980:***
  During a prayer meeting, God gave me a prophecy that there would be a change of Government by soldiers of the Ghana Army through coup de tat, unless Ghanaians repented. (This was fulfilled on December 31, 1980, when the AFRC Regime, led by Flt. Lt. J.J. Rawlings took over the seat of the government of Ghana.
- ***Sunday January 1, 1981:***
  While listening to a sermon by Very Rev. Entsua-Mensah, at Takoradi Bethel Methodist Church, the Holy Spirit declared through me at end of the service that there would be fire outbreak in Ghana and the only safe place to go for protection is the Lord Jesus. For He alone is our Hiding Place. This came to pass in February 1983.
- ***1982:***
  While I was praying, I had a vision that Ghanaians, who had left for Nigeria in search of a better living condition, would return home. It was fulfilled in February 1983.
- ***May 1987:***
  While praying about my application for admission to Wesley Theological Seminary in Washington, D. C., I had a vision that I had been admitted and was going to meet the Dean of Students in her Office. Truly, the following year,

on August 20, 1988, I stepped into the office of the Dean of Students, and was admitted to do Master of Theological Studies, leading to Doctor of Ministry Degree in May 1993.

- ***February 2, 1997***
During the night, the Lord told me in a vision: "go, gather people, who are scattered to come together to study my Word and worship Me. Do it, looking unto your Tutor." And that brought into being, after several weeks of prayer and fasting, Calvary Redeeming Methodist Church, which began its first worship in my living room in Chevy Chase, with 8 members on Sunday, May 4, 1997. Now, we are over one hundred and twenty in membership. Glory be to God!
- ***January 24, 2002***
The message of this book as already indicated in the introduction, came to me in a vision, which I received from the Lord during my devotion in the early hours of the morning. Then fterwards, God told me to put it in writing, which was not easy for me to begin with, but, by depending on the power, wisdom and guidance of the Holy Spirit, this book has been completed for the whole world to read. This is further proof of the power and faithfulness of God to His Word, that we "*can do all things through Christ who strengthens* [us]" (Philippians 4:19).

Indeed, God is faithful, and will always honor His Word to all who sincerely trust in Him. Therefore, without any doubt or fear, I am convinced that the message of this vision would be fulfilled as God has always done according to His Word. That is why He told me to put it in writing that all may read and turn from their sins to Christ, the friend of sinners (Luke 15:1-7). I want to encourage you, friend, to put your faith in Jesus Christ. If you are willing and ready, I want to invite you right now to pray the following prayer with all your heart:

> *O God, my heavenly Father, thank you for creating me in your image. Thank you for all the spiritual and material provisions you have in store for me through your Son, Jesus Christ. I believe He died on the Cross for all my sins, and that He rose again from the dead. I bessech you, O God, to fogive me all my sins. I humbly invite your Son, Jesus Christ, into my heart, to be my Savior and Lord all the days of my life.*
>
> *Thank you, Father, for accepting me as one of your children, through Jesus Christ, my Lord. Amen!*

If you have sincerely prayed the above prayer, believing with all your heart, then you must be certain that you are a changed person, and that your name is recorded in "*the Lamb's Book of Life*" (Revelation 21:27). It does mean that henceforth, Christ is in you, and you are in Christ (ref. John 15:3-4; Revelation 3:20); His abiding promise is that "*I am with you always*" (Matthew 28:20). *Believe that He is able to save to the uttermost all who come to Him, and wholeheartedly trust in His finished work on the Cross* (John 1:12, 10:27-30; Acts 16:31).

May I remind you, if I may, that I am a living witness, and so is the entire universal Church (which is His body), of what God's saving Grace, through faith in Jesus Christ, can do. All that God had done through this ministry, plus the writing of this important vision into a book must encourage all skeptics as to what God can do with anyone who trusts in Him.

The message of this book, "*Living by the Power of God*" is summed up in the two Akan words: "*Gye Nyame*" (Except God), which is to say: "*Unless God sustains us by His infinite power, no human being or any living thing, including the universe, can exist, because it is God, who upholds His own creation and nobody else*". Again, only God, and God alone, and no one else, can fill the emptiness of our aching heart. Hence, the book is subtitled, "*Without our Maker, we cannot make it.*" Habakkuk puts it this way, *"Has not the Lord Almighty determined that the people's labor is only fuel for the fire, that the nations exhaust themselves for nothing?"* (Habakkuk 2:13).

Jesus confirmed Habakkuk's message when He declared: *"Without Me, you can do nothing."* (John 15:5). The truth, which has been emphasized over and over again in this book, is that God made us (humans) in His image, in order that we might have a personal relationship with God, and depend on Him in all our ways. We were not intended to leave God out in any aspect of our lives in the pursuit of our goals on earth, lest we perish. But, being humans with free will, we went our own way instead of God's way, and were separated from God since the Fall of our first parents—Adam and Eve (Genesis 3).

Nevertheless, out of God's infinite love and compassion for lost humanity, God came to our rescue by sending His only Son, Jesus Christ, whose substitutionary death on the cross, has paid for our sins, as the holy and righteous demands of the Law require (Romans 6:23; Hebrews 2:2). By Christ's sacrifice, *"God has made us, (who believe) accepted in the beloved"* (Ephesians 1: 6). It means, therefore, that all who believe in Christ have forgiveness of sins, and new-life in Jesus Christ, and will not be condemned to hell fire. All believers will be in heaven with the Lord and be rewarded for their fruitful life in Christ through the work of the Holy Spirit (John 14: 1-3; Matthew 25:40-43, 44-46; Galatians. 5:22; 2 Corinthians 5:17; Revelation 22:12-15).

It is the prayerful, yearning of my heart that as you come to the conclusion of this urgent message of God, you will join me and all others concerned, to commit our lives afresh to Jesus Christ, our Lord. Do not let this day pass by or the sun go down without making a decision about your destiny, namely to take hold of the unlimited, unconditional, and eternal love of God through faith in Jesus Christ.

God is looking for people like you and me, who are ready to offer themselves as God's sanctified vessels to reach out to the lost, and to bless your family, community, nation and the world at large. Or we can also be a tool in the hands of Satan for destruction. Let me give you an example here: for the past one year or so, an unseen arsonist has risen up against the community of the Washington Metropolitan Area, burning down people's houses, not because the victims had done him some wrong; but simply because he is full of anger and wickedness, and is being used as an agent of the Devil, who "*comes to steal, to kill, and to destroy*" (John 10: 10). By November 20, 2003, the arsonist had burned down 32 houses in Washington, D.C., Maryland, and Virginia. There has been one dead, and many are reported injured in these arsons. What does he gain by being so wicked and so destructive to innocent people in society? We pray that he is arrested and convicted, soon, to curtail his dangerous pranks in the night. God knows him and his every move and will shortly lay hands on him to bring him to justice.

Now, friend, having come thus far through this book, I am confident that you are aware of the truth that our choices ultimately affect our detiny. We also know that in spiritual matters, we cannot be neutral; we can either be on the **right** side or the **wrong** side of the journey of life. The choice is in our hands. If we choose God by faith in Jesus, He will be with us forever here on earth and hereafter in heaven. But, if we decide to live on our own terms and be our own captain, then we leave ourselves open for Satan to dominate and destroy us in the end. You can make this day, a day of salvation for you. In this connection, I humbly, but seriously, appeal to all—black or white, man or woman, adult or youth, to choose Christ, who is "*the Way, the Truth and the Life*," (John 14: 6). It is only through Christ, and no one else, that we all, together with members of our families can be saved, and live in "*righteousness, peace and joy in the Holy Spirit*" (Romans 14:17) for ever with all the apostles and fellow believers in the Kingdom of God and His Son, Jesus Christ.

As it is declared in the Holy Scriptures, "*In the time of my favor I heard you, and in the day of salvation, I helped you. I tell you, now is the time of God's favor, now is the day of salvation*" (2 Corinthians 6:2). Since you are now fully aware of the situation we are in as human beings, particularly, as Africans, may I invite you to participate in the following tasks:

- Join me in thanking God for His goodness in giving me this vision to share with all people.

- Pray to God to forgive you all your sins; and accept Jesus Christ as your personal Lord and Savior. Here is the promise of the Lord to all, who sincerely turn to Him with a repentant heart: "*Behold, I stand at the door and knock: if any man hears my voice, and opens the door, I will come in and eat with him and he with me*" (Revelation 3:20). That is Christ's assurance of your salvation by grace through faith in Him (Ephesians 2: 8).
- Pray for the salvation and well-being of your family, both far and near.
- Let us join together to intercede for Africa, in particular, and the world, in general, that the leaders will submit to God of all power and wisdom, through faith in Jesus Christ. That they will be guided and controlled NOT by any other power such as political, economic, technological, or demonic influence, but solely by the eternal power of God, the Holy Spirit, our Comforter and Advocate (John 14:26; Romans 8:26).

If, together, we make this our daily concern in prayer, we shall certainly become partners with God, and shall experience a miracle of New Life in the members of our families and communities, and be able to defeat the diabolical works of the enemy, the Devil.

Albert Einstein said, "There are two ways to live your life. One is as though nothing is a miracle. The other is as though everything is a miracle." Since miracles do not happen by chance, except by the power of God, who made heaven and earth, including everything in it, it follows, therefore, that God loves His creation, and is actively engaged in it, miraculously accomplishing His purpose of redemption among humanity day by day through His Son, Jesus Christ. Surely, I believe that Albert Einstein might have made the above statement, based on his own observation of these irrefutable truths revealed by the Holy Spirit in diverse ways to humanity.

Thus, we shall, with God's power, fulfill God's eternal, and loving purpose for humankind, both spiritually and physically, in this life, and in the world to come. As you may have known by now, God's marvelous work of salvation in this world can be accomplished through those who have His Holy Spirit, and act in faith and obedience to His Word. Furthermore, it is good to be reminded that our life is, but a shadow that passes away (James 4: 14). In order for us to be counted worthy of the Lord, we must live in Christ and He in us by means of the power of the Holy Spirit. With Christ as our Lord and Savior, "*the Spirit testifies with our spirit that we are God's children*" (Romans 8:16).

Let's pause here briefly to examine this: if the word "Christian" is broken into two syllables, we have "Christ", and "ian". Thus, without the word 'Christ', the word 'ian' has no meaning in itself. Therefore, the letters 'i', 'a', 'n' read as follows: *"**I** **a**m **n**othing."* So the full statement reads: *"Without Christ (in me), I am nothing."* But, regardless of my race, color, gender, status or rank in sociey, *with Christ, I am a Christian—a precious somebody—namely, a child of God—the object of God's love—sealed by the Holy Spirit—* (Ephesians 1: 13), bound for heaven by virtue of God's grace through faith in Jesus Christ, our Savior and Lord (John 1: 12, 14: 3; Ephesians 2: 8;). Hence, Jesus declared: *"He who believes in me will live, even though he dies; and whoever lives and believes in me will never die"* (John 11:25-26). Knowing His victory over death, Jesus assured His followers, *"because I live, you also will live*" (John 14: 19b). Therefore, with "*Christ in you, the hope of glory*" (Colossains 1:27), you are fully certain of eternal life together with Chrst in the kindgom of God.

Now, let's take a moment to ponder deeply over these words of Jesus. Make sure that you are truly a child of God by committing your life to Christ so that from this day forward, He may be *"the authur and perfecter of your faith*" (Hebrews 12: 2) journey. Let's be reminded that without Christ, we are nothing. *"For dust we are, and to dust we shall return"* (Genesis 3:19). Besides, *"we brought nothing into the world, and we can take nothing out of it*" (1Timothy 6:7). Think seriously about this: if "*God, who formed the man* [the human being] *from the depth of the earth and breathed into his nostrils the breath of life"* (Genesis 2:7) were to stop the air we breathe for just a second, how terrrible the consequences would be? I suppose that all human beings, including every living thing—birds of the air, fish in the sea, trees of the forest, grass of the field, flowers of the garden, as well as, even the minutest creature like the ant, would be dead. But, for the sake of God's infinite goodness and mercy toward humanity, as revealed in the life, atoning death, resurrection, and the ascension of His son, Jesus Christ, including the gift of the Holy Spirit, God does not consume us.

Therefore, out of His unconditional love, God is graciously inviting right now, all those who have not yet become His children to be part of His uncountable family in His eternal kingdom through faith in His Son, Jesus Christ (Revalation 3:19-21, 7:9-17). This is an unspeakable privilege and we must not let it slip through our fingers. We must altogether seriously heed God's gracious call to all people—black or white, rich or poor, male or female, old or young, including, even our little children (Mark 10: 13-15):

> *Gather together and come; assemble, you fugitives from the nations. Ignorant are those who carry about idols of wood, who pray to gods that cannot save. And there is no God apart from me, a righteous God and a Saviour; there is none but me. Turn to me and be saved, all you ends of the earth; for I am God, and there is no other* (Isaiah 45:20, 21c, 22).

Finally, having discussed all this, I consider it essential to conclude this message at this juncture with a prayer for all who read this book, so that they may be richly blessed by its contents. It is the prayer St. Paul offered daily to God on behalf of the Ephesian Church:

> *I keep asking that the God of our Lord Jesus Christ, the glorious Father, may give you the Spirit of wisdom and revelation, so that you may know Him better. I pray also that the eyes of your heart may be enlightened in order that you may know the hope to which He has called you, the riches of His glorious*

> *inheritance in the saints, and His incomparably great power for us who believe. That power is like the working of His mighty strength, which He exerted in Christ when He raised Him from the dead and seated Him at His right hand in the heavenly realms, far above all rule and authority, power and dominion, and every title that can be given, not only in this age, but also in the one to come. And placed all things under His feet and appointed Him to be head over everything for the Church, which is His body, the fullness of Him who fills everything in every way* (Ephesians 1:17-23).

I humbly, but seriously, invite you to join me in praying this prayer every day for ourselves and for all others—believers and non—believers alike. Let us look to the Lord as He continues with His wonderful work of transformation in our lives, our families, communities, cities, countries in Africa in particular, and the world at large. We should never forget to rely on the Lord daily in all we do, keeping in mind His Word, and sharing the same with people: *"Unless the Lord builds the house, its builders labor in vain. Unless the Lord watches over the city, the watchmen stand guard in vain."* For, *"apart from me,"* He says, *"you can do nothing"; "but with God, all things are possible"* (Psalms 127:1; John. 15:5; Luke 18:27); and that *"everything is possible for him who believes"* (Mark. 9:23). For it is *"not by might nor by power, but by my Spirit,' says the Lord of Hosts"* (Zechariah 4:6). That means, it is only the Spirit of God in us that reveals to us God's purpose for our lives, and gives us power to fulfill the same (see also John 16:12-14; Acts 1:8).

With these words of the Holy Scriptures, reminding us of our need of the Lord, let us stay away from every form of tradition that hinders our faith in Christ. As you have personally read the book, you can bail me out that this book is not against tradition, as some-one may wrongly assume. Rather, it offers a better way of **living our lives, not by tradition, or by any other means, but by the power of God**, which honors both God and our ancestors. It is such holy living that will lead us as a people and nation to possess and enjoy all the spiritual and material blessings of God (Deutronomy 28:1-14) without conflicting with the Holy Scriptures. Therefore, we must trust and obey the Lord, and keep on loving Him and our neighbors as ourselves, feeding fat on His Word and praying without ceasing till the last day of our lives. For, it is written, *"you were slain and with your blood, you have purchased people for God from every tribe and language....and nation. You have made them to be a kingdom and priests to serve our God*" and community (Revelation 5: 9-10). Moreover, we *"know that our labors in the Lord shall not be in vain, if we do not lose heart.*" (1 Corinthians. 15: 58; Galatians 6: 9). In the end, we shall each receive "*a crown of life*" as a reward for faithful service (Revelation 2:10) and join *"the loud voices in heaven*" to proclaim:

> ***Worthy is the Lamb, who was slain, to receive power and wealth and wisdom and strength and honor and glory and praise***!
>
> *The kingdom of the world has become the kingdom of our Lord and of His Christ, and He will reign for ever and ever* (Rev. 5:12, 11:15).